A Shameful Business

A Shameful Business

*The Case for Human Rights
in the American Workplace*

James A. Gross

ILR Press
AN IMPRINT OF
CORNELL UNIVERSITY PRESS
ITHACA AND LONDON

Copyright © 2010 by Cornell University

First published 2010 by Cornell University Press
First printing, Cornell Paperbacks, 2010

Printed in the United States of America

Library of Congress Cataloging-in-Publication Data

Gross, James A., 1933–
  A shameful business : the case for human rights in the American workplace / James A. Gross.
       p. cm.
  Includes bibliographical references and index.
  ISBN 978-0-8014-4844-7 (cloth : alk. paper)
  ISBN 978-0-8014-7644-0 (pbk. : alk. paper)
  1. Employee rights—United States.   2. Human rights—United States.   3. Industrial relations—United States.   4. Labor laws and legislation—United States.   I. Title.
  KF3455.G76   2010
    344.7301—dc22   2009029432

Cornell University Press strives to use environmentally responsible suppliers and materials to the fullest extent possible in the publishing of its books. Such materials include vegetable-based, low-VOC inks and acid-free papers that are recycled, totally chlorine-free, or partly composed of nonwood fibers. For further information, visit our website at www.cornellpress.cornell.edu.

Cloth printing   10   9   8   7   6   5   4   3   2   1
Paperback printing   10   9   8   7   6   5   4   3   2   1

To my beloved grandchildren, Jimmy, Erin, Alexa, Matthew, Katelynn, Chapin, and Christian, who will help make the world more just

Also to Margaret Sipser for her discerning comments at every stage of the manuscript and unwavering inspiration and encouragement

Contents

A Shameful Business

INTRODUCTION

The concept of workers' rights as human rights has emerged recently in discussions concerning the state of U.S. labor relations, but it has not influenced the making and implementation of labor policy at any level. Labor relations in this country, particularly union-management relations, is thought of as just another kind of power struggle between special interest groups.

Increasingly around the world, however, the right to form labor unions and to bargain collectively, the right to workplace safety and health, and the right not to be discriminated against in employment are considered human rights—not merely rights granted by statutes or collective bargaining contracts. Yet, it is commonly asserted that our own labor laws and standards, for example, are equal or superior to international human rights standards, particularly the labor standards set forth in International Labour Organization (ILO) conventions. One objective of this book is to test that assertion by reexamining

I am indebted to Jeffrey Hilgert, a Ph.D. candidate at Cornell University, for his help and insightful suggestions. Jeff has already begun to make great contributions to the advancement of workers' rights as human rights. I am also indebted to Rhonda Clouse, friend and colleague, for her suggestions and for transforming my handwritten yellow sheets into this book.

certain aspects of U.S. domestic labor relations—freedom of association, racial discrimination, management rights, workplace safety and health, and human resources—using internationally accepted human rights principles and values as standards for judgment. In that regard, there is extensive discussion concerning what changes need to be made to bring U.S. domestic labor law, policy, and practice into conformity with human rights principles. That discussion, however, does not address nor was it intended to address, the complex implementation issues confronting human rights and human rights institutions and organizations in this country and around the world.

The human rights principles used in this book as standards of judgment have been set forth in internationally accepted and approved declarations, covenants, and conventions. Those principles are stated in general terms in the United Nations (UN) Universal Declaration of Human Rights (UDHR), more specifically in the UN International Covenant on Civil and Political Rights (ICCPR) and the International Covenant on Economic, Social, and Cultural Rights (ICESCR), and most specifically in the ILO Conventions, Nos. 87 (Freedom of Association and Protection of the Right to Organise), 98 (Right to Organise and Collective Bargaining), 155 (Occupational Safety and Health), 187 (Promotional Framework for Occupational Safety and Health), and 111 (Discrimination-Employment and Occupation).

The UDHR, although not a binding treaty, has been the foundation of much of the post–World War II codification of human rights covenants, conventions, protocols, and regional treaties. It asserts in Article 1 that "all human beings are *born* free and equal in dignity and rights" (emphasis added). *Human rights* are literally the rights one has simply because one is a human being. They are the rights needed to have one's essential humanity respected and preserved. The drafters of the UDHR intended to assert moral rights of the highest order that all human beings had and were entitled to enjoy without permission or assent and that were beyond the power of any person, group, government, or other entity to grant or deny. This concept of human rights poses a direct challenge to existing institutions, practices, and values generally and to labor-employment systems, in particular. Although the UDHR offers no *specific* definitions of the individual and collective rights of human beings, it posits a set of values, a new ethic of human rights, in sharp contradiction to the values that powerfully influence the United States' labor-employment system.

The UDHR drafters included in the document not only civil rights such as the right to liberty, freedom from discrimination, equality before the law, and due process but also economic and social rights including the right to social security; the right to work; protection against unemployment; just pay; the right to form trade unions; the right to rest and leisure; the right to a standard of living "adequate for the health and well-being of himself and of his family, including food, clothing, housing and medical care"; and the right to an education "directed to the full development of the human personality." As stated in Articles 22 and 26, these economic, social, and cultural rights are considered indispensable for the free and full development of the human personality mainly because a unity of civil, political, economic, social, and cultural rights is necessary for a fully human life.

The UDHR and the UN's ICCPR and ICESCR together constitute an International Bill of Rights. The United States signed and ratified the ICCPR but with so many reservations that the U.S. domestic law has never been changed to ensure compliance with this Covenant's obligations. The United States has not ratified the ICESCR. Ironically, however, the Preamble of the ICCPR, as well as the Preamble of the ICESCR, states unequivocally that "in accordance with the Universal Declaration of Human Rights, the ideal of human beings enjoying civil and political freedom and freedom from fear and want can only be achieved if conditions are created whereby everyone may enjoy his civil and political rights as well as his economic, social and cultural rights."

The workers' rights discussed in this book—the right not to be discriminated against on or off the job; the right to a safe and healthful workplace; the right to exercise freedom of association to join labor organizations and to bargain collectively with their employers; and the right to be treated with respect and dignity and not be treated as a resource to be used and manipulated—reflect the unity of economic and cultural and civil and political rights.

A related standard, which might be more familiar to many U.S. citizens is the "American Creed" which professes values of the essential dignity and equality of all people and inalienable rights to freedom, justice, and fair opportunity. This standard is connected to the human rights standard in that all individuals must matter if they are to live a fully human life. This standard also highlights the gap between values preached and values practiced.

The first chapter of this book addresses different conceptions of rights and justice and the values underlying those conceptions, not only to identify different standards of judgment but also to emphasize the consequences for workers and employers of utilizing those different standards.

The use of human rights principles as the standard for judgment is also intended to bring about change by changing the argument. Despite fatalistic commentaries about the futility of trying to change the way things are, history shows us that no one group or ideology dominates forever. There are many reasons for that, but one is the ability of challengers to redefine a policy issue and thereby create new perspectives on old issues. These new perspectives come about, at least in part, by questioning the values on which the prior resolutions of those old issues have been based. This book does that. The intention is to influence the practice of labor-management relations and the formulation and implementation of labor policy.

Another theme of this book, therefore, is *choice*—choices among different value judgments about the worth of human life; about workers' right to participate in the decisions that affect their workplace lives; the sources of worker and employer rights; and the basis for the distribution of workplace benefits and burdens. These are deliberate and conscious choices by legislators, governmental agencies, judges, and labor arbitrators—not choices dictated by some unalterable economic laws. These choices over the years have given property rights, economic growth, economic competition, productivity, profits, wealth, and economic power dominance over workers' human rights.

More specifically, as detailed in these chapters, these deliberate choices constitute not only violations of workers' human rights but also crimes against humanity in that they have dehumanized workers and turned them into usable and disposable things. The chapter on racial discrimination (Chapter 2) describes the destruction of the human spirit, how racial discrimination leaves scars even on those who survive it, and how race still matters in this country in the distribution of benefits and burdens. This chapter deals directly with the worth of an individual human being, a concept central to human rights. It also demonstrates how racial discrimination in the United States has denied collective rights and led to a distorted and unjust distribution of benefits and burdens at the workplace and in the larger society. Race relations in the United States is used to highlight the gap between human rights standards and a contrary value that only certain lives matter too often practiced in this country. That gap is discussed at first using race as an illustration but then is traced throughout the book using many other examples such as worker safety and health.

Three chapters (Chapter 3, 4, and 5) discuss the clash of the right of freedom of association with management rights and the unregulated market philosophy that constitutes the business creed. Those chapters show how that clash has been resolved judicially, legislatively, and otherwise in ways that facilitate employer resistance to workers' exercise of their freedom of association, give management rights dominance over workers' rights, leave workers dependent and powerless to protect themselves, promote and protect the rights and freedoms of employers, and enable employers to retain unilateral control over workers and workplaces. This has prevented workers from making claims of their human rights effective or even known and leaves them dependent on the interests of their employers and the state.

Chapters 6 and 7 show how workers' right to life has been sacrificed to economic development; how workers are confronted with the dilemma of choosing to work and risking life and limb or choosing not to work and risking their jobs; how the denial of freedom of association prevents workers from taking control of their own workplace safety and health; how the government has failed to protect workplace safety and health; and how labor arbitrators give preference to management rights and objectives even over workers' rights to protect their own lives by refusing to perform work they believe threatens their health or safety.

Chapter 8 reveals the role of human resources in manipulating workers as human capital objects or organizational assets for others to use; using behavior-influencing techniques to discourage workers from exercising their freedom of association thereby keeping them powerless and dependent; and blinding workers to what their rights are or that they are being manipulated.

The concluding chapter (Chapter 9) provides detailed justification for the crimes against humanity charge; calls for the economy to be used to provide more human lives for people rather than for people to be used as resources for the economy; explains why it is crucial to reform and revitalize domestic labor laws and policies to bring them into conformity with human rights principles even in a globalizing economic system; identifies and discusses several fundamental implications for the U.S. National Labor Relations Act if it is to conform to international human rights law; calls for U.S. judges, administrative agency members, labor arbitrators, and labor-lawyer practitioners to end their isolation from human rights law and to utilize human rights standards in their decision making and advocacy; urges a new vision for the labor movement to become part of the worldwide human rights movement; and echoes the Rev. Martin Luther King, Jr., in calling for a radical revolution of values that would change us from a thing-oriented society to a person-oriented society.

Each of these subjects is discussed in historical context to demonstrate that these violations of workers' human rights did not begin in the 1980s but rather have their beginnings in the origins of the country. The historical context also gives a more realistic understanding of what change will require. The historical context also emphasizes that in this country there have always been countermovements based on values contrary to the unregulated market philosophy that has been dominant except for relatively brief periods—such as the early Wagner Act period, 1935–1939. Those alternative and contrasting values are discussed as are their implications for labor policy and practice.

Some have feared that insistence on the individual person's human rights would subvert worker solidarity, undermine freedom of association, and even end up reinforcing the libertarian individualism central to the unregulated market philosophy. This book demonstrates to the contrary that workers' human rights are inextricably connected to workers coming together to exercise their right of freedom of association through organization and collective bargaining. Only then can they exercise control over their workplace lives. The discussions in this book make that point in many ways but perhaps most compellingly in chapters 6 and 7 on workplace health and safety.

The purpose of human rights is to eliminate or minimize the vulnerability that leaves people at the mercy of others who have the power to hurt them. An anonymous auto worker expressed this vulnerability most pointedly and poignantly[1]:

> What is it that instantaneously makes
> a child out of a man?
> Moments before he was a father, a husband,
> an owner of property,
> a voter, a lover, an adult.
> When he spoke at least some listened.
> Salesmen courted his favor.
> Insurance men appealed to his family responsibility
> And by chance the church sought his help....
> But that was before he shuffled past the guard,
> climbed his steps,
> hung his coat and
> took his place along the line.

Ending that workplace vulnerability, as Senator Robert Wagner and many before him understood, requires not only enforceable individual rights but also worker organization and collective action.

This book expresses a point of view. This is not so-called disinterested scholarship. How can one be disinterested about human rights or the gruesome violations of those rights that cost workers their livelihoods and even their lives? How can one be disinterested about good and evil or life and death or health and sickness? As demonstrated in the following chapters, moreover, academics have not been disinterested but rather have served business interests and continue to serve business interests as researchers and consultants. As confirmed in this book, many of them have been and continue to be complicit with some of the most grievous violations of workers' human rights. Objectivity, however, is to be distinguished from disinterestedness. Every effort has been made to present relevant evidence thoroughly and accurately.

Using a human rights standard of judgment and identifying and analyzing the values underlying labor relations rules and policy choices should broaden the industrial relations research agenda and require new approaches to that research. That could make industrial relations research truly interdisciplinary because it requires understanding history, law, philosophy, ethics, economics, religion, and the international and comparative aspects of all those disciplines. This will also require broadening the methodology of industrial relations research beyond quantitative techniques and opening for examination subjects previously not considered because they were not quantifiable. It would reintroduce concepts such as justice and injustice, good and evil, moral and immoral to a field that has come to disparage the "normative" as unscientific and subjective.

To be more than pious talk, however, humans' rights must be protected by the rule of law and be made enforceable through public and private institutions such as legislation, judicial and administrative agency decisions, and collectively bargained contracts between employers and representatives of their employees. Before that can happen, these rights also need to become part of all peoples' values through teaching and education. The essays that compose this book are intended to engage people in a thoughtful and provocative discussion of values and conceptions of rights and justice as a first, essential step toward the determination of what kind of people we choose to be and what kind of society we choose to have. No choices are more important.

1

Justice and Human Rights

In a land of compromisers, deal makers, and lobbyists where accommodation and expediency drive the political and economic systems, talking justice can be at best a nuisance and at worst dismissed as unrealistic. Yet, justice is universally invoked by all manner of people with all manner of grievances and objectives, all convinced (or claiming to be convinced) that their causes are just. As one philosopher put it, justice has proved "sufficient motivation for the most sublime sacrifice as well as the worst misdeeds."[1]

Despite this professed dedication to justice, history is proof enough that human life is readily sacrificed, diminished, or wasted in the pursuit of some political, military, economic, or even religious interest. This, with some notable exceptions, is the story of the human predicament, over which little control is exercised. Can justice be more than an irrelevant abstraction—and a hypocritical abstraction at that—to those who in their daily lives suffer deliberate brutalities and systematic intimidation and exploitation and have few adequate defenses against even the often cruel randomness of life? So, why bother about justice when it appears futile to think the world can be changed? The short answer, discussed at length in this chapter, is that it would be irresponsible and unjust to act as if we could not or should not eliminate or prevent at least some injustices. Moreover, "despite terrible odds in a cruel world, integrity lives and insistence upon justice can be an incredibly powerful weapon in the fight against tyranny."[2]

There have been many conceptions of justice, including the greatest good for the greatest number; obedience to the law (whatever the law); an eye for an eye and a tooth for a tooth; from each according to his or her ability, to each according to his or her need; and do unto others as you would have them do unto you. Whatever the conception, *justice* is normally understood to be a body of rules and principles used to adjudicate conflicts of interests and disputes about rights as well as to distribute benefits to and to impose burdens on those in a society. Justice is also commonly understood to require effective and impartial institutions to guarantee the enforcement of those rules and principles. The common conception of justice, therefore, is a legalistic one, defining injustice as illegality or unlawfulness. This legalistic approach to justice, although important, does not reach or even begin to identify more than a portion of the injustice being committed. There are many victims of exploitation, arrogance, or neglect who have no recourse to the formal justice system because what was done to them, no matter how unjust, was not illegal.

Someone has to decide, moreover, what is legal and illegal. The powerful in every society have far greater means to establish and control the rules and principles of legal justice. Their views and values dominate legislation and the administration of laws as well as decisions concerning the allocation of scarce resources. Consequently, they have a strong interest in limiting enforceable claims of injustice to situations involving alleged violations of laws or other formally established rules—which they had a disproportionate influence in developing. This legalistic conception of justice, moreover, draws attention away from the exercise of power and leaves many victims of exploitation, arrogance, and neglect with nothing but cries of injustice to try to gain our attention.

This inequality is the origin of injustice. As Judith Shklar has written:

> For while we internalize the ethics of inequality and accept it as right and just, we do not lose our natural ability to feel deprived, humiliated, and offended when our expectations as human beings are not met, when our claims are ignored, when our sense of our dignity and all our sensibilities are affronted, and when we are despised and rejected. And many of our expectations are rooted in nature, not in culture. So deep is our sense of injustice that it embitters our lives day in day out. Most of us do not do anything about it and follow rules meekly, but that hardly improves us or our situation. Our sense of injustice may be dormant, but it cannot go away entirely.[3]

These injustices may never be put right unless their infliction breaks some law or fails to follow some established procedures. We need, therefore, a broader conception of justice that includes the legal model with its rules, adjudications, and institutions but also listens to the voices of *all* suffering victims. It is a justice that "looks straight into the faces of those who suffer rather than staring steadfastly at a distant body of impersonal rules" and "requires not only that such suffering not be inflicted but also that it not be ignored."[4] Three questions asked by Rabbi Hillel over 2,000 years ago provide a good starting point for an exploration of this broader conception of justice: If I am not for myself, who will be for me? If I am only for myself, what am I? If not now, when?[5]

Rabbi Hillel's first question raises issues of individual worth and responsibility for one's self. Any society worthy of being called civilized respects the dignity of human persons. In a just society there can be no throw-away people. But why are human beings special? Most religions teach that humans are more than animals because they were created by God in God's own image and endowed with an eternal soul, a spirit that gives them a richer and nobler existence than the mere physical. With or without acceptance of religious underpinnings, human beings certainly are knowers, judges, creators, and communicators. Unlike other entities in nature, they are capable of understanding what they are doing; of making their own rational choices and decisions based on considerations of alternatives; of making value judgments; and of determining for themselves the goals or purposes they want to pursue. Because of these characteristics alone, each and every human being has "worth" or dignity regardless of their achievements, race, creed, ethnicity, or gender. To treat a person as less than a person or as less worthy of consideration than other people is to deny them what they need in order to have their essential humanity respected and preserved. This is profoundly unjust. Justice is giving human beings their due because justice is concerned with the dignity of human beings.[6]

In a democracy, in particular, all individuals must matter if they are to be allowed to live the fully human lives the democratic system is supposed to cherish. But as fundamental as human worth is to justice, its expression appears futile—like crying in the wilderness of an often brutal world where might makes right, nothing matters but the exercise of will and the power to carry it out, and human relationships are manipulative rather than respectful. Still, all men and women are entitled to whatever they need to live good human lives. That means being able to "stand up 'like a man,' to look others in the eye and to feel in some fundamental way the equal of anyone."[7] It is the antithesis of so much of today's human condition: people dependent and passive bearers of the consequences of power exercised elsewhere by someone other than themselves.

Consequently, it is not possible to talk about justice without talking about rights. To have a right is to be in a position to make justified demands of others who, in turn, have a duty to respond in ways that uphold that right. The existence of certain rights depends on their acceptance by the particular communities involved. Those rights are mutable in that they are subject to power and negotiation. In that sense, might makes a right. Many of these rights are legal rights set forth in laws and contracts that were the products of power and negotiation in the legislative and other bargaining processes. Those rights are interpreted and enforced by courts, administrative agencies, or arbitrators. Such rights, therefore, are established by external authority and enforced by sanctions.

For the same reasons that justice needs to be understood as involving more than legal justice, the concept of rights needs to be understood as involving more than legal, or contractual, or common law, or even constitutional rights. *Human rights,* for example, are moral rights that all human beings have simply because they are human, not because those rights are earned or acquired by special enactments or contractual agreements. Human rights are moral rights of the "highest order."[8] Put another way, even if slavery (or racial discrimination of any sort) was permitted or even sanctioned by custom, common law, federal and state law, executive order, or by collective bargaining contract, it would be a violation of core human rights principles: that every person possesses human rights equally; that every human being is sacred; that human beings are ends in themselves, not objects to be used for others' purposes; and that because every human being is sacred "certain things ought not to be done to any human being and certain other things ought to be done for every human being."[9]

In the Arthur Miller play, *Death of a Salesman,* an aging salesman, Willie Loman, after thirty-four years of work for the same company, attempts to bargain with his employer—offering to accept lower pay in return for being brought in off the road and given a job in the office. Loman's powerless "bargaining" turns into futile and pathetic groveling to save his job; pleading for "respect," "comradeship," and "gratitude"; and begging for consideration based on unwritten "promises," economic need, and the fact that he had "put thirty-four years into this firm."[10] At the low point of his humiliation, Loman cries out partly in protest and partly in grief, "You can't eat the orange and throw the peel away—a man is not a piece of fruit."[11]

Loman had no claims against the company based on legal rights, contractual rights, court precedent, or constitutional rights. He asserted a moral right, however, based on the value of human life. He claimed that it was unjust for others to be indifferent to his suffering and to treat him as if he were expendable and counted for nothing unless he had something to sell. Loman was asserting his human rights at his workplace.

There has been a limited conception of human rights in the Western tradition which emphasizes the individual and the individual's rights that need to be protected against abuse by the state. According to that conception, the corresponding duty on the state and other individuals, therefore, is simply a duty of self-restraint. From that perspective, moreover, the essential rights of man were "negative"; they were the civil and political rights that defended individual freedom from state interference. This tradition helps explain why civil and political rights have dominated human rights discussions. Until recently, the international human rights movement and organizations, human rights scholars, and even labor organizations and advocates have given little attention to worker rights as human rights.[12]

The inclusion of economic and workers' rights (such as the rights to work, to pay ensuring human dignity, to form and join labor organizations, to rest and leisure, to food, clothing, and housing, to medical care, and to education) in the traditional Western conception of human rights has been controversial. Some opposed the idea of economic rights because it led those "'destined to travel in the obscure walk of laborious life' [the common people] to believe that they were entitled to things which they could not possibly have."[13] Only one economic right was recognized and accepted in the West: the right to property.[14] A growing acceptance of economic rights as human rights coincided with the rise of working class movements and the insistence "that the propertyless were entitled to all the same rights as the propertied."[15]

What is commonly referred to as the International Bill of Rights sets forth "an interdependent and interactive"[16] system of political, civil, and economic rights. The United Nation's Universal Declaration of Human Rights (UDHR), adopted in 1948, includes economic and social rights (Articles 22–26, for example) as well as political and civil rights.[17] The preamble of the International Covenant on Civil and Political Rights (ICCPR), moreover, asserts the interdependence of political and economic rights: "The ideal of free human beings enjoying civil and political freedom and freedom from fear and want can only be achieved if conditions are created whereby everyone may enjoy his civil and political rights, as well as his economic, social and cultural rights."[18] Put most simply, it means that for those without bread, freedom of association, freedom of speech, and political participation are in reality meaningless as many are coerced into giving up their liberty to secure their subsistence. The United States' position on the question of economic rights has fluctuated from the time of Franklin D.

Roosevelt's Economic Bill of Rights[19] to the Reagan administration's rejection of economic rights as rights of any sort.[20]

Certainly, the right to physical security and the right to minimum economic security or subsistence are indispensable to the enjoyment of all other rights, including political and civil rights. They are so indispensable that even the threatened deprivation of these basic rights is a powerful weapon against those less powerful who try to exercise their other rights. The right to physical security—the right not to be subjected to murder, torture, mayhem, rape, or assault—is commonly acknowledged. Enormous amounts of money, time, and human effort are spent in this country on police forces, jails, guards, criminal courts, schools for training lawyers and police and the rest of the vast system for the preservation, detection, and punishment of violations of physical security.

There is a striking similarity, however, between assaults on physical security and assaults on subsistence rights due to inadequate food, clothing, and shelter; polluted air and water; inadequate health care; or inadequate opportunity or ability to support oneself. One is no more dead from a gunshot than from starvation or preventable disease. Yet, subsistence rights are much more accepted and protected in traditional societies generally characterized as backward or underdeveloped than in our own country where "liberalism has had a blind spot for severe economic need"[21] and those who assert subsistence rights are often looked upon with suspicion, contempt, hostility, and resentment.

Even if physical security and subsistence rights were respected and protected, however, more is required for a life to be truly human than enough food and drink, clothing, and shelter to survive. Prisons can provide those essentials. To rise above these minimal levels of human existence, people need, among other things, to have rights to education for the full development of their human personalities and abilities; the political liberty of an enfranchised citizen; freedom of thought, conscience, and religion; freedom of opinion and expression; freedom of assembly and equality before the law, being presumed innocent until proved guilty with equal entitlement to a fair and public hearing by an independent and impartial tribunal; equal opportunity free of discrimination; and freedom of movement and residence within the borders of each nation. A fully human life also requires rights to meaningful work and to safe and healthful conditions of work; to pay sufficient to ensure a life of human dignity for a worker and his or her family; protection against unemployment; the right to form and join labor unions; and ownership of property alone or in association with others. In sum, people need to exercise both political and civil rights and economic rights in order to live fully human lives.

Economic rights as human rights more particularly workers' rights as human rights constitute the theme of this book and are discussed extensively. Suffice it here to quote Eleanor Roosevelt, who played a major role in drafting the Universal Declaration of Human Rights. She warned that human rights would have little meaning unless they were enforced in the places where people lived, worked, and went to school:

> Where, after all, do universal human rights begin? In small places, close to home—so close and so small they cannot be seen on any maps of the world. Yet they are the world of the individual person; the neighborhood he lives in; the school or college he attends; the factory, farm or office where he works. Such are the places where every man, woman and child seeks equal justice, equal opportunity, equal dignity without discrimination. Unless these rights have meaning there, they have little meaning anywhere.[22]

Workers' rights are human rights. *Work* is not merely an economic activity; it is a "fundamental dimension of what it means to be human."[23] Through work, men and women can express their creativity and achieve self-realization and personal fulfillment. Through work they can become integrated into the human community by contributing to and participating in the life of that community. They also depend on work to fulfill other needs such as income for subsistence, a better life for themselves and their families, to escape poverty, to obtain education and health care, to enjoy recreation, and to achieve status in their community.

Simply having a job, however, is no guarantee of human dignity. There is work that stifles creativity and personal and social development, that is inherently demeaning and inhumane, and that alienates a person from him- or herself and from the community in which they live. In the same way, unemployment and poverty should be seen as destructive of human life and human capabilities.[24] "To deprive people of jobs is to read them out of our society,"[25] particularly in a market economy where employment "is necessary to one's identity as a human being."[26] Unemployment, moreover, is intimately associated with human misery of all sorts: suicides and homicides, imprisonment, alcoholism and drug addiction, family breakups, child abuse, emotional breakdowns, and a wide range of physical maladies.

The purpose of rights, particularly human rights, is to eliminate or minimize the vulnerability that leaves people at the mercy of others who have the power to harm them.[27] It is not only the state that has the power to violate people's rights. Employers have explicit power over individual's lives and there is always the implicit power of the "free market." People can be rendered powerless not only by totalitarian states but also by those minimalist states that do not outlaw or take effective steps to prevent the violation of people's rights by private nonstate actors.[28]

So where does a decent human life start? It begins by not having to depend on others' benevolence, charity, love, pity, or devotion to duty. It begins when people understand that they inherently deserve just treatment and stop considering themselves lucky and indebted when they receive even minimally decent treatment. No one can enjoy the substance of a right when dependent on the arbitrary will of others—no matter how benevolent the others may be.

A full human life, therefore, requires participation in the political, economic, and social life of the human community; not the pseudo-participation of form with no power, but genuine effective participation where people have an influence on the decisions that affect their lives. As Henry Shue has written, "to enjoy something only at the discretion of someone else, especially someone powerful enough to deprive you of it at will, is precisely not to enjoy a right to it."[29] If the Lord giveth, then the Lord can taketh away, and victims will have no defense without established forms of participation available to them. As will be discussed, too many workers stand before their employers not as adult persons with rights but as powerless children or servants totally dependent on the will and interests of their superiors and employers.

It is a tragedy as well as an injustice that human beings are treated as things or a resource for others to use. It is an even greater tragedy and injustice that so many millions suffer poverty and helplessness patiently and dumbly because they have come to expect so little out of life. Anton Chekhov once asked his fellow Russians, "You live badly, my friends. Is it really necessary for you to live so badly?"[30] In response to Chekhov, rights can take the victim's side by restraining the powerful and reducing people's vulnerability to harm at the hands of others—particularly agents of governments and private employers. Rights are shields against coercion. They "are asserted against power abused."[31]

On the other hand, in our competition-driven society, for example, the intrinsic importance of each human life has been used to justify an unchecked individualism where rights become the egoistic demands of people preoccupied with advancing their own self-interest by having claims to private property and otherwise demanding larger portions of the available economic pie. According to this notion of justice, emphasis is placed on the right not to be interfered with while engaging in the battle royal and the unencumbered right to the prizes (if any) acquired in the struggle. In sum, persons have rights but no duties to others except noninterference with others' rights. This "one for one and none for all"[32] philosophy is articulated by novelist Ayn Rand in *The Fountainhead,* a hymn to individualism in which her heroes struggle against any restraint on their own self-interest. Architect Howard Roark, Rand's protagonist, explains to a court that he has just dynamited housing that he had designed for the poor because, as its creator, he owed it to no one:

> It is believed that the poverty of the future tenants gave them a right to my work. That their need constituted a claim on my life. That it is my duty to contribute anything demanded of me. This is the second-hander's credo now swallowing the world.
>
> I came here to say that I do not recognize anyone's right to one minute of my life. Nor to any part of my energy. Nor to any achievement of mine. No matter who makes the claim, how large their number or how great their need.
>
> I wished to come here and say that I am a man who does not exist for others.[33]

For Roark and others like him, it would be unjust to interfere with complete and unhampered freedom. At the same time, their rejection of any obligations to the common good of the community of human persons results in the isolation of each person in his or her own selfishness or helplessness. Mutual trust is destroyed. People become alienated from each other because their relationships are based on manipulation and exploitation for personal gain. When human beings become what Jacques Maritain called unchecked "little gods,"[34] then we will hear the "kettledrums of hell."[35]

In the "real world" we do not expect people to be completely altruistic and unconcerned with their own advantage. But the person who seeks only to squeeze the greatest advantage and make no concession or the slightest sacrifice for the benefit of others "reveals himself as not being one of us, but an alien instead, a potential enemy to be frustrated, circumvented, exploited or manipulated, not a fellow worker with whom we can make common cause."[36]

Rabbi Hillel asked three questions and only the first—"If I am not for myself, who will be for me?"—has been discussed. The second question is as much an integral part of justice as the first: "If I am only for myself, what am I?" As the second question implies, individualism recognizes only half of what constitutes justice. Justice does not deny self-interest or require complete selflessness. But justice is social in that it can be found only where the actions and claims of persons meet so there can be a profound opposition between freedom and justice. Human rights need to be integrated with the goals of social justice rather than to become selfish and individualized demands without corresponding duties or obligations to others.[37]

Justice is, for example, the first assault on egoism. It is the "bond of society."[38] It does not ignore social justice. It lays down how other human beings should be treated and requires consideration of and respect for the rights and interests of others. It deals with the relation of individuals and the common good. The Howard Roarks of the world would claim the freedom to act regardless of others. Why should I recognize and respect the other person or have an obligation to act in certain ways toward him or her? Because he or she is a human being, a person just like me and may not be treated as a mere means to the satisfaction of others, or in some other way as a lesser human being.

The purpose of a just society, therefore, is not to give the strong freedom to oppress the weak but to promote the good of the human community through the common good of human persons. Justice recognizes not only the fundamental rights of individual human persons but also the interconnectedness of those persons in a human community. "No man is an island entire of it selfe," John Donne wrote over four hundred years ago: "any man's death diminishes me, because I am involved in Mankinde; And therefore never send to know for whom the bell tolls; it tolls for thee."[39] Tom Joad in *The Grapes of Wrath* remembered the preacher Jim Casey and how Casey went into the wilderness to find his own soul only to discover that he had only "a little piece of a great big soul" and that "his little piece of soul wasn't no good 'less it was with the rest,' an was whole." Joad added, "I know now a fella ain't no good alone."[40] What justice requires is a coalition of all for each.[41]

Still, many see this interconnectedness of human beings as a matter of charity rather than justice and rights. In the biblical parable of the Good Samaritan, for example, two people saw but passed by a man who had been beaten by robbers and left half dead in a ditch by the side of a road. Later, the Good Samaritan bandaged his wounds, took him to an inn, and paid for his care. Those who passed him by did nothing illegal by ignoring this helpless man. If they owed the man nothing but noninterference with the exercise of his rights, they could deny any obligation to help him out of the ditch because they did not push him into it. From that point of view, they could be seen as lacking charity but not as being unjust.

But they were unjust. Providing reasonable aid to the helpless man was not an option, it was an obligation. Concern for the man is rooted in claims of justice not love or compassion. Justice in that situation required more than not committing assault and battery. The dignity and rights inherent in the human person and needed for a fully human life are the bases for three correlative duties that must be performed if these rights are to be fully honored: (1) a duty to avoid depriving anyone of their rights; (2) a duty to protect people from being deprived of their rights; and (3) a duty to aid those who have been deprived of their rights.[42]

Those who passed by the injured man were unjust because they did not carry out their duty to aid the beaten man even though they had not beaten him and had not been there to protect him from being beaten. In other words, justice required that they not be indifferent to the man, saying, in effect, "you do not interest me"; not conduct themselves as if the man was not there; not pass him by as if he were a mere thing; and not negate his existence as a person. Human beings in need of help, moreover, do not have to be assaulted to be deprived of their life or health or capacity to enjoy other rights: "To be helpless they need only to be left alone."[43]

In sum, justice combines nonexploitation with taking up the cause of those who are treated unjustly. It requires more than recognition of and respect for the rights of others; it requires active engagement in securing these rights.[44] In Memphis, on the night before he was assassinated, Martin Luther King, Jr., used the Good Samaritan parable to explain why justice required support for the striking Memphis sanitation workers. Dr. King speculated that, because those who ignored the man may have feared that the robbers were still nearby or that the man was faking injury in order to trap them, the first question each asked himself was, "If I stop to help this man, what will happen to me?" The Good Samaritan, however, reversed the question: "If I do not stop to help this man, what will happen to him?" Dr. King explained:

> That's the question before you tonight. Not, "If I stop to help the sanitation workers, what will happen to all of the hours that I usually spend in my office every day and every week as a pastor?" The question is not, "If I stop to help this man in need, what will happen to me?" "If I do not stop to help the sanitation workers, what will happen to them?" That's the question.[45]

This is *social justice,* and it concerns rights and duties in a way that is both personal and communal. It ensures the welfare of the whole community by liberating each person from economic and social subjugation and submissiveness. Social justice calls for the establishment of a "brotherly city."[46]

Rousseau said kings never cared about the condition of their subjects because they never expected to share their lot. As an illustration, in Mark Twain's *A Connecticut Yankee in King Arthur's Court,* when Sir Boss was disguising King Arthur as a petty freeman so they could go about the country and experience the "humbler life of the people," Sir Boss' biggest problem was teaching the King to "imitate the trade-marks of poverty, misery, oppression, insult, and the other several and common inhumanities that sap the manliness out of a man and make him a loyal and proper and approved subject and a satisfaction to his masters."[47] When told he should address these poor people as brother, the King was indignant: "Brother—to dirt like that?"[48] King Arthur was of the highest economic and social class, and he was isolated and alienated from others.

Yet, once among the people who were suffering the horrors of a smallpox epidemic, the King became a brother:

> There was a slight noise from the direction of the dim corner where the ladder was. It was the king descending. I could see that he was bearing something in one arm, and assisting himself with the other. He came forward into the light; upon his breast lay a slender girl of fifteen. She was but half-conscious; she was dying of smallpox. Here was heroism at its last and loftiest possibility, its utmost summit; this was challenging death in the open field unarmed, with all the odds against the challenger, no reward set upon the contest, and no admiring world in silks and cloths of gold to gaze and applaud; and yet the king's bearing was as severely brave as it had always been in those cheaper contests where knight meets knight in equal fight and clothed in protecting steel. He was great now; sublimely great. The rude statues of his ancestors in this place should have an addition—I would see to that; and it would not be a mailed king killing a giant or a dragon, like the rest, it would be a king in commoner's garb bearing death in his arms that a peasant mother might look her last upon her child and be comforted.[49]

The idea of brotherhood is often held in contempt as soft-headed. But the brotherhood of social justice is surely not "feel goodism." On the contrary, those who practice brotherhood, the otherness aspect of justice, do so knowing that in the end the world will break their hearts.[50] Love without justice is sentimentality just as justice without love is arid, inflexible, and contentious legalism. However, if social justice has to be practical to be accepted, then as Judith Shklar has written, it should be realized that "we do ensure our own future by demanding the rights of others for the possibilities of violations are universal."[51]

Injustice to others is a threat to each of us. In the memorable words attributed to Pastor Martin Niemoeller:

> In Germany they came first for the Communists, and I didn't speak up because I wasn't a Communist. Then they came for the Jews, and I didn't speak up because I wasn't a Jew. Then they came for the trade unionists and I didn't speak up because I wasn't a trade unionist. Then they came for the Catholics and I didn't speak up because I was Protestant. Then they came for me and by that time no one was left to speak up.[52]

Unfortunately, when some people are doing reasonably well for themselves, they forget their own vulnerabilities and become passive beholders of the humiliation of others. They are complacent about injustice when it is not inflicted on them. In other words, they choose peace with injustice. A commonly offered excuse or dodge is that life is unfair, a fatalistic evasion that redefines injustice as unavoidable misfortune—in effect, bad luck. The difference between misfortune and injustice, Shklar writes, "frequently involves our willingness and our capacity to act or not to act on behalf of the victims, to blame or absolve, to help, mitigate, and compensate, or to just turn away."[53] If we can prevent or oppose wrongs but are simply indifferent and do nothing, we contribute to injustice. This passive injustice goes beyond the usual legalistic or adjudicatory model that defines injustice as the violation of established rules by actively unjust people. It recognizes that the inactive or passive contribute to injustice by turning away from actual and potential victims letting matters take their course.

Labor lawyer Thomas Geoghegan writes in his book *Which Side Are You On?* that he saw a group of Korean women carrying picket signs in his Chicago neighborhood and learned he had been living next to a cramped windowless sweatshop employing Latino, Filipino, and Korean women. As he put it, "We passed them all the time and didn't even notice." The women had been fired. On his way to work each day, he and the condo owners on the Elevated platform above would look down on them with compassion, but all knew "that the women below were doomed." Geoghegan concluded: "There is just Big Business, Big Labor, and the Rest of Us. And the Rest of Us are like the Swiss, we are morally neutral with our Swiss passports. A strike even in our neighborhoods is none of our business."[54] When others' rights are being violated, moral neutrality is passive injustice.

By the end of that summer, the Korean women were no longer there, and Geoghegan never saw them again: "They probably have jobs now in other sweatshops, and they will never try this union stuff again."[55] That is one of the hidden but most pernicious consequences of passive injustice: that those suffering injustice will do nothing about it because they are afraid to stand up alone with no support from others. This means, as Shklar says, "we may never really know the extent of both the injustices and the sense of injustice that prevail among us. Much is silent, forgotten, or locked away, which allows us to resign ourselves to them."[56]

Understanding that doing nothing can contribute to injustice makes it clearer that the answer to Rabbi Hillel's third question—"If not now, when?"—is, "when they need it."[57] Rabbi Hillel's three questions, therefore, are actually one because a just person cannot say: for part of my life I will think only of myself, and I will be concerned about others only when I can get around to it. Justice, therefore, addresses not only the rights of each individual but also the duties of all to respect, protect, and advocate the rights of others. Justice is both personal and communal but community without individual rights is tyranny. The moral end of justice is human welfare—the welfare of *all* people.

Finally, "active justice"[58] requires us to use our power and ability to prevent wrongs being done to others. It is, as was said at the outset, the justice that looks into the faces of those suffering and requires more than the application of impersonal rules. Active justice is neither blind nor impassive and goes beyond established rules in the cause of human rights. It requires greatness.

Fights over rights are, at their core, fights over the redistribution of power. Discussions of justice rarely give adequate attention to the vital fact of power and the nearly implacable opposition between the demands of human rights and the determination of those holding power not to relinquish any of it. The demand for participation, for example, is one that most threatens to diffuse and limit power. Although might does not make right, it does take might to get right done. Power is needed to move active justice from talk to action where it can actually influence conduct and cause change.

To be more than pious talk, human rights must be protected by the rule of law and made enforceable through public and private institutions such as legislation, judicial and administrative agency decisions, and collectively bargained contracts between employers and representatives of their employees. In today's world that requires fundamental social and economic changes that would reach to the foundations of a society, a government, an economic system, and worker-employer relationships. Human rights constitute what has been called "a particular moral vision of human potentiality"; that is, not just living but a "dignified life, a life worthy of a human being."[59] The requirements for a fully human life are set forth "in the form of rights."[60] That vision and the rights associated with it clash with many other visions and their associated rights. The resolution of those clashes of visions and rights requires choices among alternatives. Those choices at their core are more moral choices than they are economic or political or cultural. That is why it is essential to identify and examine the values that underlie those moral choices.

Simply put, *values* as used in these essays are personal or societal conceptions of the way things ought to be. They prescribe and proscribe. They are beliefs that certain means and ends of action are desirable or undesirable. Values are used in many ways: to judge our own conduct and the conduct of others; to persuade, propagandize, or rationalize; or to control or manipulate the conduct of others. For the purposes of this book, the focus will be on values as guides for choices among alternatives and as principles underlying decision making in regard to clashes of rights at workplaces.

The sharply conflicting conceptions of workplace rights and justice and their consequences cannot be fully understood without exploring the values that underlie each. More specifically, the decision-making process—whether judicial, administrative, or arbitral—cannot be fully understood without addressing the influence of underlying values, particularly conceptions about the nature of the rights and power relationship between employers and workers. The standards of judgment these decision makers use will reveal, among other things, whether they see the workplace through the eyes of employees on the shop floor, in offices, or in classrooms—in dirty, dangerous, demanding, and demeaning jobs—or from the perspective of those who control and manage those enterprises. There is an important subjective element to the nature of the policy-making and decision-making processes. The key is to identify the values underlying these choices, to assess their influence, to determine who is benefited and who is burdened by those choices and what those choices say about the worth of the individual human being and our obligations to each other. The choices made will determine the nature of the lives people will be able to live. In other words, those choices will determine what kind of people we are and what kind of society we want to have.

In the *Grapes of Wrath,* a tenant farmer is bulldozed off his land by a driver who is just as poor and helpless as he is but desperate for the three dollars he is earning to feed his children. The two tried unsuccessfully to determine whom or what to blame for what was happening to them. As his shack was being crushed, the tenant shouted, "We all got to figure. There's some way to stop this. It's not like lightening or an earthquake. We've got a bad thing made by men, and by God that's something we can change."[61]

The chapters that follow will examine some of the "bad things" made by men in the world of work and business and will propose human rights, particularly workers' rights as human rights, as the way to prevent unjust suffering and to promote the justice required to live a fully human life.

2

"Without Distinction of Any Kind"

Race and Human Rights in the United States

On March 7, 1965, the nation witnessed on television Alabama State Troopers clubbing, bullwhipping, teargassing, and riding horses into peaceful civil rights demonstrators marching from Selma, Alabama, to the state's capital in Montgomery. They heard Sheriff Jim Clark shouting, "Get those goddamed niggers" and "Get those goddamed *white* niggers." For some reason, the events of that Bloody Sunday, as it came to be known, were less tolerable to an American public that previously had read of and seen beatings of demonstrators, unleashing of attack dogs on them, and driving them back and punishing them with gushing water shot from high-pressure hoses. John Lewis, a civil rights leader and badly beaten demonstrator at that now historic atrocity at the Edmund Pettis Bridge, speculated that these events touched a deeper nerve because the injustice was so clear and unambiguous: a malevolent force of heavily armed, hate-filled state troopers rolling over and into lines of "stoic, silent, unarmed people."[1]

President Lyndon Johnson added Selma, Alabama, to Lexington and Concord, Massachusetts, as turning points "in man's unending search for freedom." He told the people of the United States that the issue of equal rights for "American Negroes" was an issue that laid "bare the secret heart of America itself."

He also told them that they would have failed as a people and as a nation, even if "we defeat every enemy and should double our wealth and conquer the stars," if those equal rights were not respected and enforced.[2] Johnson placed an obligation on all the people to achieve that human equality: "It is all of us who must overcome the crippling legacy of bigotry and injustice." He concluded with the words of the demonstrators' anthem: "We shall overcome."[3]

Race mattered in this country long before Bloody Sunday, and it still matters today. Invidious discrimination—treating another human being as if they are less than fully human or as if they do not matter or are less worthy of consideration unless they can be used—strikes at the heart of the human rights conception that *every* life is sacred. There are no throw-away people in a human rights–based society. The doctrine of racial superiority also denies the unity of rights concept and the interconnectedness of all persons in the human community, particularly when it becomes the basis for the distribution of benefits and burdens in a society.

The white supremacy doctrine in action read blacks out of the human race. It was and continues to be a crime against humanity among the greatest of all moral wrongs. Human rights are moral rights that all persons possess because they are human. Human rights are rooted in the conviction that every human being is sacred and that because every human being is sacred "certain things ought not to be done to any human being and certain other things ought to be done for every human being."[4] At a minimum, human rights mean that every human being is entitled to whatever is necessary to develop one's capacities fully and to live life as a human being. No individual, group, business, or other institution or organization and no government ought to be permitted to have the power to decide to refuse or to grant human rights.[5]

The greatest evil and greatest human rights violation resulting from the racial superiority doctrine is its destruction of the human spirit. The United Nations (UN) International Bill of Human Rights—the Universal Declaration of Human Rights (UDHR; Articles 1 and 2)[6] and the International Covenants on Civil and Political Rights (ICCPR; Article 2)[7] and Economic, Social and Cultural Rights (ICESCR, Article 2)[8]—use identical language in affirming that "everyone" is entitled to the rights set forth in those documents "without distinction of any kind, such as race, colour, sex, language, religion, political or other opinion, national or social origin, property, birth or status."

The Declaration of Philadelphia annexed to the Constitution of the International Labour Organization (ILO) also affirms that "all human beings irrespective of race, creed or sex, have the right to pursue both their material well-being and their spiritual development in conditions of freedom and dignity, of economic security and equal opportunity."[9] ILO Convention 111,[10] condemning discrimination in employment and occupation, references the UDHR and the Declaration of Philadelphia in its detailed provisions intended to eliminate any discrimination in employment.

The denial of human rights on racial grounds in this country is not caused by impersonal forces beyond anyone's control or by bad luck. It has been caused by deliberate moral choices by many public and private groups and institutions. It was and is active injustice when the choice was and is to violate the human rights of black men, women, and children; it was and is passive injustice when the choice was and is to accommodate those violations or not to resist them in any way.

In 1965, Bloody Sunday was the latest manifestation of the doctrine of white superiority that had been in the heart of America since its beginning. Race has always mattered in this country in the distribution of the society's benefits and burdens, and it continues to matter. Before the Civil War Alexis de Tocqueville, a now famous French observer of democracy in America who traveled the country in the 1830s, wrote that nothing struck him "more forcibly than the general equality of condition among the people." He explained, however, that he meant equality among white people because "almost insurmountable barriers had been raised" between them and Native Americans and 'Africans.'" De Tocqueville, who was white, commented, "It is difficult for us, who have the good fortune to be born among men like ourselves by nature and our equals by law, to conceive of the irreconcilable differences that separate the Negro from the European in America." The oppression of slavery, he reported, had "at one stroke, deprived the descendants of the Africans of almost all the privileges of humanity."[11]

One hundred years later, Swedish economist Gunnar Myrdal in An *American Dilemma*,[12] his classic study of "the Negro in America," found that whites had continued to maintain those barriers between themselves and blacks, no longer through slavery but through systems of segregation and separation rigorously enforced by law, social sanctions, and violence. The objective was to keep black people in their "place" based on doctrines and assumptions espousing the inequality of certain human beings. Myrdal concluded that America was caught in a moral dilemma between its practice of (and tolerance of) this racial superiority doctrine and the nation's professed ideals of the dignity of the individual human being, the fundamental equality of all people, and inalienable rights to freedom and justice.

Almost twenty-five years later, President Lyndon Johnson appointed a National Commission on Civil Disorders (the Kerner Commission) to investigate the race riots that had erupted in New York, Los Angeles, Newark, and Detroit between 1966 and 1967. The Kerner Commission's core conclusion was that "our nation is moving toward two societies, one black, one white—separate and unequal." The Commission also concluded that white society was "deeply implicated" in the creation of racial ghettos: "White institutions created it, white institutions maintain it, and white society condones it." The Commission warned that unless there was "compassionate, massive and sustained" national action that made good on the promises inherent in the ideals of American society, the present course would lead to continuing polarization and the destruction of basic democratic values.[13]

Although in the next twenty years African Americans and their supporters engaged in massive direct actions to resist segregation and to refuse to abide discrimination, a distinguished group of experts that composed a nongovernmental 1988 Commission on the Cities found that the nation had ignored the conclusions and recommendations of the Kerner Commission. The consensus was that race remained what one of the experts called "the most basic divider in our cities" and that ghettoized black families had become even more separated and their already poverty-ridden conditions had further deteriorated. The Commission acknowledged that some African Americans had worked their way into the middle class but that, despite the urging of the Kerner Commission, no national commitment had been made to the creation of a "true union" that would fulfill its pledge of equality and provide social justice for all.[14]

In fact, the nation has ignored the findings and recommendations of the Kerner Commission—civil rights have vanished from national politics despite still-pervasive separation. Separate but unequal societies based on concepts of racial superiority and inferiority existed in this country even before the forced importation of blacks as slaves. At its core, this is a moral issue. No economic progress alone, even if more widespread and more substantial, can touch that moral core.

The professed principles of the "American Creed"—the essential dignity and equality of all people and inalienable rights to freedom, justice, and fair opportunity—are moral principles that constitute the ideological foundation of the nation. Although these humane ideals existed long before the United States, they have become the national conscience. The Creed is also the basis for the realization of the "American Dream," which in addition to being a dream of wealth has also "been a dream of being able to grow to fullest development as a man and woman" to benefit "the simple human being of any and every class." These are the moral promises of America.[15]

Yet, in a monstrous and immoral inconsistency—even as these promises were being written into the Declaration of Independence—white Americans had claimed for themselves alone the rights of liberty, equality, and justice. In matters of race in particular the ideals of the Creed were sacrificed when they conflicted with selfish pragmatism. The Constitution itself was a monument to pragmatic politics when in return for national union it defined a slave as three-fifths of a man thereby confirming slavery as permissible and slaves as less than fully human.

The claim that blacks were an inferior race, a separate species, became the moral apology for an institution of human inequality in a society that professed equality based on the inalienable rights of *all* men. The Creed's equality of opportunity, moreover, was twisted into the "separate but equal" justification for segregation. From the beginning of this country, therefore, human inequality was the cornerstone not only for subsequent rules of law but also for a way of life that removed blacks from the mainstream and put whatever abstract rights they were granted at the mercy of the white majority. Black men and women had no rights that white men and women were bound to respect.

Instead of moral revulsion to the basest violations of the human rights of black men and women, however, the nation instituted and practiced state-enforced segregation as a badge of servitude and inferiority and cruel evidence of man's inhumanity to man.[16] After the end of slavery, equality for the freedmen and -women was a much more revolutionary objective than obtaining their freedom.[17] To live fully human lives, ex-slaves needed more than emancipation; they needed land and economic assistance, education, voting rights, full civil liberties, and the end of discrimination against them. Instead, Americans, with the support of the nation's Supreme Court, legislated blacks into an isolated corner of society and, by continuing to deny them their human rights, kept them "in their place."[18]

The Supreme Court's 1896 decision in *Plessy v. Ferguson*[19] did not initiate this racial ostracism, but the value choices made by the majority in that case and the language used to justify those choices granted whites state-sanctioned permission to hate blacks.[20] Before *Plessy*, the Supreme Court had ruled that private railroad companies had a right under the common law to require separate but equal coaches for "the white and colored races."[21] The issue in *Plessy* was whether the Constitution of the United States prohibited the state of Louisiana from enforcing the same racial separation.

The *Plessy* Court distinguished between political equality, which it acknowledged the Fourteenth Amendment to the U.S. Constitution was intended to enforce, and social equality which it asserted the Fourteenth Amendment could not have been intended to enforce because racial segregation was "in the nature of things." Consequently, the Court said that the state of Louisiana was free to act on the basis of "established usages, customs, and traditions of the people and with a view to the promotion of their comfort and the preservation of the public peace and good order." The Court was concerned not only with the comfort of racial separatists. In a classic example of blaming the victim, it denied the charge that enforced segregation of blacks from whites pinned a badge of inferiority on blacks with a dismissive, "If this be so, it is not by reason of anything found in the [Louisiana] act, but solely because the colored race chooses to put that construction upon it."[22]

The lone dissenter, Justice Harlan, understood that the "seeds of race hate" were being "planted under the sanction of law" by permitting "a dominant race"—a self-designated superior class of citizens—"by sinister legislation" to put "the brand of servitude and degradation" on blacks under the "thin disguise of 'equal' accommodation."[23] As Harlan feared, the seeds of hate that were fertilized by the Supreme Court grew well beyond separate accommodations on railroads and well beyond the South into the North as blacks migrated there. The southern way was spreading as the American Way in race relations, although it took on more sub rosa forms outside the South except when it exploded in race riots in major cities.[24] The violations of the human rights of blacks was not peculiar to the South.

White power over blacks was enforced in many ways, not least of which was the constant threat of physical violence that permeated white-black relations. Lynching was the ultimate violent act used to remind blacks of their inferiority and their place and the cheapness of their lives. Lynching was a renunciation of blacks' humanity and human rights. The ritual horrors of lynching—a farcical judicial process, compliant law enforcement, burning the victim as he hung, cutting off his body parts for souvenirs, and often dragging the burned and mutilated body through the streets—were intended to intimidate and control through terror.[25] White superiority was imposed not only by mobs but also by individuals on an everyday basis. Writing about Jim Crow segregation laws and customs, historian C. Vann Woodward pointed out:

> The Jim Crow laws put the authority of the state or city in the voice of the street car conductor, the railway brakeman, the bus driver, the theater usher, and also into the voice of the hoodlum of the public parks and playgrounds.[26]

Separation enforced by law or custom was so pervasive that even churches that taught brotherly love and equality before God either maintained separate benches for blacks or totally excluded them[27] despite the glaring and hypocritical gap between the professed Christian creed and the practice of caste. Blacks in the

U.S. armed forces in World War II to fight against Hitler's doctrines of Aryan superiority had to serve in racially segregated units. Housing was ghettoized, and public schools segregated. Segregation at work meant no employment at all for blacks, relegation to unskilled and menial "Negro jobs," or elaborate arrangements at work to keep blacks separate from whites: separate toilet facilities, drinking water, eating areas, even separate work areas. Segregation permeated all aspects of life and death: soda fountains, bars, parks, amusement parks, playgrounds, bathing facilities and swimming areas, race tracks, theaters, barber shops, baseball parks (and professional baseball itself), interracial boxing matches, street cars, and buses, waiting rooms for bus and train passengers, public transportation, and cemeteries. When the Lincoln Memorial was dedicated in the nation's capital, blacks were put in a "special section far off from the platform and across the road."[28]

Segregation is partly economic, partly political, partly religious, partly psychological, and partly social but because all of it is rooted in grounds of black inferiority, it is interrelated and all of one piece. It is all a vicious circle wherein inadequate education, jobs, income, health care, housing, sewage, and garbage removal, street paving, police protection, disenfranchisement, and inequalities in the justice system combine to keep pushing people further down. The vicious circle is completed when the deleterious results of separation on blacks are used as reasons to justify not wanting to associate with them and to rationalize superiority to them.

The greatest evil of any racial superiority doctrine with all its cruelty and bigotry is its destruction of the human spirit. It wounds the soul, sometimes mortally: "Tell [a] race in books, in law, in courts, in education, in church and school, in employment, in transportation, in hotels and motels, in the government, that it is inferior—it is bound to leave its damaging mark upon the souls and minds of the segregated."[29] That is what makes the implementation of the doctrine of racial superiority a violation of the most fundamental human rights. When the Supreme Court decided in 1954 in *Brown v. Board of Education*[30] that the separate educational facilities in the public school systems were inherently unequal and deprived children of equal educational opportunities, Chief Justice Warren spoke directly to the core evil:

> To separate them from others of similar age and qualifications solely because of their race generates a feeling of inferiority as to their status in the community that may affect their hearts and minds in a way unlikely ever to be undone.[31]

The effects of the evil of white supremacy have not been undone. Although black men, women, and children eventually could no longer be set apart lawfully from other human beings in this country, state-sanctioned segregation was only a part of a whole system that has been built and maintained to enforce racial separation in other ways. Although overt raw racism is no longer the accepted way, racism remains and segregation continues. Other than Native Americans on reservations, African Americans, are still the most ghettoized people in the United States with nearly one-half living in communities that are 90 percent or more black. But ghettoized means more than social separation. It also means educational, economic, social, and psychological isolation and exclusion as well.

There is more than ample evidence of the continuing presence of the white superiority doctrine, for example, in the violation of children's human rights. Many children in the United States are treated not only as if their lives are cheap and do not matter but also as if they are not members of the human race. It is an uncontested principle in the international law of human rights, for example, that all children have the right to an education that has as its objective the development of a child's talents, personality, and physical and mental capacities *"to their fullest potential."*[32]

Black children concentrated in the most poverty-stricken school districts in the country still receive an education that is separate and unequal, fifty years after the Supreme Court's decision in *Brown.* There are many reasons: black children are treated as inherently inferior intellectually; overcrowded classrooms; dilapidated and unsafe school buildings; out-of-date textbooks; overburdened teachers; unqualified teachers; and teachers and administrators who are disinterested or even hostile; and few preschool opportunities. Jonathan Kozol calls it "apartheid education" with schools separated racially and economically.[33]

Almost 140 years after Emancipation, many black children "went to school with some 'trust that they [were] going to be treated fairly' only to have their wills broken and their trust betrayed."[34] Thomas Sowell has written:

> Virtually every black child who has grown up in this country over the past 300 years has been told by word or deed that he is inferior intellectually and that the expectations of those around him are geared to his lack of capacity, that when he shows progress it is something of a fluke, and that when he persists in showing progress he is something of a freak.[35]

Instead of outrage at the devaluation of the lives of other people's children, there is rejection by the "more fortunate" of any attempt to extend more justly to others the opportunities they enjoy. The denial of the education that children need to live fully human lives is not a misfortune, it is an injustice. This denial is a violation of children's rights as human beings. This violation is not caused by uncontrollable forces or bad luck. Rather, it is caused by deliberate moral choices that underlie political and economic policy choices made by certain communities pursuing their own self-interest and the self-interest of their children. There is something brutal and selfish in this nation that permits human rights violations to be committed against these children with indifference to their plight.

There is no widespread moral revulsion in the nation against these violations of children's rights or any "public conviction that the most deadly of all possible sins is the mutilation of a child's spirit."[36] These children are being read out of the human race by treating them as disposable rather than as sacred human persons with human rights and human dignity. This, too, is among the greatest of all moral wrongs.

These are fundamental issues of human rights, morality, justice, and values. A just society, particularly one with the economic resources of the United States, would not choose to reject any of its children. A just society would treat each of its children as an unprecedented wonder and would be committed to enabling them to realize their potential for living a full human life. Kozol has asked, "How does a nation deal with those whom it has cursed."[37] Howell Raines in a 1991 Pulitzer Prize–winning essay asked, "How could we not have known—and how can we not know—the carnage of lives and minds and souls that is going on among young black people in this country today?"[38]

In general, the answers most commonly given today blame the victims for their plight. These children are at fault, not the educational, or political, or economic, or social systems. The twisted conclusion is that these children are a disease in an otherwise healthy and just society.[39] When little heroes succeed despite the manmade obstacles put in their way, this is used as evidence that anyone can do it if they are willing to work hard. Those who give this answer do not ask why so many black children should have to be heroic to achieve what other children have the opportunity to achieve without heroic efforts.[40] Blaming the victim ignores not only the denial of equal opportunity but also denial of access to the qualifications needed to take advantage of such opportunities when, and if, they become available.

There are those who maintain that since the end of legalized Jim Crowism, racism has become a thing of the past in this country and, except for bigots at the fringes, the United States has become a color-blind society. Consequently, continuing inequalities between whites and blacks are due to the voluntary individual choices of African Americans who choose not to take responsibility for their own lives. They choose instead to engage in antisocial and unproductive behavior such as having babies out of wedlock, committing crimes, and dropping out of school. Given the country's color-blindness, it follows, this argument goes, that all people will rise or fall according to their own individual efforts and abilities.[41]

The often-asked question why have blacks been unable to escape from poverty and the ghetto as European immigrants who were also subjected to discrimination and poverty have done contains its own implied answer: All people in this country can "better" themselves unless they are too lazy to make the effort. Again, the implication is that the fault is not in a system that promotes and tolerates white racial superiority, within those institutions that practice it, or in those individuals who live it but instead in black people themselves, who are said to be responsible for the conditions in which they find themselves.

Immigrants to this country confronted discrimination, poverty, abominable working conditions in unskilled and often unsafe and dangerous jobs, urban slum-living, isolation, alienation, loneliness, and hostility and rejection from dominant earlier-arriving immigrants who had declared themselves Americans. As serious and unjust as those obstacles were and continue to be for recent immigrants, in the words of historian C. Vann Woodward, those immigrants "never had anything approaching the handicaps against which the Negro had to struggle to gain acceptance."[42]

Millions of immigrants could and did become assimilated or "Americanized" by abandoning or disguising their distinguishing cultural peculiarities and ethnic characteristics and adopting and conforming to the ways of those dominant in the society. Blacks, however, have been kept permanent aliens in the United States by denying them assimilation because of their race. The implication of the question about comparative achievements is unfair because it ignores the temporary nature of the discriminatory impediments imposed on successive groups of white immigrants and the permanent nature of the racial caste system imposed on blacks. The permanency of the caste was due to doctrines of white superiority based in great part on "racial purity" and an associated fear of miscegenation. That racial doctrine denied to blacks the assimilation, intermarriage, social equality, and economic opportunity that immigrants used to overcome the handicaps imposed on them. As evil as all discrimination is, no type of discrimination in this country has matched the virulence and permanence of the discrimination against African Americans.

In answering such questions, therefore, the history of a willful public and private policy of segregation, exclusion, racial domination, and white privilege must not be ignored. When those humiliations and deprivations have their desired psychological (namely, low self-esteem, self-destructive and publicly destructive behavior, and limited or no aspirations) economic, political, and social effects, those effects are twisted into proofs of laziness, immorality, unreliability, shiftlessness, stupidity, ineptness, and anything else that "confirms" black people's overall inferiority.[43] As George Bernard Shaw wrote, "The haughty American Nation...makes the negro clean its boots and then proves the moral and physical inferiority of the negro by the fact that he is a boot black."[44]

It is undeniable that some African Americans have engaged in irresponsible, destructive, and even self-destructive behavior. To focus only on that individual behavior, however, is to ignore how the past affects the present. In other words, to ignore the cumulative effects of generations of discrimination is to be deliberately ahistorical.

The history of white superiority in this country, moreover, provides a deeper understanding not only of the current economic, political, and social state of people long denied their human rights but also of how that doctrine benefited whites—the color white "improved economic opportunities and life chances."[45] If affirmative action is defined as "race and gender preferences codified into law and enforced through public policy," then affirmative action was lawfully (and de facto) in effect for whites in this country for over 330 years.[46] That is a long time to accumulate wealth and other economic, political, educational, and social power and advantages. It was also a long time for black people to be subjected to economic, political, educational, and social powerlessness, disadvantage, and deprivation. It was a "system of pervasive white privilege"[47] that had powerful, wide-ranging benefits for whites and burdens for blacks, the consequences of which did not magically disappear with the Supreme Court's decision in *Brown v. Board of Education*[48] or the passage of the Civil Rights Act in 1964.[49]

Whiteness constituted the right to exclude and to deny the opportunity to accumulate assets:

> [Whites] have accumulated wealth, power, and opportunity at the expense of the people who have been designated as not white. In this sense, the experiences of white and nonwhite Americans are intimately connected. The benefits of being white are related to the costs of being nonwhite. That is why it makes more sense to analyze racism in terms of group position rather than in terms of the bigoted attitudes of individuals.[50]

The history of the racial superiority doctrine in this country also exposes as mythology white "boot strapping," a tale of individual triumphs over adversity without government support or handouts. Among many governmental programs that favored whites, the G.I. Bill of Rights (Servicemen's Readjustment

Act of 1944)[51] after World War II "underwrote a massive shift of white men from working class jobs into higher income professional and managerial occupations."[52] Black veterans that did benefit from the Bill faced segregated and low-level occupations across the labor market and a United States Employment Service that placed them in low-skilled jobs.[53]

The Federal Housing Administration (FHA) and the Veterans Administration (VA) financed almost one-half of the suburban housing built in the 1950s and 1960s. Whites and the suburbs were favored by an FHA policy that cautioned lenders that "If a neighborhood is to retain stability, it is necessary that properties shall continue to be occupied by the same social and racial classes." The FHA also instructed lenders "to add restrictive covenants to contracts and deals."[54] These federal housing policies and urban renewal policies maintained tightly segregated neighborhoods and caused disinvestment in black communities. In addition, federal redlining discouraged private investors from making housing or business loans in segregated black communities. As one author put it:

> The lack of loan capital flowing into minority areas made it impossible for owners to sell their homes, leading to steep declines in property values and a pattern of disrepair, deterioration, vacancy, and abandonment. This meant that white-owned housing was more valuable than black-owned housing and that the value of white-owned housing largely depended on public policies that created and sustained residential segregation.[55]

In addition, whites enjoying these state-sponsored benefits were also entitled to "America's major middle class tax subsidy: the mortgage interest deduction."[56] All of these government policies guaranteed to members of a growing white middle class that, with government assistance, they would accumulate considerable wealth to pass on to their children: "The best predictor of current net worth for young black and white families is their parents' net worth, a reflection of the legacy of white privilege in labor and housing markets and access to government handouts."[57] This is not a story "of individual triumphs in acquiring human capital and slogging unassisted up the ladder of success."[58]

The deplorable state of blacks in major cities today—an urban crisis—constitutes conclusive evidence that so many remain so poor because the consequences of the white superiority doctrine are ongoing:

> The urban crisis is jarringly visible in the shattered storefronts and fire-scarred apartments of Chicago's South and West Sides; the rubble-strewn lots of New

York's Brownsville, Bedford-Stuyvesant and South Bronx; the surreal vistas
of abandoned factories along the waterfronts and railways of Cleveland, Gary,
Philadelphia, Pittsburgh, and Saint Louis; the boarded-up and graffiti-covered
houses of Camden, Baltimore, and Newark. Rates of poverty among black res-
idents of these cities all range from 25 to 40 percent. With a few exceptions, all
have witnessed a tremendous loss in manufacturing jobs and the emergence of
a low-wage service sector. Almost all of these cities…'have large ghettos characterized by extreme segregation and special isolation.' The faces that appear in
the rundown houses, homeless shelters, and social agencies in these urban waste-
lands are predictably familiar. Almost all are people of color.[59]

This situation is not the result of inevitable, impersonal forces over which
no one had any control. It is not a matter of black workers simply being in the
wrong place at the wrong time. Rather, human choices made and not made
by employers, unions, federal, state, and local governments, and various other
groups and individuals ghettoized blacks long after official state-sanctioned
segregation had supposedly ended.

The roots of the contemporary economic situation of blacks in urban centers
are deep. They can be traced not only to slavery but also to the time immediately after Emancipation when the nation that had permitted the enslavement
of black men, women, and children left them without assistance or protection
in their search for livelihoods in a labor market system foreign to them. The
federal government within ten years of slavery's end chose for political reasons to abandon the Freedmen's bureau that was once described as "the most
extraordinary governmental effort at mass uplift in the nation's history" before
the New Deal.[60]

Instead of securing economic independence, ex-slaves, without land, tools,
job skills, education, or experience in the labor market were forced back into
economic peonage through sharecropping, tenant farming, and other debt- and
lien-creating systems that returned blacks to the control of whites. This was
done in ways supported by state laws that defended landlords' interests and
were enforced by physical intimidation and violence. Blacks had neither the
economic means nor the legal security to engage in entrepreneurship.

In the mid-1940s, Gunnar Myrdal in *An American Dilemma* called the economic situation of blacks "pathological" and termed "destitute" the condition
of "masses of Negroes" in the rural South and in the "segregated slum quarters" in northern and southern cities. Even when blacks who had migrated
to the North after World War I and during World War II acquired jobs in

manufacturing industries such as steel and automobile making, they were prohibited from becoming skilled workers much less foremen or supervisors or
office workers. A black business class (small grocery stores, undertakers, bar-
bershops, rooming houses, and beauticians) and profession class (preachers,
teachers, and lawyers) had developed. Ironically, they had a vested interest in
the continuation of racial segregation because they were excluded from any
white markets.[61]

By 1960, a majority of African Americans lived in northern cities where they
made inroads into manufacturing jobs in several major industries including the
automobile industry in Detroit. They found, however, that the doctrine of white
superiority was not a uniquely southern phenomenon. Consequently, they continued to bear more than their fair share of the burdens in economic bad times
and receive less than their fair share of the benefits in economic good times.

Although the jobs they obtained provided an income unattainable in the
South, they were jobs reserved for blacks: the meanest, dirtiest, and most dangerous, unskilled, dead-end jobs with no upward mobility and most vulnerable
to layoffs and elimination due to technology. Employers, focused on profitability and worker efficiency, excluded black workers for many reasons including presumptions of inefficiency and unreliability based on racial stereotypes
and fear that "race-mixing on the plant floor would cause white workers to
strike" or otherwise disrupt the workplace. The exclusion of blacks from retail
trade salespersons or counter clerks jobs was in part due to employer fear of
alienating white customers. Because women were the major customers of most
of these stores, a black man in a sales position defied the sexual conventions
so intimately interwoven with race. Consequently, jobs for blacks in retailing
were restricted to janitorial or stockroom laborer positions. Employers accommodated their hiring and job assignment decisions to the prevailing racial doctrines in- and outside their workplaces.[62]

As in most businesses, management in the automobile industry, for example, retained its absolute management prerogative to make all hiring decisions.
The powerful United Auto Workers (UAW) union represented the workers
in the industry's factories, a substantial number of whom were black workers.
The UAW did attempt to have antidiscrimination in hiring and promotion
provisions inserted into labor-management collective bargaining contracts but
was unwilling to force the issue and risk hard-won economic gains over an issue
that did not have widespread support among the union's white members.

Although the UAW at its national level worked actively on behalf of civil rights
causes and officially deplored racial discrimination within its organization, it

rarely interfered with its local unions that either acquiesced in or practiced racial discrimination. Both employers and unions, therefore, made preeminent their economic and institutional interests even when that required accommodation to violations of black workers' human rights.[63]

The UAW's decisions reflected many years of organized labor–black worker relations. The American Federation of Labor (AFL), for example, deliberately rejected the social reformist approach of earlier unions in favor of business unionism that concentrated on protection of the wages and job control of certain skilled trades and crafts. The triumph of the AFL signaled the end of aspirations of labor solidarity or industrial worker brotherhood. The economic self-interest of each craft union became the paramount value. It was the basis of a job consciousness or job control that limited the number of members admitted to the various trade unions and surrounded each job with a protectionist "web of rules." This was no toiling masses ideology.

Although the AFL officially opposed racial discrimination in the trade union movement, it refused membership to black workers. Many national unions affiliated with the AFL excluded black workers by constitutional provision, or limited their black membership to segregated or auxiliary local unions. Black workers in these segregated locals were supposed to be protected by the same national unions that claimed jurisdiction over their work but refused to admit them to membership. The AFL was a major accommodationist.

When the Congress of Industrial Organizations (CIO) split from the AFL in 1935, it organized the predominantly unskilled workers in the mass-production industries. Practical necessity dictated that it organize the substantial number of black workers already employed there. Although civil rights was a more important part of the CIO's philosophy, and it presented itself as being motivated by social idealism, its constituent unions never risked their institutional survival or the economic interests of the majority of their members to live up to those professed ideals. For example, when the CIO decided in 1954 that reunification with the AFL was necessary for its survival, it backtracked on several issues that had most sharply divided it from the AFL, including its active organizing of black workers.[64] Discrimination against black workers continued after the merger.

Prior to the merger in 1954, the AFL had expelled member unions that were "Communist-dominated" and other members unions that were "corrupt." In both cases, the Federation was responding to widespread and hostile public opinion and the threat of repressive labor legislation. The survival and growth of the Federation had been seriously threatened. The AFL responded differently, however, after the merger with the CIO when A. Philip Randolph, civil rights activist and president of the all-black Brotherhood of Sleeping Car Porters union, challenged AFL President George Meany to expel unions that barred black workers from membership and had racially segregated local unions. Meany and the AFL-CIO refused.[65] The violations of the human rights of black workers, unlike communists and corruption, did not pose a threat to the more important interests of the AFL-CIO.

For a brief moment in the early 1950s, after the deindustrialization of Detroit had begun, UAW Local Union 600 at Ford's River Rouge plant and the National Negro Labor Council challenged management's claimed inalienable property right to relocate plants and work as it wished. Their resistance was based on assertions not only of workers' right to work but also of management's corporate responsibility to its workers and the Detroit community. They rejected the traditional assumption that an employer's only, or at least greatest, obligation was to its shareholders.[66] A. Philip Randolph once said that property rights did not include the right to humiliate him because of the color of his skin and that the "sanctity of private property takes second place to the sanctity of the human personality."[67]

In the temperate words of a historian who studied Detroit's urban crisis, the UAW "was increasingly unwilling to challenge corporate leadership openly on controversial issues such as plant location policy and discriminatory hiring policy." He added, "The reluctance of the International (and most other unions) to challenge sacrosanct business practices limited the possibilities of resistance to deindustrialization."[68]

The consequent loss of manufacturing jobs in Detroit and other major cities hit the poorest, least skilled, and least educated workers hardest; namely, black workers and their families. This was no economic misfortune; it was the inevitable consequence of human choices to violate the human rights of black people or to accommodate those violations or not to resist them in any way. It was of one piece from slavery to Jim Crow separation doctrines; to state-sanctioned segregation in every aspect of human life; to separation enforced by public lynchings and other means of physical and psychological intimidation; to the denial of adequate health care and even a basic education; to consignment to "Negro jobs" and the denial of workplace rights, dignity, and economic opportunity by corporations, other businesses, and even unions that professed to promote and protect workers' rights; to the ghettoization of housing often enforced by violence, unsavory real estate practices, and neighborhood associations of ethnic working and middle-class whites who used "homeowners' rights" as a rallying cry to keep blacks out of their neighborhoods. (Consequently, today's city ghettos "have replaced Jim Crow as the most important contemporary source of racial poverty and isolation.")[69]

Many of these "homeowners' rights" people are the descendants of immigrants against whom blacks are compared unfavorably. These immigrants and their descendants have done their share of discriminating against others, especially blacks. In a current-day repeat of the "blame the victim" approach, they and people who believe as they do deplore "forced housing," "welfare queens," and black crime and have become a powerful conservative political force in opposition to school integration, spending on the "undeserving poor," and government-enforced affirmative action programs. The vicious circle has been completed once again. How ironic and morally twisted it is to contend that blacks' persistent poverty is "their own damn fault."

Not all whites are racists, and whites do not have a monopoly on racism. Brutality and compassion and honesty and dishonesty are found among all races, and not all blacks are long-suffering noble victims. Despite the focus of this essay on the violations of the fundamental human rights of black men, women, and children in this country, it is a fact that black people as a whole are better off politically, socially, and economically than they were in and immediately after slavery, during state-sanctioned segregation, before the civil rights protests of the 1960s and 1970s, and before subsequent governmental poverty and equal opportunity programs. More precisely, however, that progress has been made by what W. E. B. du Bois called the "Talented Tenth," those exceptional highly educated and skilled blacks whose advancement was most aided by affirmative action policies. That is why the subjects involved in the debates over affirmative action as well as in key court decisions concern admission to college, law school, and medical school and well-paid professional business or high-skilled jobs.

Does race still matter? Well, do whites want to be black or would they be indifferent to that possibility?[70] We all know which race is preferred by whites even if the choice is between being a less-well-off white or a much better-off black. Over one hundred years ago, one of Homer Plessy's attorneys in his brief to the Supreme Court maintained that "most white persons, if given a choice, would prefer death to life in the United States as a *colored person.*" He called whiteness the "most valuable sort of property, being the master key that unlocks the golden door of opportunity."[71]

Whiteness is still a treasured asset that provides advantages, privileges, and benefits that blackness does not.[72] White privilege has been described as "so woven into the unexamined institutional practices, habits of mind, and received truths that [white] Americans can barely see it," and it has created "one group's perspective [that] pervades almost everything from culture to law."[73] At the same time, whiteness is also a treasured aspect of self-identity that means inclusion in the dominant group regardless of one's economic or social class, power, money, or influence. In sum, "the advantage of being white is so extreme, so overwhelming, so immense, that to use the word 'advantage' at all is misleading since it implies a kind of parity that simply does not exist."[74] Understanding that is to understand racism as not limited to manifestations of a bigoted if not pathological hatred of blacks but as including "a system that normalizes, honors, and rewards whiteness."[75]

Neither economic nor political progress has changed what it means to be black in this country. August Wilson in his play, *Radio Golf,* has one of his characters express this fact pointedly:

> No matter what you always on the edge. If you go to the center and look up and find everything done shifted and the center is now the edge. The rules change every day. You got to change with them. After a while the edge starts to get worn. You don't notice it at first but you're fraying with it. Oh, no, look...We got a black mayor. We got a black CEO. The head of our department is black. We couldn't possibly be prejudiced. Got two hundred and fourteen people work in the department and two blacks but we couldn't possibly be race-conscious. Look, we even got a black football coach. You guys can sing. You can run fast. Boy, I love Nat King Cole. I love Michael Jordan. I just love him. We got a black guy who works in management. Twenty-four million blacks living in poverty but it's their fault. Look we got a black astronaut. I just love Oprah. How do you guys dance like that? After a while that center starts to go. They keep making up the rules as you go along. They keep changing the maps. Then you realize you're never going to get to that center. It's all a house of cards. Everybody resting on a slim edge. Looking back you can see it all. Wasn't nothing solid about it. Everything was an *if* and a *when* and a *maybe.*[76]

Economic and political progress, moreover, has not erased the scars inflicted by white superiority on all black people, even those who have progressed. For example, Maya Angelou, internationally respected poet, playwright, and author, recalled her childhood fantasy of becoming white because whites looked at her with "such loathing" when she walked in the white part of town.[77] She did not "shrivel up" as she often thought she might do but instead used her rage to "grit her teeth," straighten up, and keep going. She described how her pen still "scrapes across those scars." She also confessed that she was still unable to go "down inside to look at those scars" because she might "dissolve" because the "power of hate is almost as strong as the power of love."[78]

For every Maya Angelou, many more have had the life within them suppressed and have manifested their rage in ways different from the way she chose. Deliberately and systematically suppressing the life in black men, women, and children is and has been a crime against humanity. Is there no answer to it? In his "I Have a Dream" speech on the steps of the Lincoln Memorial in 1963, Martin Luther King, Jr., spoke of his dream "that one day this nation will rise up, live out the true meaning of its creed: 'We hold these truths to be self-evident, that all men are created equal.'"[79] In his "I've Been to the Mountaintop" remarks in 1968 on behalf of the Memphis sanitation workers the night before he was assassinated, Dr. King made it clear that "We are saying that we are determined to be men. We are determined to be people. We are saying that we are God's children. And that we don't have to live like we are forced to live."[80]

As King knew, economic and political progress alone cannot touch the immoral core of the white supremacy doctrine. It was during that strike that the black sanitation workers carried the powerful message on their picket signs: "I AM A MAN." Lyndon Johnson was right when he said that the issue of equal rights for black people in the United States was an issue that laid "bare the secret heart of America itself." He was also right when he told the American people that, no matter what progress they and the country made economically, or scientifically, or in world affairs, they would fail as a people and as a nation if equal rights for black men, women, and children were not respected and enforced. It has been forty years since Johnson's speech to the nation, and the human rights of black men, women, and children are still being violated. It is reasonable to ask, as a character in one of John Okada's books did, is "there no answer to the bigotry and meanness and smallness and ugliness of people?"[81]

Human rights for all black Americans can occur only when there is a moral revulsion[82] to the white supremacy doctrine and a commitment to the fundamental moral principle underlying human rights that *all* human beings are sacred.

3

The Market Economics Values underlying U.S. Labor Law

Property Rights over Workers' Rights

Every economic system and every legal system are sets of rules and regulations. Without agreement on rules, a civilized society presumably would degenerate into anarchy and the strong would take what they want from the weak. The fact is, however, that the strong do take from the weak even with economic and legal rules and regulations in place. That fact alone confirms that justice and legality are not necessarily synonymous. Justice demands, therefore, that we identify the values underlying all these rules and determine who is benefited and who is burdened by those rules and what those rules say about the worth of an individual human being and our obligations to each other.

Every economic system also embodies value judgments about the individual person, law, private property, liberty, and the role of government. The rules of any economic system are value-laden. Every economic system is also the embodiment of decisions about economic justice and economic rights. Because those rules have to be made and enforced by somebody or -bodies, power and conflict figure prominently in rule making and rule changing. It could not be otherwise because economics concerns choices about how scarce resources are going to be used to produce what goods and services and on what basis those goods and services will be distributed among individuals and groups in the society. In other words, economics is the study of who gets what and why. Its rules help determine the material welfare of mankind and, therefore, to a great extent determine what kind of life people will have.[1]

Yet, the neoclassical economics, more commonly known as free market economics, that is dominant in this country and increasingly around the world, attempts to hide its value judgments under the cover of what purports to be a science.[2] The abstract and mathematical aspects of this so-called science make it appear to be even more objective and morally neutral.[3] However, as one eminent economist acknowledged, "No other discipline attempts to make the world act as it thinks the world should act."[4] In fact, prescription dominates description in free market economics contrary to all other social sciences that study human behavior. The best example is classical economics' basic assumption that defines human behavior as rational only when a person acts to maximize his or her personal satisfaction (or income or utility). Each human being is an amoral, hedonistic, pleasure-maximizing, acquisitive animal—or, as preferred by economics, "homo economicus."

Every discipline that studies human behavior other than classical market economics has discovered that human motivation is complex. Individual economic self-interest is a motivation for human action, but it is hardly the only reason people do what they do in the economic world. People also act for self-esteem; duty; friendship; altruism; compassion; adventure; curiosity; habit; peer pressure; interdependence; coercive comparisons with others; ethnic, racial, religious, and cultural values; and even by mistake. Human choices, moreover, are the consequences of interaction between society and the individual.

Many years ago Swedish economist Gunnar Myrdal observed that "seldom in the history of mankind has a social philosophy been so naïve about its own psychological foundations as this one [classical market economics], whose honest pretension it was to be so enlightened and so rational."[5] If free market economics is understood for what it is, a political and social philosophy, then *homo economicus* is not naïve at all because the point of this value-laden system of economic thought is to prescribe for reality rather than to describe it. Classical economics has implications far beyond the realm of economic theory. As one economist put it, market economics is a political philosophy, "often becoming something approaching a religion."[6]

The real power of this economic, political, and social philosophy, therefore, is not in its ability to explain the real world. In other disciplines, for example, a theory is rejected or modified when it is inconsistent with reality. In a bizarre twist, classical market economics characterizes real world inconsistencies with its doctrine as market imperfections that should be eliminated to bring the real world into conformity with market theory. In other words, "the theory is always right." If that was the extent of it, it would amount to not much more than "playing in a sandbox of abstraction."[7]

The powerful influences of today's classical economics, however, lie in the values that undergird its philosophy. Those values, particularly in the United States, have become the articles of faith on which business has fashioned a creed justifying what it does, and in which lawmakers and judicial and quasi-judicial decision makers root their decisions. The general public, moreover, embraces these values because they believe them to be American values, consistently individualistic and consistently anticollectivist. The dominance of these values throughout most of U.S. history has had telling consequences for workers' rights and other issues of economic justice in this country.

The essential freedoms in this country have become free enterprise; private property; free trade; competition between and among consumers, workers, and business; all operating in a deregulated economy free of government "intrusion" where the invisible hand of competition provides the greatest good for the greatest number. When a society is dominated by the values of business, the economic system lays down the law to that society, which becomes subordinate to the laws of the market.[8]

The laws of the market are rooted in the basic philosophy that self-interest is what motivates people to act; that competition, not the state, is the regulator of self-interest; and that, consequently, it is necessary for the government to leave the market alone and not meddle in it because that invisible hand of competition will lead people in the direction of the best interests of the whole society. These are the very values and prescriptions that are accepted by much of the public in the United States as the essentials of freedom.

Advocates of this philosophy focus on the potential power of the state to suppress the freedom of individuals. They claim that men of manufacturing and commerce have "separated the economy from the state not only to unleash the power of individual imagination but to limit the state from within and to check it from without."[9] There is a moral choice being made here, and those who choose this laissez-faire economic philosophy "do not fear unrestrained economic power as much as they fear political tyranny."[10] In sum, it is modern conservatism: "the fear of the state, the elevation of individual liberty above all other values, [and] the insistence that personal freedom is inseparable from economic freedom."[11]

In 1944, in a best-selling book that many postwar conservatives treated as "a philosophical and even programmatic bible,"[12] Austrian economist Friedrich Hayek warned that submission to collectivism or "'conscious' direction of all social forces" rather than submission to the "impersonal and anonymous mechanism of the market" would (as his book was titled) be the *Road to Serfdom*.[13] He wrote:

> It was men's submission to the impersonal forces of the market that in the past has made possible the growth of a civilization which without this could not have developed; it is by this submitting that we are every day helping to build something that is greater than any one of us can fully comprehend.[14]

He went on to say that the refusal to yield to those impersonal forces

> …fails to see that unless this complex society is to be destroyed, the only alternative to submission to the impersonal and seemingly irrational forces of the market is submission to an equally uncontrollable and therefore arbitrary power of other men. In his anxiety to escape the irksome restraints which he now feels, man does not realize that the new authoritarian restraints which will have to be deliberately imposed in their stead will be even more painful.[15]

Because we are discussing values, rights, and justice, it is necessary to question why any human being should submit to either political tyranny or to the allegedly impersonal forces of the market. It needs to be made clear, moreover, that the choice is not between governmental involvement or no governmental involvement. No economic system can function without rules: "Without governmental regulation there are no property rights and without property rights there is no free market."[16] Even laissez-faire has to be enforced by the state. If private property limits the power of the state as some market advocates maintain, the irony is that those property rights depend on the government for their promotion, protection, and enforcement.

A market society serves the market economic system not only by protecting property but also by maintaining law and order, providing national and civil defense, constructing public works, and providing a legal framework to facilitate and implement the system (e.g., to enforce contracts). A market society also serves the market system by inculcating moral and cultural values such as self-restraint, hard work, respect for authority, discipline, thrift, and acquisitiveness. A free market economy, in other words, requires a substantial amount of government involvement. There is objection to only certain kinds of government involvement in the market economy, therefore, depending on who is benefited and who is burdened.

The antiregulatory free market doctrine seized on by business for obvious reasons maintains, moreover, not only that if left alone the market can best deal with economic problems but also that government intervention is either the cause of the problem or will make things worse. There are many alleged examples, such as claims that occupational safety and health regulations increase production costs, reduce productivity, and do nothing to improve safety and health; environmental regulations increase costs, decrease productivity, and cause unemployment; regulations to protect consumers not only increase costs but violate their freedom of choice; minimum wage laws and some other forms of protective labor legislation, by increasing employers' costs, increase unemployment particularly among the least skilled and poorest paid; and social welfare programs cause dependence and destroy self-reliance and incentives to work. These regulatory programs and others like them are said to require high taxes that discourage individual and corporate productivity and a huge government bureaucracy that by its nature is wasteful and inefficient.[17]

The free market philosophy, harnessing the value of individualism exalted by mainstream U.S. society, installed the individual consumer as sovereign rather than the state and made consumption, rather than state power, the objective of economic activity. Those satisfaction-maximizing, never-satiated individuals, by voting with their dollars, would determine what would be produced; in other words, for what purposes scarce land, labor, and capital would be used. Even ignoring the power of advertising to create consumer demand, reality once again dispels the apparent democratic, almost populist, appeal of that concept of consumer sovereignty because it is in reality not a one-person, one-vote system. Obviously, some consumers wield a disproportionate power because they have many more dollar votes than others, some of whom have very few or no votes. This weighted voting system means not only that some are benefited and some are burdened by this unequal power to influence economic decisions about the use of scarce resources but also that those who have greater power in the economic system are doubly benefited because this economic power "can be used to buy political power to change the rules of the economic game"[18] to their even greater benefit. The separation of economics and politics is only in theory, not in fact. Even taken at face value, therefore, this economic philosophy that purports to make the individual person paramount and free of domination by the state is inherently undemocratic.

The competitive market philosophy ignores the reality of power and conflict because, purportedly, rigorous competition would drastically limit the exercise of private economic power and thereby eliminate the possibilities for its misuse. No business would be large enough to influence prices in the market or to harm consumers or suppliers or the wages or physical well-being of workers. As John Kenneth Galbraith pointed out over fifty years ago, "To minimize the exercise of private power, and especially the opportunity for its misuse, was to remove most of the justification for the exercise of government authority over the economy."[19]

There is another powerful implication of this philosophy that denies even the existence of economic justice or injustice. The each-versus-all individualism that drives the free market approach to life induces people to be preoccupied with their own private self-interests and, ultimately, to accept even the harsh economic and social consequences of the market as the inevitable results of impersonal forces beyond their control or comprehension. The claim that the market system is impersonal makes it more plausible to argue that the market can be neither just nor unjust. This is because the market's apportionment of benefits and burdens is supposedly the result, not of some person's or group's deliberate allocation of income and wealth to particular people, but of the interaction of a multitude of circumstances not known in their totality to anyone or controlled by anyone. The consequences for people in the system, therefore, are neither intended nor foreseen. It is absurd, the argument goes, to demand justice of such a process because there is no answer to the question of who has been unjust. There is no individual group of people against whom a sufferer (or loser) would have a just complaint. In fact, justice and injustice are not only allegedly irrelevant but, in the words of a foremost advocate of free market theory, "'social justice' is simply a quasi-religious superstition."[20] Here is the complete separation of ethics from economics.

Exponents of this free market approach also claim that it maximizes individual liberty. Given the nature of the free market, the bad things that happen to individuals in their working lives are merely misfortunes beyond anyone's control. The unfortunate, however, are perfectly free to go where things are better—and they will, we are assured, because we are all rational satisfaction maximizers. If an individual does not respond to market "incentives," then that individual and no one or nothing else is to blame. In other words, the fault cannot lie with the functioning of the economic system itself, the power structure of the society, or the unfairness of the distributions of the society's benefits and burdens. Finally, government regulation only restrains the freedom of individual employers and employees and prevents the market from producing and allocating most efficiently and from achieving the greatest public good.

The economic and social philosophy of laissez-faire economics is, therefore, an elaborate and interconnected set of values in which *freedom* is the economic freedom of the entrepreneur; *democracy* is a governmental system that gives maximum protection to property rights; *progress* is economic growth; *individualism* means the right to use one's property as one desires and to compete with others; and *society* is a market society that promotes and does nothing to interfere with the competition in which the fittest win out. This is at best a utopian view of freedom and at worst a deliberately misleading one. No society of any sort is possible without power and compulsion. Unrestricted private enterprise can violate human freedom as effectively as any state. Freeing property from state control does not free ordinary people from the tyranny of property[21] or the tyranny of being left alone when in need of help. Why object to the power of the state to coerce individuals but not to employers' explicit powers over individuals' lives or to the implicit coercive power of the free market?[22] Inactive government also tolerates, if not encourages, gross inequalities of social status and wealth so that life, liberty, and the pursuit of happiness become matters not of justice and rights but of economic fortune.[23]

Regulation both extends and restricts freedom; only the balance of the freedoms won and lost is significant. Karl Polyani said this about the reaction of what he called the "comfortable classes" to regulation:

> They are naturally less anxious to extend freedom in society than those who for lack of income must rest content with a minimum of it. This becomes apparent as soon as compulsion is suggested in order to more justly spread out income, leisure and security. Though restriction applies to all, the privileged tend to resent it, as if it were directed solely against themselves. They talk of slavery, while in effect only an extension to the others of the vested freedom they themselves enjoy is intended. Initially, there may have to be reduction in their own leisure and security, and, consequently, their freedom so that the level of freedom throughout the land shall be raised. But such a shifting, reshaping and enlarging of freedoms should offer no ground whatsoever for the assertion that the new condition must necessarily be less free than was the old.[24]

In other words, "regulation and control can achieve freedom not only for the few, but for all."[25] Consequently, to turn against regulation is to turn against reform so that the idea of freedom

> denigrates into a mere advocacy of free enterprise.... This means the fullness of freedom for those whose income, leisure and security need no enhancing, and a mere pittance of liberty for the people [trying] to make use of their democratic rights to gain shelter from the power of the owners of property.[26]

Because there can be no economy, market-driven or otherwise, without government, the issues are not whether there should be regulation or no regulation but how much and what kind of regulation and who is benefited and burdened by that regulation. Every society governs itself and develops systems of law for social control "to keep the peace, settle disputes and suppress deviance."[27]

The basic foundation of law, whether made by legislators or judges, is moral choice. The choice of an economic or labor policy is more than a choice among conflicting interests and varying degrees of power among interest groups. At their core, these are choices of values: about justice and human and civil rights; about the worth of individuals and their right to participate collectively in decisions that affect their lives and the lives of their families and communities; about how and on what basis the benefits and burdens of work and business will be apportioned; and about how power, freedom, and equality are or are not harmonized with justice at workplaces.[28]

The orthodox doctrine of the rule of law, particularly when commonly expressed as "a government of laws and not of men," was (and apparently still is in some quarters) that judges do not create law but merely discover pre-existing legal rules and principles and apply them to new situations.[29] Just as there are supposedly impersonal, objective, scientific, and unalterable laws of economics, so too, in this conception of justice, coldly impersonal and objective judges speak the words of an objective truth "which they have no choice except to utter."[30]

The problem with this theory is that in practice judges are human beings. As former Supreme Court Justice Benjamin Cardozo said of himself and his fellow judges, "We may try to see things as objectively as we please. Nonetheless, we can never see them with any eyes except our own."[31] "Below this consciousness," Cardozo identified other forces influencing judicial decision-making: "the likes and the dislikes, the predilections and the prejudices, the complex of instincts and emotions and habits and convictions, which make the man whether he be litigant or judge."[32] The lesson to be learned, Cardozo said, is that "the whole subject matter of jurisprudence is more plastic, more malleable, the molds less definitely cast, the bounds of right and wrong less preordained and constant" than the doctrine of the rule of law had led people to believe.[33]

He concluded that there are few rules but mainly "standards and degrees." Cardozo attributed "a certain lack of candor" in the reluctance to discuss subjectivity in judicial decision-making to a fear that judges would lose respect and confidence if it were admitted that they were subject to human limitations.[34] Recognition of judicial discretion and the influence of personal values in decision-making choices among applicable sets of principles does not mean that there is a government of people who can do whatever they choose to do. There are limits to a judicial or quasi-judicial decider's discretion. The clearer and more comprehensive the statutory, regulatory, or contractual language at issue, the less latitude for the exercise of subjective choice. Conversely, judicial or quasi-judicial discretion is at its greatest in cases involving ambiguous language and in situations where the statute, regulation, or contract is silent concerning the matter in dispute. In those situations, more than one outcome is legally possible. In every case, however, some exercise of discretion or activism is unavoidable. In varying degrees, therefore, judges, administrative agencies, and arbitrators make law whenever they decide a dispute because they must choose among conflicting alternatives.[35]

Common law judges, for example, were powerful forces in the major transformation of the legal and economic systems that took place after the American Revolution. It was a transformation that "enabled emergent entrepreneurial and commercial groups to win a disproportionate share of the wealth and power in American society."[36] Common law is a system of judge-made law consisting of the accumulated decisions of courts rather than legislative enactments. The central role of these common law judges in the nineteenth century contrasts sharply with the far lesser influence of legislation in this country's earliest labor history. Both the early legislation and the subsequent common law, however, served the needs of the market economy and were consistent with the market economy's underlying values.

For the first two centuries of U.S. history, there was a severe shortage of labor in a land of otherwise plentiful resources. Colonial governments encouraged immigration to increase the pool of competent labor and developed two systems for the control of white labor: free labor and indentured servitude. Slavery controlled black labor. Free skilled labor was so scarce and thus so expensive that the first wage legislation in the colonies established maximum not minimum wages. Consequently, a bound labor system was devised to ensure a supply of cheap labor. Apprenticeships in certain trades provided training in return for services. Redemptioners or "free-willers" found themselves as servants for a period of years in return for their passage to America. England also sent convicts to the colonies as indentured servants.[37]

Employment law was based on England's long-established law of master and servant. Although it may be an exaggeration to characterize indentured servants as, in essence, temporary slaves, the personal property of their master, subordination to legitimate authority was an essential component of the law of master and servant. It was a legal relationship made for an agricultural economy and was modeled on a household where the master's role and authority were the same as a father's, and the servant's obligations "were as total, as moral, and as personal as [a] son's."[38] The legal obligations of master and servant, including the terms and conditions of employment, were fixed by law. By law, the master had the right to command and discipline the servant, and the servant had a duty to obey; their relationship was not terminable at will, as both were expected to honor their commitments until the end of the term of service; and the legal obligation to render personal service was enforced as a property right. Although not clearly defined, the master had a duty to provide subsistence and lodging to the servant, to teach the apprentice, and to care for the servant when ill. The likelihood of a servant's obtaining court enforcement of a master's responsibilities was slim, however, because servants were excluded from juries, ordinary workers had little chance to serve on one, and magistrates were "mainly at the service of the master."[39]

This form of employment law in colonial America was a comprehensive system of governmental regulation based on obligation not freedom of choice. The rules of master and servant did not liberate, free from constraint, or encourage choice. In the words of an eminent historian of the colonial period:

> Prior to *laissez faire* capitalism, both business and labor considered governmental regulation the normal order. This was particularly true in the age of colonial settlement, an era when business enterprise was regulated in the interest of a political program. Then the entrepreneur was not free to carry on his business as he saw fit, nor was the worker free to withhold his labor or to demand any working conditions he wished.[40]

In an increasingly market society after the Revolutionary War, judge-made law secured economic and political power for entrepreneurs and merchants. It also facilitated a redistribution of wealth in their favor at the expense of workers, farmers, consumers, and other less powerful people. As Justice Cardozo understood, "The decisions of courts on economic and social questions depend upon their economic and social philosophy."[41] The prevailing economic philosophy of common law judges was always one of free enterprise.[42]

In striking parallel to the promulgation of the values of market philosophy under the cover of allegedly objective and scientific economic laws, a major intellectual effort was also made at this time and later to separate law and politics, law and power, law and morality, and law and the subjectivity of values.

Theories were developed on the scientific nature of the law, as were intellectual systems "which gave common law rules the appearance of being self-contained, apolitical, and inexorable, and which by making 'legal reasoning seem like mathematics' conveyed 'an air...of...inevitability' about legal decisions."[43] Judges were "making discretionary policy determinations under the guise of doing science."[44]

But neither the law nor economics can be separated from politics, power, morals, or values. Because the law can serve as an instrument of great power, there are always struggles to control the law and its operations. The legal system always "works" in the sense that it does the bidding and reflects the goals and policies of those "whose hands are on the controls."[45] In part, that explains the pitched battles throughout U.S. history over how judges are to be chosen, what judges are chosen, and what those judges believe.[46]

The United States was an underdeveloped, laissez-faire driven country in the nineteenth century. Although there was government involvement at all levels, it was promotional rather than regulatory, satisfying its most powerful business constituents' interests in wanting business and the economy to grow. Judge-made law also gave public force in support of the private decision-making that was at the heart of the market economy. In brief, the courts, sharing the spirit of economic development that seized U.S. society in the early years of the nineteenth century, changed the doctrine of property rights from an agrarian conception of an absolute dominion over land that conferred on its owner the power to prevent others from interfering with it to the conception that the "essential attribute of property ownership was the power to develop one's property regardless of the injurious consequences to others."[47] Property's value was as an instrument to achieve the overriding objective of promoting economic growth. As one judge explained, "We must have factories, machinery, dams, canals and railroads. They are demanded by the manifold wants of mankind, and lay at the basis of all our civilization."[48]

In this age of engines and machines, common law judges created or adapted rules supportive of the growth of business. One important way was to limit employers' liability for injuries to employees so that enterprise in general and developing railroads in particular would not be economically drained by lawsuits for personal injury. Consequently, judges developed new doctrines—the *fellow servant rule* (under which an employee could not sue his employer for the injuries caused by the negligence of another employee); *contributory negligence* (under which an employee could not recover from an employer if he was negligent himself no matter how slight); and *assumption of risk* (under which an employee could not recover if he had put himself voluntarily in a dangerous position—which practically excluded workers in mines, railroads, and factories merely by accepting those dangerous jobs). The value choices of judges who chose the promotion and protection of economic growth and profitability over the safety and health of human beings in their work were translated into the objective language of the rule of law.

These value choices were generally implicit. In a famous case in 1866 (*Ryan v. New York Central Railroad*),[49] however, the judge made no effort to camouflage his values in deciding to relieve entrepreneurs of liability:

> But no corporation can be ruined without bringing ruin to some of the noblest and most meritorious classes of the land. Those who first gave the start to such corporations are men of bold and enterprising qualities, kindled no doubt, in part by self-interest, but in part also by the delight which men of such type feel in generous schemes for the development of public resources, and the extension to new fields of the wealth and industry of the community.[50]

He went on to deplore the consequences for workers, "the bone and sinew of the land," of imposing liability costs on their employers:

> We hear sometimes of the cruelty of the eviction of the laborers from their cottages and a landlord's caprice. But there are no evictions which approach in vastness and bitterness to those which are caused by the stoppage of railway improvements or of manufacturing corporations; in few cases is there such misery to the laboring classes worked, as when one of these great institutions is closed.[51]

The rapidly developing railroad interests, however, led others to deplore the "organized lawlessness under law" of the men who controlled "hundreds of miles of railway, thousands of men, tens of millions of revenue, and hundreds of millions of capital":

> These modern potentates have declared war, negotiated peace, reduced courts, legislatures and sovereign states to an unqualified obedience to their will, disturbed trade, agitated the currency, imposed taxes, and, boldly setting both law and public opinion at defiance, have freely exercised many other attributes of sovereignty.[52]

The triumph of a market economy also required a transformation of contract law; accordingly, judges chose or created well-suited doctrines. Earlier contract law doctrine was hostile to a market economy because it was based on objective standards of value, that is, an equitable conception of contract in which the justification for a contractual obligation was the inherent justness or fairness of an exchange. Unequal bargaining power was considered an illegitimate form of duress. The market economy required a different ethos. Judges in the nineteenth century rejected the old doctrine and asserted the view that all value was subjective, and, therefore, the only source for the legal obligation of contract was the convergence of the wills of the contracting parties—the "meeting of the minds."[53]

As with free market economics, the common law contract doctrine came to epitomize a separation of law and morals. Contract became bargaining for advantage—a depersonalized exchange purged of all but economic calculation between the parties to an agreement. Because contractual justice was no longer concerned with the subjective content of an agreement, courts enforced what people had voluntarily agreed to thereby giving those parties power to remake law according to their own desires.

In 1905, the concept of freedom of contract was elevated "to the level of a sacred constitutional principle"[54] in *Lochner v. New York*[55] when the Supreme Court ruled that a law limiting bakers to a sixty-hour work week was an unconstitutional attempt by the legislature to protect the health of workers. The Court rejected legislative attempts at regulation that interfered with contractual freedom for the purpose of redistributing economic power. The *Lochner* decision confirmed the triumph of free market values. The market, not the state, was the "natural and neutral institution" for distributing benefits and burdens on the economy.[56]

This new common law doctrine of freedom of contract was supposed to be liberating and rights-endowing: Parties could decide for themselves whether to enter into a contractual relationship and what the terms of a contract would be; voluntarily entered into contractual commitments were limited to specific promises and for a specified period of time; contracts established a mutually beneficial arrangement based on self-interest and reciprocity; and only the parties to a contract were entitled to its benefits and could be required to meet its obligations.[57] When the new doctrine was extended to treat the employment relation the same as any other contract, however, the result was not liberating or rights-endowing for workers. In part, this was due to the values of the judges who interpreted and applied that doctrine. These judges, overwhelmingly "solid independent men of middle-class," were "terrified of class struggle, mob rule, the anarchists and their bombs, railroad strikers, and the collapse of the social system as they knew it."[58] They also feared that legislatures would be used to redistribute wealth for egalitarian ends.[59] Yet, their decisions were written—and the history of their decisions has often been written—as if they were not influenced at all by free market ideology or by the political and economic struggles going on around them but only by objective rules.

Those supposedly objective rules ignored the reality of the power imbalance inherent in the employer-employee relation. Even as corporations and trusts became at least as powerful as modern states, courts, including the Supreme Court, continued to recite the fiction that in making employment contracts the parties had an equal right to obtain from each other the best terms they could obtain through private bargaining. When employers used their control of workers' means of livelihood to exploit wage earners' need to earn a living on any terms available, courts claimed to see no duress or even unfair economic advantage but only the "inequalities of fortune" that are the necessary result of the exercise of the right of private property and the freedom to contract. These courts aided and abetted a great economic transformation whereby "control of the means of livelihood of vast masses of people had fallen into the hands of a relatively few."[60]

Relative economic power and comparative degrees of mutual dependence are major determinants of just how free freedom of contract is. It defied reality then and it denies history now to maintain that these employment contracts were voluntary exchanges of freely bargained promises. It was not only the unique nature of the power that employers had over their employees and potential employees, however, that made the employment contract what, in a great understatement, has been called "a very special sort of contract."[61] No individually or collectively bargained employment contract can anticipate all the problems and disputes involved in interpreting and applying such an agreement, particularly in constantly changing economic conditions. These disputes are ever-recurring at workplaces, moreover, because employers unilaterally make work rules and unilaterally enforce them. True contract doctrine would not permit one of the parties to a contract to be the sole judge of whether some action violated that contract or was beyond its scope but would rely on the adjudication of disputes by a body independent of the contracting parties.

But appeals to courts or arbitrators to decide employment disputes would mean that employers would no longer have unfettered control of their workers. Consequently, employment contract doctrine gave employers a legal basis for the prerogatives they demanded and free market ideology claimed were essential. That was accomplished by importing into employment contract doctrine the law of master and servant in a way that not only preserved the masters' authority but also absolved employers of the duties masters owed their servants. The wage contract was considered not only a commodity purchase and sale like any other but employees, in addition, were now obliged to render obedience and personal deference to their employers. Again, treating the legal enforcement of a traditional relation of subordination as a bargain between equals defies reality and history.

In theory, contract was to be a liberating substitute for regulation by government. In practice, however, the employment contract substituted comprehensive employer regulation of the employment relationship. In sum, the employment contract became "a legal device for guaranteeing to management the unilateral power to make rules and exercise discretion."[62]

These market philosophy–imbued common law doctrines became the still-embedded roots of dominant present-day assumptions in this country that the nature of the employer-employee relationship is one of employer dominance and employee subservience. These value presumptions still underlie U.S. labor law. Although there is a fair amount of protective labor legislation, the presumptions of superior–subordinate have been used to block workers from exercising any effective control within the enterprise.

Flowing from these value assumptions, for example, is another current common law rule first set forth in the late 1800s known today as the *employment-at-will doctrine*. This variation in the freedom of contract doctrine states that, absent some explicit agreement to the contrary, every employment relationship is an employment-at-will that can be terminated by either party at any time for any reason or no reason. The employment-at-will doctrine remains embedded in U.S. labor law.

The Supreme Court elevated the doctrine to the level of a sacred constitutional principle in *Adair v. United States*[63] in 1908 when the Court held unconstitutional a statute prohibiting the discharge of railroad employees for membership in a union. This case concerned enforcement of a "yellow dog" contract, which required present or prospective employees to promise, as a condition of employment, not to join a union, to leave any union they had joined, and not to try to organize fellow employees. Employers who used yellow-dog contracts dictated to wage earners what organizations they could or could not belong to if they wanted a job. In the Supreme Court's value scheme, the employee's legal right to quit an employer who did not employ union members was equivalent to the employer's legal right to discharge an employee for being a member of a labor organization: "The employer and the employee have equality of right, and any legislation that disturbs that equality is an arbitrary interference with the liberty of contract which no government can legally justify in a free land."[64] This set of values still prevails in the employment-at-will doctrine, although it is now unlawful to discharge an employee for union membership.

The Supreme Court, in *Adair,* not only sanctioned employer power to deny workers freedom of association under the legal fiction of freedom of contract but also upheld the use of injunctions against unions that attempted to induce breaches of those contracts. It was the final touch in a common law system of private self-determination or, more precisely, private power, freed from the dangers of regulation or collectivism.[65]

Business, particularly corporations that introduced revolutionary changes in production and distribution processes, only increased their control of the economy from the earliest days of U.S. economic development, to the Gilded Age of the late nineteenth century, and through the 1920s—that is, until the Great Depression that began in 1929. Until then, the business of America was business, and the values of the market philosophy were pervasive and dominant. There was abiding faith (as long as that faith paid off for believers) in the market power of organized business. That market power and control was supplemented by corporate control of the industrial and labor relations system made possible in great part by common law judges and the judiciary in general.

The ascendancy of corporations and the dominance of the economic philosophy and legal values that legitimized and aided their rise, however, were challenged continually by those who advocated reform or fundamental change based on different values and conceptions of rights and justice. Various humanist movements actively deplored the widespread poverty in cities and rural areas—a new slavery—with many people living in slums while others enjoyed unprecedented prosperity, consumption, leisure, and ostentatious excess. They exposed all the causes that "without justice or mercy condemned little children to man-made hells."[66] (In 1918, the Supreme Court found unconstitutional a state law that prohibited the transportation in interstate commerce of goods produced in any factory where children under 14 were employed.)[67]

These challengers did not see poverty as a personal failure but rather as a failure of a society in which some people were helpless and defenseless against the potentially life-ruining consequences of the self-interest–driven choices of the more powerful or—as some preferred to put it—against economic "misfortunes." These challengers believed it was the obligation of the state, what many envisioned as a public-service state, to make a better life for the poor, to redistribute income, to protect workers, and to end political corruption in the cities.

A Christian Social Gospel movement preached that the only natural law was the law of brotherhood not the law of greed and dog eat dog. One of the movement's most important leaders, Walter Rauschenbusch, pointed to capitalism as the cause of the evils affecting U.S. society and concluded that "if we can trust the Bible, God is against capitalism, its methods, spirit and results."[68] The Social Gospel was the religious dimension of the Progressive political movement that sought to assert public control of private economic power as part of the substitution of a positive state for laissez-faire. The Progressive movement has been described as a "potpourri of social theories and beliefs" and as a "crusade in which farmers, wage earners, and small businessmen all marched together."[69]

Even a group of distinguished economists rebelled against the traditional market economics core of that profession, and during the Progressive era and beyond sought to slay *homo economicus,* reunite ethics with economics, and reject the mechanical theories and laws of classical economics. Many of them concluded that it was unrestrained private enterprise that posed the greatest threat to freedom and maintained that human progress could not be attained without state involvement.[70] In an affluent society, they argued, "people go hungry not because of any inexorable laws but only because we choose to do as we do in respects that are quite amenable to alteration."[71]

Workers, more than any other group, were the victims of abuses of power. Consequently, one of the most important challenges to corporate dominance was the struggle for power between employers committed to preserving absolute control and organized workers just as committed to getting some control over their wages, hours, and conditions of work. These labor unions ranged in objectives and approaches from the International Workers of the World ("It is the historic mission of the working class to do away with capitalism"),[72] to the Knights of Labor (one big union where "an injury to one was an injury to all"),[73] to the American Federation of Labor (separate trade unions seeking job control through collective bargaining within the existing private enterprise system with "no ultimate ends" but "fighting only for immediate objects").[74]

American business "never willingly conceded any of its prerogatives to workers and unions or to political reformers," and employers "waged bloody battles with even the most 'responsible' and 'conservative' of trade unions."[75] As William Leiserson wrote about labor law in the 1920s:

> The law recognized the equal freedom of employers to destroy labor organizations and to deny the right of employees to join trade unions. An employer could coerce or threaten his employees to keep them from organizing. He could

discharge them if they joined a union, and he could refuse to hire anyone who was a member .... Under such circumstances to speak of labor's right to organize was clearly a misuse of terms. All that employees had was a right to try to organize if they could get away with it; and whether they could or not depended on the relative economic strength of the employers' and employees' organizations.[76]

The strife-ridden history of union-management relations in the United States provides ample evidence that the dominant value choice was that the exercise by workers of their right to freedom of association was to be made dependent on the relative power of capital and labor. The list of the great and violent strikes for organization is a memorial to crushed attempts by workers to organize and participate in the decisions that affected their lives on and off the job: the railroad strikes of 1877, the Homestead steel and Coeur d'Alenes mining strikes in 1892, the 1902 anthracite coal strike, and the 1919 steel strike. These strikers and others over all these years faced federal troops, state militias, martial law, privately and publicly protected nonunion strikebreakers, and government protection of employer property.

These challenges failed in that the state and private employers combined to deny workers the exercise of their right of freedom of association. They succeeded, however, in making the public aware of the extent to which property rights dominated human rights in this country and of the fact that workers, at least some workers at some times, would demand their human rights.

These strikes and the political, social, economic, and moral turmoil that surrounded them generated not only expressions of discontent with the established order but also proposals for change. During the Homestead strike, for example, Senator John Palmer of Illinois argued during Senate debates that large corporations were "clothed with a public interest," that "human rights should not be sacrificed to establish property rights," and that the organization of workers "should be promoted as a matter of public policy."[77]

Since the judiciary had effectively blocked Congress from enacting laws regulating private employer–employee relations, Congress used its power to investigate to raise its own challenges to the denial of workers' freedom to associate. In 1902, a nineteen-volume U.S. Industrial Commission report (that covered every sector of the economy and every region of the country) concluded:

> [B]y the organization of labor and by no other means, it is possible to introduce an element of democracy in the government of industry. By this means only the workers can take part in determining the conditions under which they work.

This becomes true in the fullest and best sense only when employers frankly meet the representatives of workmen and deal with them as parties equally in the conduct of affairs.[78]

In 1916, another U.S. Commission on Industrial Relations issued an eleven-volume majority report considered by at least one labor historian as "perhaps the most radical document ever released by a federal commission."[79] It condemned employers' denial of workers' human rights and recommended welfare programs to protect workers and their families "against unemployment, illness, and indigent old age, as well as to redistribute wealth and income."[80] The Commission majority also proposed, as the major objective of federal labor policy, laws to protect the right of workers to join unions and bargain collectively.

The truly radical aspect of the Commission majority's report was not just its call for federal law to protect workers' right to organize but rather its understanding that the exercise of that right meant more than wages, hours, and working conditions, as essential as those are; it meant the human right to be a free man and woman even at the workplace:

> The struggle of labor for organization is not merely an attempt to secure an increased measure of the material comforts of life, but is a part of the age-long struggle for liberty; that this struggle is sharpened by the pinch of hunger and the exhaustion of body and mind by long hours and improper working conditions; but that even if men were well fed they would still struggle to be free. It is not denied that the exceptional individual can secure an economic sufficiency either by the sale of his unusual ability or talent or by sycophantic subservience to some person in authority, but it is insisted that no individual can achieve freedom by his own efforts. . . . It is evident that there can be at best only a benevolent despotism where collective action on the part of the employees does not exist.[81]

Through the first third of the twentieth century, few were listening to those who criticized the established economic or labor-management systems or the dominant values. It took the crushing failure of the unregulated market system in the Great Depression of the 1930s to shake people's faith in business values, particularly the allegedly self-generating force of economic growth. As John Kenneth Galbraith observed in *The Great Crash,* there have been few opportunities like 1929 to see behind the barrier of the "thickly stuffed shirt":

> In the autumn of 1929 the mightiest of Americans were, for a brief time, revealed as human beings. Like most humans, most of the time, they did some very foolish

things. On the whole, the greater the earlier reputation for omniscience, the more serene the previous idiocy, the greater the foolishness now exposed. Things that in other times were concealed by a heavy façade of dignity now stood exposed, for the panic suddenly, almost obscenely, snatched the façade away.[82]

The prolonged desperation of the economic crisis made people receptive to almost any kind of remedial action, including unconventional experiments in economic policy by the federal government. When Franklin Delano Roosevelt was inaugurated as President of the United States in 1933, the nation was suffering through the fourth year of its most disastrous economic depression. The first one hundred days of Roosevelt's New Deal administration produced an extraordinary series of reforms designed to bring about economic recovery. By 1935, events had imposed policy on the President, and he signed the National Labor Relations Act (NLRA, or Wagner Act) on July 5, 1935.

Even then, the Wagner Act received only a "tepid public blessing" from Roosevelt, while Senator Robert F. Wagner, who sponsored the legislation, hailed the new law as a "bulwark of industrial peace and justice."[83] For Wagner, the right to organize and bargain collectively was "at the bottom of social justice for the worker" and was essential for a free and democratic society. He believed that "the struggle for a voice in industry through the process of collective bargaining is at the heart of the struggle for the preservation of political as well as economic democracy in America." He opposed the tyranny of both free-market laissez-faire, in which "men become the servile pawns of their masters in the factories," and the authoritarian "super government."[84]

The Wagner Act established the most democratic procedure in U.S. labor history for the participation of workers in the determination of their wages, hours, and working conditions. The Wagner Act was not neutral; the law declared it to be the policy of the United States to encourage the practice and procedure of collective bargaining and to protect workers in their exercise "of full freedom of association, self-organization, and designation of representatives of their own choosing, for the purpose of negotiating the terms and conditions of their employment or other mutual aid or protection."[85] The Wagner Act constituted a fundamental change in public policy, particularly in regard to the role of government regulation of labor relations. After the Wagner Act, the issue of union recognition was no longer to be decided by economic warfare but, rather, by peaceful government elections to determine employee desires.

The Act also made serious inroads upon the traditional conception of employer property rights. It outlawed employer interference with, restraint of, or coercion of employees in the exercise of their right to organize, to bargain collectively, and to engage in concerted acts such as strikes and picketing. It also prohibited company-formed and controlled representation plans that gave employees the forms of organization but not the substance. Discrimination in hiring or firing or in any condition of employment to encourage or discourage membership in a labor organization, as with the yellow-dog contract, was also prohibited as was retaliation for filing charges or giving testimony under the Act. In addition, it was an unfair labor practice for an employer to refuse to bargain with the representative chosen by a majority of employees in an appropriate bargaining unit. All these 1935 rights and protections remain legislatively intact today, and the government still retains the power to prosecute violations through unfair labor practice proceedings.

The Roosevelt administration and Congress not only statutorily recognized employee rights but also developed a comprehensive system of administrative law and administrative agencies to implement New Deal legislation. The Wagner Act created the National Labor Relations Board (NLRB) to determine appropriate units for collective bargaining, to conduct secret ballot representation elections to determine if a labor organization had majority support, and to prosecute the unfair labor practices provisions of the Act. The NLRB continues to perform these functions.

Although Congress approved an extensive role for the federal government in regulating labor relations, the Wagner Act was not a radical break with the well-rooted freedom of contract concept. Aside from requiring employers and unions to bargain with each other in good faith, the government neither compelled the parties to reach an agreement nor scrutinized the terms of any agreement reached. The Wagner Act preserved the principle of freedom of contract but adapted it to the new collective nature of the employer-employee relationship. It contemplated, not isolated individuals forced by their powerlessness to accept whatever terms of employment an employer dictated, but organized employees exercising collective bargaining power to negotiate the conditions of their own employment on an equal basis with the collective power of employers. The realization of their human rights at the workplace, however, was dependent on their collective bargaining power to negotiate these rights into enforceable contracts.

The Wagner Act promised a protected *opportunity* for workers through power-sharing to participate in making the decisions that affect their workplace lives. What was then called *industrial democracy* was to replace employers' unilateral determination of matters affecting wages, hours, and working conditions. The Wagner Act had the potential to bring about a major redistribution of power from the powerful to the powerless at U.S. workplaces covered by the statute.

The promises made in the Wagner Act embody fundamentally different values and conceptions of rights and justice than those underlying the allegedly free market system. The provisions of the Wagner Act confirmed that workers were human beings—not mere resources—and that human beings were not to be submissive to employers, markets, or governments. Those provisions promoted individual rights and responsibility, social obligations, and a democratic approach to employment decisions.

The values underlying the Wagner Act, and most but not all of the Act's provisions, are the values most consistent with human rights values. At its core, for example, was the promotion and protection of the freedom of association that Human Rights Watch has called "the bedrock workers' right under international law on which all other labor rights rest."[86] The right to bargain collectively follows directly as an inherent aspect of the freedom of association. Consequently, the Wagner Act was intended to enable workers to obtain sufficient power to make the claims of their human rights both known and effective so that respect for their rights was not dependent solely on the interests of the state, their employers, or others. The Wagner Act was a moral choice against servility. Servility is incompatible with human rights. Wagner knew that a human being has a right to be free from domination regardless of the source and understood that government support and protection are essential to the exercise of participatory rights at the workplace. The fundamental rights that people need to live a human life, therefore, include not only those a government must not invade but also those a government must promote and protect.

Common law judges balanced conflicting rights and interests using a cost-benefit as well as a market philosophy standard to make policy-based choices. Those choices gave property rights and economic development priority over any other rights. When the human rights of workers are involved in that balancing, however, decisions that violate those human rights are unacceptable and impermissible regardless of any of the following justifications for these decisions: the economy would grow faster as a result; work would be done more efficiently, competitive positions would improve, and profits would increase; property would be protected; that's what the majority of people want; or certain groups might be better off.

Given the earlier discussion of discrimination and human rights, a good example of such a decision (in addition to the many examples in this chapter) would be denying black children equal education in order to keep peace in a community. In such cases involving human rights, the function of the courts or any other administrative agency or arbitral decision-maker "is not to balance one set of claims against the other to see which side has the net gain," but rather "to come out actively and aggressively" as adversaries of those who threaten fundamental human respect-based rights.[87]

If the core values of the Wagner Act are understood for what they actually are—that is, human rights values—it changes the scheme for giving certain rights priority over other rights. If freedom of association is recognized as a human right, for example, then it gets first priority. That does not mean that property rights, efficiency, or management rights are forsaken; it simply means that those rights are no longer entitled to receive the first priority that courts, administrative agencies, and labor arbitrators have historically given them. It would mean that the fundamental human right of freedom of association should prevail over property rights of the employer at the workplace. It does not today for reasons discussed in the next two chapters.

4

PROPERTY RIGHTS OVER FREEDOM
OF ASSOCIATION RIGHTS

Congressional and Judicial Value Choices

Before the Great Depression and the Wagner Act, business in this country dominated almost every aspect of American life, not only factories and the government but also the society's values. Employers identified business values with the larger society's "traditional" American values of consumption, material possessions, and individualism. The widespread suffering during the Great Depression, however, generated and spread different values of social justice, equal rights, economic equality, industrial democracy through collective action at the workplace, government regulation of business, and a government on the side of the powerless rather than the powerful.

This crisis of faith was an even more momentous threat to business control because it occurred in seemingly out-of-control years of historic and violent labor unrest, including the seizure of industrial plants by sit-down strikers; violent class conflict; sweeping union organizing drives that spread unionism throughout the country's major industries; public exposure by a Senate investigating committee (the La Follette Committee) of employers' use of espionage, strikebreaking, armed violence, and private police to stop unionization; a Supreme Court decision upholding the constitutionality of the Wagner Act; and a National Labor Relations Board (NLRB) that in its first five years of administering the Wagner Act engaged in "the most high powered and effective law enforcement in our history":[1]

> The years 1929–1941 constituted the age of trauma for the American businessman. His image as the decisive figure in the society was shattered. He was blamed for the stock market crash and the joblessness of the Great Depression; his enterprise was subjected to new and more rigorous government regulations and taxation; and his unilateral control over his workforce was challenged by the union supported by federal policy.[2]

Although employers' responses to unionism varied, their basic philosophy remained unchanged: Unions would threaten management's rightful authority to manage. Unions were an intruding outside influence, and the consequences would be that "the boss was no longer the boss."[3] The chairman of the first Wagner Act NLRB, J. Warren Madden, understood why employers objected to what he called the serious inroads NLRB decisions made upon the traditional conception of employer rights in the ownership of property:

> When an employer was told that he could not discharge a workman because he had joined a union, a serious inroad was made upon a traditional and important component of his ownership... Employers, almost unanimously, did not welcome the change. I have never been able to see why they should have welcomed it. I cannot remember instances when any other elements of our population have surrendered with pleasure powers and prerogatives which were traditionally theirs.[4]

A company attorney arguing against one of these NLRB decisions told the court, "I feel like a traveler walking on a familiar road and finding all the signposts reversed."[5] American employers saw those signposts as the values that people used to understand and judge their own worlds and the world around them. Business immediately set about reorienting workers away from their only recently developed loyalties to organized labor and the state by reshaping these values. The objective was to restore economic growth as the paramount goal and to link economic success with the American way of freedom, individualism not collectivism, nationalism, free enterprise, and abundance created by ever-increasing productivity. Reshaping society's values was a key component of regaining employers' decision-making power free of interference from unions or the state.

This was not business' first foray into selling free-enterprise values to solidify their power and justify their actions. The selling began in earnest after

the individual entrepreneur who toiled side by side with workers had been replaced by large corporations that had developed peace zones or trusts when the
war of the marketplace became too costly and risky. Those entrepreneurs, characterized later by muckrakers as robber barons, needed to reconcile the values
they preached of the free individual competing in the atomistic free market
with the reality of concentrated corporate economic and political power.

That was accomplished by combining Darwinian survival of the fittest theories and Christian principles into a justification of wealth and power. Darwin
and Jesus were woven together and, in turn, interpreted through a combination of laws: the Scientific Law of Competition and the divinely ordained Law
of the Accumulation of Wealth to fashion what steel baron Andrew Carnegie
called the Gospel of Wealth.

The bedrock message of this Gospel according to Carnegie was rugged individualism and freedom of action mainly in the economic arena guided by the
unregulated market philosophy that life is a race in which the prizes should go
to the swiftest of foot. The fittest survive the competitive struggle in the marketplace, whereas the weak and the incompetent do not. That industries were
economic aristocracies and that management power was supreme within this
economic domain was not to be deplored but rather celebrated as the best evidence that control of the economy was in the hands of the best and the brightest.
Power should be in the hands of the strong. Losers in the market competition,
moreover, had nothing to blame but their own shortcomings. In sum:

> But whether the law [of competition] be benign or not, we must say of it…It is
> here; we cannot evade it; no substitutes for it have been found; and while the law
> may sometimes be hard on the individual, it is best for the race, because it ensures
> the survival of the fittest in every department. We accept and welcome, therefore,
> as conditions to which we must accommodate ourselves, great inequality of en-
> vironment; the concentration of business industrial and commercial in the hands
> of the few; and the law of competition between these, as being not only beneficial,
> but essential to the future progress of the race.[6]

The iron law of competition was the basis not only for the distribution of
power and the justification for its unequal concentration in the hands of a triumphant few but also for the distribution of wealth and the justification for its
unequal accumulation in the hands of the same triumphant few:

> The millionaires are a product of natural selection.…It is because they are thus
> selected that wealth—both their own and that entrusted to them—aggregates

under their hands.... They get high wages and live in luxury, but the bargain is a good one for society.[7]

This "scientific" version of the market philosophy was intended to reiterate the argument that government meddling would have detrimental economic consequences by interfering with the natural order ordained by the law of competition. Government meant politics, moreover, and "politics lifts mediocrity into the saddle" in violation of the law of competition.[8]

It was also an economic system ordained by God. Christian love was best expressed by the benevolent use of power—a stewardship wherein the wealthy became trustees for their poor brethren, "bringing to their service his superior wisdom, experience, and ability to administer, doing for them better than they would or could do for themselves."[9] George Baer, president of the Philadelphia and Reading Railroad Company, captured the essence of the Gospel of Wealth in a letter he wrote during a long and bitter strike in 1902:

> The rights and interests of the laboring man will be protected and cared for— not by the labor agitators, but by the Christian men to whom God in His infinite wisdom has given the control of the property interests of the country, and upon the management of which so much depends.[10]

In sum, the Gospel of Wealth was a value-based justification of the way things were. The prophets of this Gospel taught that workers should remain unorganized; that business, because it was controlled by a "natural aristocracy of ability,"[11] should be free from government regulation; and that the prosperity of enterprise "was the way, the truth and the consummate social good."[12] People were poor, therefore, not because of any fault in the system but because they were personally defective in capacity or morals or both. As Carnegie phrased it, "The laws of individualism will continue, but the millionaire will be but a trustee for the poor."[13] George Fitzhugh in his 1857 book, *Cannibals All or Slaves without Masters,* a defense of southern slavery, agreed that men were not born equal: "Some were born with saddles on their backs, and others booted and spurred to ride them."[14] In the words of Jacques Maritain, the blessed rich were "Little Gods."[15]

Business' selling techniques were more sophisticated after the Great Depression, but the core message remained unchanged as did the values underlying that message. World War II and postwar foreign policy events combined to give business the opportunity to regain lost faith and reacquire some of its lost power. Employers attributed the wartime "miracle of production" and economic mobilization to the "initiative, ingenuity, and organizing genius of private enterprise" and to rugged individualism[16] despite the fact that much wartime success was due to government planning and regulation.

After the war, communism and communist subversion became the greatest perceived threats to the country. Business exploited the nation's anticommunist fervor by warning "of the decline of America's values, morals, and freedoms due to government's and labor's attacks on the free enterprise system."[17] Just as employers had done after World War I, business used fears of radicalism and collectivism to portray unions as subversive, un-American, and dictatorial and work stoppages as leftist-inspired attempts to destroy the U.S. economy. Business cast the situation as a life-or-death struggle to save the "American way of life," and business portrayed itself as leaders in the fight against communism, "Big Labor," and "Big Government" and as defenders of real American values of individual initiative and opportunity, free market competition, free enterprise, and economic prosperity.

Organized business initiated a national campaign to sell the free enterprise system that reached not only into factories but also into schools, churches, and communities. From the earliest years of public education in this country, employers contributed to schools financially and otherwise. They recognized that schools were strategically placed institutions not only for developing skills useful to business but also for inculcating business-approved values. Schools helped develop future employees in part by teaching values "of hard work, industriousness, and punctuality."[18]

After the Depression, business worked to restore its influence over education. In addition to financial support, corporations increased direct contacts with teachers and administrators (who were "instrumental in shaping young minds") and with students, both as a recruitment technique and to instill in them the values of business. The most coordinated effort was made to teach economics in public schools. Business organizations such as the National Association of Manufacturers (NAM) developed their own curriculum and required schools that used it to adopt it without modification and teachers to attend workshops to become familiar with the material. (In 1956, NAM claimed to have "trained" 2,000 teachers.)[19]

Although businesses concentrated on elementary and secondary schools, corporations also increased their financial support for colleges and universities to help create what General Electric called the climate needed for the continued progress of competitive free enterprise. Business foundations and individual firms sponsored seminars, exchange programs, and conferences that "brought faculty from public and private higher educational institutions into personal contact with the business community."[20] The NAM and the Chamber of Commerce (C of C) told their members that money invested in education was the same as money invested directly in a business enterprise.[21]

Business also sold the concept of free enterprise at its workplaces with the ultimate goal of convincing workers that what was good for their companies was good for them. What became known as human relations resurrected industry's earlier welfare capitalism experiments with less authoritative, more consultative management styles including personnel relations and employee representation plans, safety campaigns, lunch rooms, in-plant doctors and nurses, stock purchasing plans, pensions, house-ownership plans, and industrial recreation such as picnics, clubs, and athletic teams.[22] The objective was to win workers' loyalty to their companies by expressing their employer's concern for employee welfare and by getting workers "to accept what management wants them to accept *but* to *make* them feel they made or helped to make the decision."[23] Management intended to make its authority more accepted and legitimate without limiting "the prerogative of ownership and management or altering the essential purposes of the enterprise."[24] The human relations strategy, moreover, was coupled with economics education programs for workers, all designed to win support for free enterprise. All of this was meant to increase productivity and to have workers conclude that unions and government were not only unnecessary but could jeopardize the benefits their employers were giving them by making things more difficult for their employers.

The selling of the market economic philosophy also reached into communities, using public relations firms, advertising experts, popular magazines, radio programs, and motion pictures. One phase "was an aggressive public relations effort threatening the decline of American values, morals, and freedoms due to government's and labor's attacks on the free enterprise system."[25] The second phase, similar to the human relations tactics used at workplaces, sought to convince communities that business was a good neighbor providing, among other things, taxes and a payroll on which the community depended.[26]

All of this was intended to restore voluntary acceptance of employer unilateral decision-making power. The Wagner Act, with its fundamentally different values of human rights and worker participation in workplace decision making, was a threat to historically rooted management prerogatives. The NLRB's vigorous, uncompromising, and literal enforcement of the law in the Act's early years proved how serious the threat was. The challenge for business was to get the Wagner Act repealed or amended and to discredit the NLRB and the New Deal. That required selling free enterprise in different ways and at different levels.

As I have recounted elsewhere,[27] the NLRB from 1935 to 1947 was subjected to intense hostile pressure from the NAM, the C of C, trade associations, and powerful corporations that worked closely with an alliance of conservative southern Democrats and Republicans, a generally hostile press, and even the American Federation of Labor (AFL), which was convinced the Board favored its rival, the Congress of Industrial Organizations (CIO). Organized business and its allies used House and Senate committee investigations of the NLRB as effective weapons to generate amendments to the law, intimidate the NLRB, and put political pressure on the White House to appoint Board members acceptable to business. A House Special Committee (the Smith Committee) was most effective:

> The NLRB was the focus of changes that threatened not only the power positions of American industry and its leaders, but also the power position of traditional AFL craft unions and their leaders. Howard Smith's Special Committee to investigate the [NLRB] was a major political effort to regain, maintain, and increase the power of American industry and business and the AFL. The Smith Committee would be a watershed in the history of the NLRB and American labor policy.[28]

Although World War II delayed legislative changes, the Labor-Management Relations Act of 1947, better known as the Taft-Hartley Act, was a legacy of the Smith Committee.[29] The passage of the Taft-Hartley Act was an acceleration, but not the beginning, of a process that has turned a policy that encouraged the replacement of employer autocracy with a democratic system of workplace power-sharing into the protection of employers' unilateral decision-making power over matters directly affecting people's workplace lives. Almost forty years after Taft-Hartley, for example, a House Labor Committee concluded not only that the labor law had failed to achieve its purpose of encouraging collective bargaining but also that the law itself was being used "as a weapon to obstruct collective bargaining."[30] That has occurred for many reasons but two have important connections to issues of values.

Even before Taft-Hartley, employers wanted to eliminate from the Wagner Act the language declaring it to be the policy of the United States to encourage collective bargaining, the core purpose of the law. The Hartley House bill (as did the Smith bill years before) did eliminate that statement, but the compromise between the House and Senate (Taft bill) retained the Wagner Act statement of purpose but added the Hartley bill's statement of purpose that did not mention collective bargaining. The added statement said, among other things, that the law's purpose was to protect the rights of individual employees.

When the Hartley statement of purpose was coupled with language added to Section 7 of the Act, affirming worker's right to refrain from collective bargaining, what emerged was the concept of government as a *neutral* guarantor of employee free-choice between individual and collective bargaining—a concept clearly inconsistent with the Wagner Act's concept of the government as the promoter and protector of collective bargaining.[31] Although there is no necessary conflict between the encouragement of collective bargaining and the protection of individual rights, at the time Taft-Hartley became law, experts predicted correctly that the new language would be read as statutory justification for the promotion of individual bargaining and resistance to collective bargaining. In sum, the same law has been read as promoting collective bargaining and as facilitating resistance to it.[32]

The second major objective of organized business after the Wagner Act was to restore what employers called their freedom of speech. The first Wagner Act NLRB required employers to maintain strict hands-off neutrality in regard to their employees' organizing efforts. The Board reasoned that since the employment relationship involved a complete economic dependence of the employee upon the employer, any antiunion speech or literature from the employer was inherently coercive and violative of the employee's statutorily guaranteed free choice. As Judge Learned Hand phrased it, "What to an outsider will be no more than the vigorous presentation of a conviction to an employee may be the manifestation of a determination which is not safe to thwart."[33]

Senator Wagner, who was too ill to attend the debates on the Senate floor in 1947, warned that the "free speech" language in the Hartley bill was intended to deny workers their right to organize:

> Moreover, all the propaganda to the contrary notwithstanding, the phenomenal growth of labor organization has taken place without any diminution of the employer's constitutional right to free speech in labor relations. The talk of restoring free speech to the employer is a polite way of reintroducing employer interference, economic retaliation and other insidious means of discouraging union membership and union activity thereby greatly diminishing and restricting the exercise of free speech and free choice by the working men and women of America. No constitutional principle can support this, nor would a just labor-relations policy result from it.[34]

However, Section 8(c), the so-called employer free speech provision, was added in 1947 as part of the Taft-Hartley Act:

> The expressing of any views, argument, or opinion, or the dissemination thereof, whether written, printed, graphic, or visual form, shall not constitute or be evidence of any unfair labor practice under any provisions of this Act, if such expression contains no threat of reprisal or force or promise of benefit.[35]

Section 8(c), as Wagner warned, has become "the primary instrument used by employers to discourage unionization and collective bargaining."[36] There was a certain degree of semantic fraud in referring to representation election campaign cases as issues of employer free speech. The phrase concealed the real policy issue: the extent to which, if at all, an employer was to be permitted to exert economic power through speech in regard to employees' choice of and participation in unions. Employer antiunion speech during representation campaigns creates a clash among at least three important rights: the right of freedom of association, the right of freedom of speech (not only an employer's but also a union's and the employee's), and property rights. Each of these rights, moreover, is a human right. The dominant hierarchy of rights established by Congress in Section 8(c) of the Taft-Hartley Act and by subsequent judicial and NLRB decision-makers gives employer speech and property rights dominance over workers' freedom of association.

In enacting Section 8(c) (and other provisions of the Taft-Hartley Act), Congress went beyond the notion of protecting an individual employee's right to choose or reject unionization and collective bargaining. Congress knowingly created and sanctioned an employer statutory right to resist and obstruct workers' exercise of their right of freedom of association at the workplace. This deregulation of employer speech did not create equality between unions and management or result in a more informed electorate in representation elections; it did what it was intended to do: increase the ability of employers to use their economic job-control power to squash unionization efforts. This is particularly true for employers who, often with expert counsel, know how to dress up their threats as predictions, possibilities, or statements of legal principles.

By the mid-1950s, as in the pre–Wagner Act days, economic power controlled the outcome of representation elections and employers had overwhelming advantage in power struggles over workers' exercise of their freedom of association. The exercise of this coercive power over employees struck at the core purpose of the law: the freedom of association. The first chairman of the

Wagner Act NLRB, J. Warren Madden, told a congressional committee eight years before Taft-Harley, "Upon this fundamental principle—that an employer shall keep his hands off the self-organizing of employees—the entire structure of the act rests. Any compromise or weakening of that principle strikes at the roots of the law."[37] Without the congressionally approved and NLRB- and judiciary-enforced employer free speech incursion into the core of the Act, the law's basic value of freedom of association could not have been as seriously undermined as it has been in this country. Except for the brief interlude of the Wagner Act, therefore, employer property rights values have dominated the freedom of association in this country. Court and NLRB decisions concerning access to employer property to communicate with employees about unionization are good examples.

The Supreme Court's 1945 decision in *Republic Aviation Corp. v. NLRB*,[38] however, conflicts with traditionally dominant rights of property to the extent that it permits employees to solicit union membership and to distribute organizational literature in nonwork areas, on nonworking time, as long as it does not interfere with production, discipline, or safety. The Wagner Act NLRB, with some limitations, extended the *Republic Aviation* standard to permit non-employee union organizers access to employer property. The Board concluded that "to differentiate between employees soliciting on behalf of the Union and non-employee union solicitors would be a differentiation not only without substance but in clear defiance of the rationale enunciated by the Board and the courts for permitting solicitation."[39] The Board also pointed out that "normally an employer cannot forbid union solicitation on company property during nonworking time even where there is no showing that solicitation away from the plant would be ineffective," because the "place of work has been recognized to be the most effective place for the communication of information and opinion concerning unionization."[40]

NLRB v. Babcock & Wilcox Co.[41] was one of those cases where the Board had permitted access to employer property by nonemployee union organizers. It was to become a landmark decision in U.S. labor law. The Supreme Court overruled the Board and pronounced that the distinction between employees and nonemployees was "one of substance." In a unanimous decision, the Court ruled that "an employer may validly post his property against non-employee distribution of union literature if reasonable efforts by the union through other available channels of communication will enable it to reach the employees with its message."[42]

In the years since *Babcock & Wilcox,* the alternative channels of communication rule has been applied by the courts and the NLRB "to exclude virtually all non-employee organizational activity from private commercial property."[43] But in this case, as in some other landmark cases,[44] the Supreme Court simply announced a rule with no persuasive justification for the alleged distinction of substance between the status of employees and nonemployees. As one commentator pointed out: "The real issue raised by *Babcock* is whether, in light of the undisputed right of employees to receive information on their rights under the NLRA, *any* employer property interest is sufficiently important to justify exclusion of non-employee organizers from the workplace."[45]

The Supreme Court in its 1992 decision in *Lechmere, Inc. v NLRB*[46] expanded the "use of property rights to exercise sovereignty over workers."[47] In *Lechmere,* the employer asserted the right to exclude nonemployee union organizers without any claim that the union activity interfered with production, services, security, or other business functions. A majority of the Court held that the Taft-Hartley Act conferred rights "only on employees not on unions or their non-employee organizers."[48] The Court also ruled that the exception to the rule barring nonemployee union organizers from employers' premises is a narrow one. The exception did not apply "wherever non-tresspassory access to employees may be cumbersome or less-than-ideally effective but only where the *location of a plant and the living quarters of the employees* place the employees *beyond the reach* of reasonable union efforts to communicate with them."[49] The Court's examples confirmed the rarity of the exception: logging camps, mining camps and mountain resort hotels.

The Court went on to say that the "union's burden of establishing such isolation is...'a heavy one.'"[50] As another commentator noted, the "Court allowed this naked property right to trump the substantial statutory interests of organized employees in spreading information about and seeking support for unionization, and of unorganized employees in receiving that information."[51] It meant that nonemployee union organizers would almost never have the right to enter private property to communicate with unorganized employees. The advocates of Section 8(c) had claimed that the provision would protect "one of the fundamentals of liberty."[52] Clearly, they meant the liberty of employers to oppose their employees' freedom of association.

In *Lechmere,* the only apparent employer interest was in preventing the organizers' message from reaching the employees—the broadest power to interfere with the freedom of association. *Lechmere* defies the intent of the law to encourage collective bargaining. As already noted, the NLRB and the Supreme Court in *Republic Aviation* recognized years ago that the workplace is the most effective place for the communication of information and opinion about unionization. That is where sustained face-to-face contact is readily available as part of a concerted effort to persuade fearful employees that the benefits will outweigh the risks of supporting the union. It is also the one place where employees gather as a group. Employers' essentially unfettered power to exclude union organizers from workplaces not only deprives employees, who might otherwise fear or not know how to use the workplace forum, of the assistance of experienced and knowledgeable voices but also demonstrates to employees their employer's unchallenged power over the workplace.

Over the years, the courts and government agencies have placed many limitations on employers' use of their property, including requiring access for various inspectors and prohibiting employers from denying access to workers or customers because of their race. Only in regard to union organizers has the government and its agencies enforced a ban against access to the workplace despite the public policy encouraging collective bargaining and worker freedom of association. It may be because the exercise of the right of freedom of association at the workplace threatens power-sharing that employers, with the aid of Congress, the courts, and the NLRB, have resisted access with such determination.

The workplace is also the only place in this country where people can be compelled to listen to a speech under threat of disciplinary penalty. Under the "captive audience" doctrine fashioned by the first Republican-appointed majority NLRB over fifty years ago, an employer is permitted to hold a captive audience (compulsory attendance) meeting at the workplace on working time (no nonwork area, nonworking time issues here), deliver an antiunion speech (appropriately phrased), and terminate the employment of any employee who refuses to attend, refuse access to union organizers, and even stifle any dissenting views.

This is another area of the decisional law governing organizational campaigns that has changed since the earliest NLRB decisions that promoted self-organization and collective bargaining. One year before the passage of Taft-Hartley, the Board in *Clark Brothers Co.*[53] ruled that requiring employees to listen to antiunion speeches on company property during work time, a captive audience speech, was per se a violation of the Act. As the legislative history of Section 8(c) shows, Congress wanted to eliminate the *Clark Brothers* doctrine. Subsequent to the Taft-Hartley amendments, in a line of cases from *Bonwit Teller, Inc.*[54] to *Metropolitan Auto Parts, Inc.*,[55] the NLRB modified its position and decided that it was not the employer's captive audience speech that was illegal but the employer's denial of an equal opportunity for the union to speak.

The first Republican-appointed NLRB after Taft-Harley rejected that doctrine in 1953 in *Livingston Shirt Corp.*[56] The majority talked of property rights, employer free speech, and the preeminence of the individual's right to choose not to join a union. The NLRB ruled that it was not an unfair labor practice for an employer to make a pre-election speech on company time and premises to employees and to deny the union's request for an equal opportunity to reply.

Board Member Murdock's dissent in *Livingston Shirt* was based on a very different conception of the purpose of the Taft-Hartley Act. He maintained that the congressional policy was one of encouraging collective bargaining. Murdock said that "practically every employer speech on company time and property is designed to perpetuate individual bargaining and to discourage collective bargaining."[57] To the extent legally possible, Murdock said, the Board should effectuate that congressional policy "by seeing that the parties who seek to implement that policy by bringing collective bargaining to the employees have an equality of opportunity to have their arguments reach the employees in the same effective forum used by those who would defeat collective bargaining."[58] Judicial and administrative deference to employer property rights promotes employer speech, restricts employee speech, interferes with the exercise of the right of freedom of association, and prevents the promotion of workplace democracy.[59]

The first Wagner Act NLRB required employer neutrality in regard to employee organization because of the inherently coercive power that employers have over their employees. That coercive employer power remains. The issue of employer speech and worker freedom of association is a choice to unleash or restrict that power. Judge Learned Hand, in an early employer speech case, said that words "in their aggregate take their purport from the setting in which they are used, of which the relation between the speaker and the hearer is perhaps the most important part."[60] The relation of employer-speaker to employee-hearer at nonunion workplaces is one of employment-at-will, meaning that the employee-hearer continues to be an employee only at the will of the employer-speaker. A representation election, therefore, is not the same as a political election. Employers have the power to deprive employee-voters of their jobs or, in many other ways, to make their workplace lives worse or better.

The coercive effect of this power imbalance at the workplace has been made greater by widespread utilization by employers of consultants that now compose a multimillion-dollar union-busting or "union free" industry. Their tactics include use of employer free speech designed to exploit the speaker-hearer relationship:

> "Personal" communication methods, such as individual meetings with employees, are management's most effective method of conveying their anti-union message

to employees. Consultants require supervisors to talk daily to employees, on a one-to-one basis, and record their reactions to the conversations. These meetings become more frequent, and consultant pressure on supervisors and supervisor pressure on employees intensifies as the campaign progresses. Supervisors clearly have the ability to make employees' working lives pleasant or miserable and, because there are no witnesses to these meetings, it is difficult for the union to establish violations of the law, such as threats or promise of benefit.[61]

The purpose of these and other communications from the employer is to persuade workers that the choice they are making is not between union or no union but "between the union and their jobs."[62] Captive audience speeches constitute an important part of these antiunion campaigns. Consultants stress that management's great advantage "lies with its exclusive and ultimate access to employees at the workplace."[63]

Whether through the selling of the values of free enterprise and the market philosophy through propaganda-based communication or through the use of the coercive force of job control via the employer free speech provision of the law, U.S. employers long before and long after the Wagner Act have done whatever was necessary to combat any encroachment on their power. A union research director who attended a "union free" seminar captured both the history of the clash of values and the use of values to justify employers' retention of total control of the workplace:

> Anyone who thinks that…Corporate America has accepted trade unionism as a fact of life with which they can live should attend a seminar like this. Our enemies now wear button-down collars and Brooks Brothers clothes. They are well educated and speak the jargon of social science management. They are lawyers, psychologists and human resource specialists using the latest, most sophisticated methods. Yet, their goals are not different from those 19th century industrialists who espoused the Gospel of Wealth and gave American labor history such names as Haymarket, Homestead and Pullman. I have to agree with one thing stressed [by the seminar leaders]. This is not a game, it is war and the side which attempts to play fair and follows the rules is going to end up the loser.[64]

In its 2000 report on the state of workers' freedom of association in the United States, Human Rights Watch found that it was "a right under severe, often buckling pressure when workers in the United States try to exercise it."[65] Human Rights Watch added that the freedom of association was "under sustained attack in the United States" and that the "government is often failing its responsibility under international human rights standards to deter such attacks and protect workers' rights."[66] This is more than a violation of a statutory right, it is a violation of a human right.

A human being has a right to be free of domination regardless of the source. Servility is incompatible with human rights. Servility, or what some call powerlessness, leaves human beings dependent on the benevolence, pity, charity, or arbitrary power of others. A full human life requires the kind of participation in the political, economic, and social life of the human community that enables people to have an influence on the decisions that affect their lives. That includes workers' participation in workplace decisions that affect their lives and livelihoods. Realistically, that can be accomplished only through exercise of their right to freedom of association.

In the United States, workers are considered to have only those rights set forth in statutes or collective bargaining contracts. Outside the United States, the right to form labor unions and bargain collectively, the right to workplace safety and health, and the right not to be discriminated against are considered human rights. Article 20 of the Universal Declaration of Human Rights (UDHR)[67] issued by the United Nations in 1948 asserts the right to freedom of association, including in Article 23(4) the right to form and join trade unions. The International Covenant on Civil and Political Rights,[68] which the United States ratified in 1992, incorporates in Article 22 the language of the UDHR: "Everyone shall have the right to freedom of association with others, including the right to form and join trade unions for the protection of his interests." Article 8 of the International Covenant on Economic, Social and Cultural Rights,[69] which the United States has not ratified, also affirms the "right of everyone to form trade unions and to join trade unions of his choice."

Over forty years before the UDHR, the International Labour Organization (ILO) had incorporated into its Constitution the right of freedom of association. Social justice for all countries and all individuals has always been the stated prime objective of the ILO, and freedom of association holds a special place in the ILO's standards as a fundamental human right necessary for social justice. The ILO's 1948 *Convention concerning Freedom of Association and Protection of the Right to Organize* (no. 87)[70] establishes and defines the right of workers (and employers) to set up and join organizations of their choosing. It calls on states to take all necessary measures to ensure that workers (and employers) can exercise freely their right to organize. The ILO's 1949 *Convention concerning the Application of the Principles of the Right to Organize and to Bargain Collectively* (no. 98)[71] asserts the right of workers to be free of antiunion discrimination, to organize, and to engage in collective bargaining.

Recently, the ILO has sought "consensus" on what it terms "core principles." In 1998, it issued an ILO Declaration on Fundamental Principles and Rights at Work.[72] In that Declaration, all members of the ILO (which includes the United States), whether or not they have ratified the relevant ILO Conventions, pledged to respect, to promote, and to realize, in good faith fundamental rights, specifically:

(a) freedom of association and the effective recognition of the right to collective bargaining
(b) the elimination of all forms of forced or compulsory labour
(c) the effective abolition of child labour, and
(d) the elimination of discrimination in respect of employment an occupation

Employers in this country have committed and continue to commit widespread violations of the human right and statutory right of freedom of association at the workplace. Equally reprehensible is the fact that the U.S. government legitimizes these violations. As one scholar noted, "Few advanced democratic societies condone open opposition by employers to unionization".[73] While Section 8(c) of the Taft-Hartley Act permits employers to oppose employees' organization, Article 11 of ILO Convention no. 87 requires that each member-state of the ILO take all the necessary and appropriate measures to ensure that workers and employers may exercise freely the right to organize." The U.S. Council for International Business, however, has urged the U.S. government not to ratify that Convention (the United States has not) because "Article 11 has been interpreted as foreclosing any interference in [union] organizing rights, such as employer 'free speech' under Section 8(c) and other acts of interference permitted under the NLRA would be illegal under Convention 87."[74] Employers and the U.S. government are joined in discouraging and violating workers' freedom of association. The U.S. government bears ultimate responsibility for the failure to promote and protect freedom of association at this country's workplaces. The fact that it simply permits private power to be exercised does not absolve the government of its responsibility to intervene when that private power is used to interfere with a human right such as the human right to freedom of association.

In 1992, the United Food and Commercial Workers and the AFL-CIO filed a charge with the ILO's Freedom of Association Committee claiming, among other things, that the Supreme Court's *Lechmere* decision would have a "devastating impact" because the Court had "declared that private property will assume absolute priority over rights of freedom of association, wherever union organizers were involved."[75] The Freedom of Association Committee, in its recommendations, requested the U.S. government "to guarantee access of trade union representatives to workplaces, with due respect for the rights of property and management, so that trade unions can communicate with workers, in order to apprise them of the potential advantages of unionization."[76] That recommendation has been ignored.

What would need to be done to comply with the Freedom of Association Committee's recommendation? There are various policy choices that could be made to promote and protect freedom of association. Any policy choice, in my opinion, must begin with the repeal of Section 8(c) of the Taft-Hartley Act. Given the inherently coercive control that employers have over employees' jobs, the first Wagner Act NLRB's requirement of strict employer neutrality in representation election campaigns is most consistent with the statutory encouragement and protection of the exercise by workers of their right of freedom of association and with respect for that right as a human right. Another policy choice would permit employers to voice opposition to unions but only outside the coercive workplace setting while allowing nonemployee union organizers access to the workplace to promote freedom of association.[77]

Rather than repeal Section 8(c) or restrict employers' speech, Human Rights Watch advocates more speech for workers not less for employers. That approach would include nonemployee union organizer access to the workplace.[78] An employer would be permitted to deny or limit access to labor organizers only if the employer can show that it is necessary to do so to prevent interference with production, to maintain discipline or safety, or for some other substantial reason. That standard, which is the *Republic Aviation* standard, would promote and protect freedom of association and at the same time enable an employer to protect the production process and exclude those who interfere with it. Even if nonemployee organizers were treated the same as employees at the workplace, the *Republic Aviation* standard would provide the same protections to employers. *Babcock & Wilcox* and *Lechmere,* therefore, are not only destructive of the freedom of association but also are unnecessary to protect employers' legitimate interests. Those decisions simply assert the predominance of a property right in a way that denies the exercise of the freedom of association.

In regard to captive audience meetings, this more speech approach maintains that this fundamental violation of human rights at the workplace could be ended with no significant damage to employers' legitimate interests. For example, the NLRB could return to its earlier doctrine requiring employers who deliver captive audience speeches to provide equal opportunity for a union to address employees on the employers' premises. That doctrine is most consistent with the "marketplace of ideas" conception of free speech, including the need for an informed electorate. Human Rights Watch recommends a "principle of proportional access" when employers force employees into captive audience meetings at the workplace.[79] However, I am not enthusiastic about the more employee speech to balance employer speech approach when applied to representation election campaign speech in general and captive audience speech in particular. Employers should remain neutral concerning their employees' exercise of their freedom of association because their control of employees' livelihoods makes what they say and do inherently coercive.

More important, however, no matter what the sales pitch has been—from the Gospel of Wealth to a life-or-death social Darwinistic struggle to anticommunism to free enterprise and the American Way of Life—the underlying objective of U.S. business has always been retention of total decision-making over the enterprise, including at the workplace. Because the freedom of association is a human right, however, there is no justification for permitting employers to deny that right, to discourage its exercise, or even to try to persuade their employees not to exercise it.

5

Expanding the Zone
of Management Control

Devaluing the Freedom of Association

Employers' freedom of enterprise, freedom of contract, freedom of property, and freedom of speech and workers' freedom of association inevitably result in a clash of rights and values. Although portrayed in the abstract as freedoms, when these freedoms are exercised in the workplace they cause a struggle for power—on employers' part to retain sole control of the enterprise including the workplace, and on workers' part to reallocate power not only to prevent or limit the employer's control but also to secure control over their own workplace lives. Choices have been and must continue to be made to determine how this power struggle gets resolved and which rights are predominant. Those choices have been and will be influenced, if not determined, by the values of those making those choices.

As discussed in Chapter 4, after World War II, management retained its workplace sovereignty and regained much of its lost authority, staying union-free with the assistance of Congress with the Taft-Hartley Act, White House–appointed National Labor Relations Boards (NLRBs), and value choices by the courts. The other major challenge to management sovereignty came from workers who organized. Discussions of this challenge have focused on the so-called inherent rights of management rather than on workers' inherent rights. Much of the challenge, phrased in today's bloodless but value-laden legal terminology, was over the "scope of collective bargaining." Bluntly, however, it was an issue of power that employers camouflaged with the concepts of the future of the free enterprise system, property rights, the market economic philosophy, and fear of communism, socialism, and government regulation, portraying themselves as defenders of the American Way of Life.

A labor-management deadlock over the issue of what decisions were exclusively the function and responsibilities of management and, therefore, not subjects of collective bargaining with a union scuttled President Truman's National Labor-Management Conference in 1945. As illustrative of the inherent rights of employers, management members of the Committee on Management's Rights to Manage claimed as exclusively their own the determination of the following: products to be manufactured, location of the business, plant layout and equipment to be used, methods of production, financial policies, prices, selection of employees for promotion, job duties, work assignments, production standards, scheduling of operations, and the maintenance of discipline. Management committee members did acknowledge that discharge for cause and management's application of contractual seniority provisions could be subject to review by mutually agreed on grievance procedures. In other words, management acts and the union reacts, but there is no codetermination.

Union members of the Committee took the position, not reassuring to employers, that "the responsibilities of one of the parties today may well become the joint responsibility of both parties tomorrow."[1] A few years later, Charles Wilson, the president of General Motors warned that stretching collective bargaining to include "any subject that a union leader may desire to bargain on"[2] was a foreign concept and would result in unions running the economy and stifling progress. His forebodings reflected the emotional and ideological as well as the power aspects of the issue:

Only by defining and restricting collective bargaining to its proper sphere can we hope to save what we have come to know as our American system and keep it from evolving into an alien form, imported from east of the Rhine. Until this is done, the border area of collective bargaining will be a constant battleground between employers and unions, as the unions continuously attempt to press the boundary farther and farther into the area of management's functions.[3]

Employers offered various justifications for their control of their enterprises. They were uniform, however, in expressing their "timeless faith" that their power to make business decisions free from union (or government) encroachment was rooted in common law property rights. Either as owners of that property or as agents for shareholders, employers and management were free to decide how that privately held property was to be used.[4]

That is not a persuasive justification for controlling employees, however, because property rights confer control only over things not over human beings who happen to be employees. Business ownership does not confer on the owner the right to force or compel employees to obey—except in a system of slavery where people are owned as property. Employers need to induce people to work and comply with their business decisions, while at the same time people need to work and to keep their jobs to survive economically. This is another way of saying that at some level, unless workers are coerced by their economic dependence, employers in some form must bargain with their employees.[5]

Inducements to have workers comply, however, can be positive, conferring benefits for compliance, or negative, imposing burdens and costly consequences for noncompliance. The nature of the inducement at workplaces is the consequence, among other things, of the relative power of employers and workers. In principle, however, there is nothing in property rights that precludes workers from demanding more money or something more than money as a condition for supplying their labor and cooperation with management. It is the something more than money aspect of bargaining that most threatens employers' control of the workplace. According to bargaining theorist Neil Chamberlain, workers may impose any conditions for their cooperation except those prohibited by law:

> There is nothing that can prevent them from demanding as the price of their cooperation, that management must give them a voice in matters of production, or sales, or location or even the selection of supervisory personnel. Whether they can win such demands depends, of course, upon the degree of their bargaining power—but it is equally true that whether management can avoid such demands, if made, depends not on its legal status as owner or agent or private property, but on its bargaining power.[6]

It is not merely a matter of relative power, however. As will be discussed in this chapter, the Supreme Court has told employers that they have no statutory obligation to bargain with a union about some of the specific subjects of bargaining identified by Chamberlain in the just-quoted passage.

Employers in their own definitions of the scope of their rights often refer to the "inherent rights" of management. Although it is far less common now than in the Gospel of Wealth days to hear that management sovereignty at the workplace is divinely ordained, one labor scholar calls the inherent prerogatives notion the "Genesis theory" of management rights:[7] "In the beginning" (when there was perfection in the Garden of Eden), there was management and management had all the rights. As readers of the bible know, the devil (unions and government regulations) invaded the Garden and brought imperfections. These imperfections were manifested in collective bargaining contracts, labor laws, and some court and administrative agency and arbitration decisions giving meaning to those laws and contracts. The end result is the concept of reserved management rights; that is, all rights remain in management's exclusive domain except those management agreed to limit in a collective bargaining contract or those expressly limited by law.

The nature of the management function is also used as justification for the maintenance of exclusive employer rights. According to this approach, only management is in the central position to coordinate the bargains that have to be made not only with various interest groups within the enterprise but also with stockholders, customers, suppliers, the community, unions, and local, state, and federal government. The contention is that this is a function that cannot be delegated to or shared with a union. With some not so faint echoes of the Gospel of Wealth in the background, management is once again the steward of these various groups that have an interest in the success of the firm.[8]

Even setting aside that in pursuing these bargains management is not a neutral coordinating agent without any profit objective of its own, it does not follow that because of its multiple responsibilities of ownership, management has the right to keep certain subjects off the table when it bargains with unions. That would be just as logical (or illogical) as an employer telling an important customer that the customer has no right to demand any changes in the employer's product.[9]

What does follow from all of these management rights assertions is that there is no room for democracy in business. Many years ago economist F. W. Taussig wrote that workers can have little freedom in industry:

> In ever growing measure the modern development of industry has necessitated direction and discipline—single-minded management.... The liberty of the individual workman is necessarily restricted.... This limitation of freedom is often regarded as a special characteristic of employer capitalism and private property. But it is the inevitable result of highly organized production.[10]

A military analogy is often used to justify management control. At the workplace, there are supervisors who decide and subordinates who carry out, and in private enterprise, management is the decider. There had to be a single authority and a single chain of command: "industry could not, any more than an army could, take orders from every private in the rear ranks and operate successfully."[11] With unintended irony, Michael Novak in his paean to capitalism writes that what the founders of democratic capitalism (his term) feared most was "the gathering of all power into one."[12] Yet, whatever the need for democracy elsewhere in the society, Novak maintained that "to organize industry democratically would be a grave and costly error, since democratic procedures are not designed for productivity and efficiency"—the essential objectives of organizations "whose goal it is to increase the wealth not only of the United States but of the world."[13]

During most of the 1960s, after the Republican Eisenhower administration and during the Kennedy-Johnson era, NLRBs appointed by those Democratic administrations reestablished as the national labor policy the federal government's encouragement of collective bargaining and the organization of employees into unions. In a case involving the *Fibreboard Paper Products Corporation,*[14] for example, the NLRB ruled in 1962 that the employer had a statutory obligation to bargain with its employees' union about the company's decision to contract out all of its bargaining-unit maintenance work and to terminate the employment of all bargaining-unit employees. The Board reached that decision even though the company's motivation was economic (saving $225,000 a year) rather than discriminatory. The Board ordered the employer to reinstate its maintenance operation and to fulfill its statutory obligation to bargain with the union. A Republican-appointed Board member dissented, warning that if this decision was not overruled all economic actions taken by management "whether it be the discontinuance of an unprofitable line, the closing of an unnecessary facility, or the abandonment of an outmoded procedure" would be subject to mandatory bargaining.[15]

Employers knew that this decision, if carried to its logical conclusion and extended to its full reach, could restrict management power and flexibility substantially. As *Fibreboard* worked its way to the Supreme Court in the mid-1960s, conservative columnists, such as Arthur Krock of the *New York Times,* said that the Court's ruling on the rights of corporation management would determine the future of American free enterprise.[16] Management spokesmen predicted that the Board's *Fibreboard* rule would put U.S. industry at a serious competitive disadvantage and retard economic expansion by prohibiting the movement of capital to lower wage areas; prohibiting employers from obtaining the lowest cost of production; preventing the discontinuance of unprofitable lines or products; inhibiting automation, mergers, and consolidations; and removing a natural economic regulator on the abuse of union power—the elimination or movement away of bargaining-unit jobs whenever a union forced too costly a deal on an employer.[17] Other employer representatives spoke publicly of the Board's attempt to "committeeize" the management of U.S. business or to "foist" the codetermination of fundamental business decisions, conjuring up un-American substitutes for the capitalistic system.[18] Even employers who ostensibly had accepted unionization and collective bargaining resisted mightily any encroachment on what they considered the exclusive rights and privileges of management.

The NLRB expressed a sharply different understanding of collective bargaining and management rights in its brief to the Supreme Court in *Fibreboard*. Contrary to management's claims about its rights, the NLRB argued that the national labor policy "does not undertake to assign prerogatives to management or labor, nor does it specify a list of subjects of joint concern."[19] The Board defined a broad scope for collective bargaining, saying that the national labor policy was concerned with methods for resolving "*whatever*" conflicts of interest arose between labor and employers, "at least when they directly relate to tenure of employment."[20] The NLRB's statement of its position was widely quoted publicly and in management circles and was understood by employers to portend "codetermination":

> It may be objected that the literal reading [of the statute] would give labor unions a statutory right to bargain about a host of subjects heretofore regarded as "management prerogatives," including prices, types of product, volume of production, and even methods of financing. Such is doubtless the logical, theoretical consequence of giving effect to the literal sweep of words, although the Board has never gone so far. As a practical matter, however, the scope of collective bargaining is confined by the range of *employees' vital interests*.[21]

At the same time that the new Board majority was expanding government regulation of collective bargaining, a group of distinguished academic experts in a study sponsored by the Committee on Economic Development (CED), recommended deregulation of the duty to bargain: "The present national policy calling on the parties to bargain in good faith has developed into an unwarranted intrusion into the business of the parties and a source of voluminous and wasteful litigation. The subjects to be covered, the procedures to be followed, the nuances of strategy involved in bargaining are best left to the parties themselves."[22] NLRB staff members, who had seen subcontracting, plant removals, and shutdowns used to avoid collective bargaining and destroy newly organized unions, disagreed with that recommendation. As they put it, "we witness daily, in the cases we process, the efforts of respondents to avoid and evade their duty to bargain by a variety of devices and stratagems. Without the governmental interference complained of by the [CED group], we are convinced that good faith bargaining would be a rarity."[23]

Another highly publicized and debated management rights dispute, involving the Darlington Manufacturing Company of South Carolina, raised the question of whether an employer could close an entire plant to avoid unionization. The issue was particularly important to employers who had moved south in search of nonunion and low-wage labor as well as to employers threatening to close up if unionized. It was equally critical to the Textile Workers Union of America (TWUA) and other unions still trying to organize southern mill hands. In the words of one TWUA representative, *Darlington* had been used "as a propaganda weapon against us in every election since the plant closed. We have lost elections because employees are fearful of mill closings, dismissals, and long periods of unemployment."[24]

In 1956 the TWUA began an organizing campaign among the employees of Darlington, one of twenty-seven mills and seventeen companies, all unorganized, composing the family-owned Deering Milliken Company, headed by Roger Milliken, whose mills had long been a target of the union. The Darlington plant employed approximately six hundred people in a city of five thousand. Milliken stated openly that his antiunion feelings were a major reason for the shutdown of the Darlington mill, warning that management did not intend to share its prerogatives with labor union leaders. Despite the company's vigorous resistance, including threats to close the mill if the employees voted for the union, on September 6, 1956, the TWUA won a representation election, but by only eight votes, 256 to 248. As he threatened, Milliken closed the mill the same day the employees voted for the union. Company officials told the employees that the decision to liquidate was caused by the election and encouraged them to sign a petition disavowing the union. Eighty-three percent did, but Milliken was unmoved: "As long as there are 17 percent of the hard core crowd here, I refuse to run the mill."[25] The plant ceased operations in November, and all mill machinery and equipment was sold at auction in December.

Darlington claimed the absolute right to go out of business for whatever reason, even if antiunion animus was one of the reasons. The NLRB firmly rejected Darlington's contention, holding that a plant shutdown resulting in the discharge of employees that is even partly due to employees' union activities was an unfair labor practice, even if Darlington's economic reasons for closing the mill were genuine.[26] They called Darlington's conduct contrary to the fundamental spirit and purpose of the statute. Darlington, the majority said, had destroyed the possibility of collective bargaining by shutting its plant after the employees had exercised their statutory right to choose a union representative.

The NLRB found Darlington to be only one part of a single employer, Deering Milliken Company and its affiliated corporations. Acknowledging the futility of ordering discriminatorily discharged employees reinstated to a closed plant and emphasizing the suffering of more than five hundred discharged employees "thrown into the ranks of the unemployed in a very small city," the Board held Darlington and Deering Milliken liable for back pay until the discharged employees were able to obtain substantially equivalent employment. The Board also ordered Darlington to reinstate the discriminatorily discharged employees if the plant resumed operations. In the event Darlington remained closed, however, the Board ordered Deering Milliken to offer employment to the discharged employees in its other mills in South Carolina and adjacent states and to put those for whom no work was currently available on a preferential hiring list to be the first hired when equivalent positions did become available. The Textile Workers union was dissatisfied, however, because it wanted the Board to order Deering Milliken to reopen the Darlington Mill and offer reinstatement there.[27]

Darlington hired an unusual advocate to argue its case before the Supreme Court, North Carolina's Democratic senator, Sam J. Ervin, Jr. Although no law prevented members of the Senate or House from trying cases in court, "purists looked askance at a U.S. Senator representing a private client against the U.S. Government—to say nothing of the fact that Ervin's constituents include thousands of North Carolina textile workers."[28] Ervin had helped prepare himself by attending the oral arguments before the Supreme Court in the *Fibreboard* case.

Not only was there no conflict of interest in his representing Darlington, Ervin told the Supreme Court, it was actually "harmonious" with his obligations as a senator because that office required him to uphold the Constitution and the right to go out of business at any time was a constitutional right. During his argument before the Supreme court on behalf of Darlington, Ervin quoted form the Bible, claimed that free enterprise in the textile industry rode on the case, said he was "fighting for the economic freedom of all Americans," and concluded by thanking the Court for its patience in listening to "this country lawyer."[29]

The Kennedy-Johnson Board's rulings making fundamental management decisions subjects of mandatory bargaining were the most controversial and the most strongly opposed by employers because they directly threatened management power. Many employers accepted unionization and collective bargaining but intended to keep control over the scope and manner of collective bargaining. They vigorously resisted Board decisions requiring the surrender of their prerogatives and permitting union "encroachment" into matters previously determined unilaterally by management. These decisions drew the battle line between the Board and U.S. industry because they enforced the Taft-Hartley Act's conception of joint union-management participation contemplated originally by Senator Wagner and incorporated into Taft-Hartley.

Management charged the NLRB with nullifying congressional intent, harassing free enterprise, and forcing codetermination on U.S. industry. Many employers supported legislation to transfer the NLRB jurisdiction over unfair labor practices to the federal district courts. Employers also stressed the need to maintain management rights, prerogatives, power, and flexibility in the new worldwide economic competition in which survival depended on unencumbered and creative management responses. Employers were particularly interested in becoming more efficient through technological change, ending inflationary contract settlements with unions, and in other ways seeking to overcome the labor cost advantage enjoyed by foreign competitors.

As employer opposition to self-organization and collective bargaining intensified, the Kennedy-Johnson Board remained determined to promote collective bargaining as the objective of the Wagner-Taft-Hartley Act and as an essential element of economic democracy and to encourage as well as protect employees in the exercise of their statutory right to self-organization. In response to management's accusation that the Board, through decisions such as *Fibreboard,* was trying to bring about union-management codetermination in the business enterprise, Board member Gerald Brown replied that "since the Wagner Act, the national policy of the United States has been to promote collective bargaining"; the "purpose of collective bargaining in our democratic society is to achieve 'codetermination'" of "wages, hours, and other terms and conditions of employment as a means of avoiding economic warfare."[30]

Although employers were unanimous in their opposition to NLRB rulings that threatened their decision-making prerogatives, several top-level corporate executives were dissatisfied with the disorganized and uncoordinated nature of their anti-NLRB protests. They wanted not only a unified effort but also a major change in the "climate of public understanding" and the mobilization of public opinion necessary for legislative support. In the mid-1960s, twelve top management executives formed a steering committee which eventually became known as the Labor Law Reform Group. Soon added were a Blue Ribbon Committee of more than one hundred management lawyers representing the country's most powerful corporations, a Legislative Committee for lobbying members of Congress, and a Trade Association Coordinating Committee representing approximately forty important associations.[31]

Phase one of this labor law reform project consisted of a section-by-section analysis of the Taft-Hartley Act with the objective of developing proposals for amendments. All the changes sought by the employer coalition could best be summarized by its desire to eliminate from the law the affirmation that it was the policy of the United States to encourage the practice of collective bargaining. The NLRB, they charged, had used this policy statement in the Act's preamble as a mandate to foster unionism. Rooting out this statement of purpose, which had been carried over from the Wagner Act, would make the protection of employee choice to join or refrain from joining a union—not the encouragement of collective bargaining—the undisputed purpose of Taft-Hartley. In sum, the goal was to help employers keep free of unions or, if unionized, to retain unilateral control over the workplace.

Phase two consisted of attitude surveys to determine the most effective way to develop public opinion favorable to management's proposed legislative reforms. The third and final phase involved the use of a sophisticated public relations campaign to mobilize opinion. The world's largest public relations firm, Hill & Knowlton, was hired to spearhead the campaign to develop public acceptance of management's proposals for labor law reform. Hill & Knowlton, in the words of *Fortune* magazine, was well known "as a conservative organization favoring big business and opposing labor."[32] (Two vice presidents of Hill & Knowlton wrote the book that became the basis of the Marlon Brando movie *On the Waterfront,* which concerned union racketeering on the New York docks.)

The advertising agency fashioned a message portraying the NLRB as "an outrage against America's traditional sense of fair play" and showing management in the underdog position, unions preventing economic progress, and every person a loser as a consequence. Once again management was selling free enterprise, this time through sophisticated public relations experts who had cunning (some might say insidious) ways of getting the message into people's minds: providing data and story lines to authors who were regular contributors to "think" publications such as *Harper's, Commonweal,* and The *Atlantic*

Monthly; preparing scripts for radio commentators; working with television writers "to focus gentle derision" on organized labor in T.V. dramas and comedy series; and influencing publishers and authors of junior and senior high school textbooks and courses to use Hill & Knowlton prepared materials.

The Labor Law Reform Group did not reveal its identity or its work because employers knew that the Senate Subcommittee on Separation of Powers, chaired by Senator Ervin, was scheduled to begin hearings. Employers saw these hearings as an excellent forum for management to present its labor law reform proposals. It was decided that employer testimony would carry more weight if offered by witnesses identified only as representatives of their own companies rather than as members of an organized employer effort to rewrite the labor law and defang the NLRB.

Although Ervin claimed that his committee would focus on the major role in governance played by all administrative agencies, the NLRB was the only agency scrutinized. Ten of the fourteen management attorneys who testified during the Committee's hearings, which began in 1968, were affiliated with the Labor Law Reform Group (LLRG) but none of them revealed that for the record. Witnesses associated with the LLRG hit hard at the Kennedy-Johnson Board's *Fibreboard* doctrine. Frank O'Connell, for example, accused the Board of a calculated imposition by "administrative fiat" of a policy of codetermination. Codetermination, O'Connell told the committee, was an alien doctrine, fundamentally contrary to the structure of U.S. industry because it involved the worker in the management of the enterprise. It had its deepest roots, O'Connell said, in socialism, particularly in Germany where it was a matter of national policy legislatively imposed on industry. "In a capitalistic free-enterprise economy," O'Connell testified, "critical decisions on the use of capital and on the sound management of the business must be made by the owners and managers of that capital and by them alone."[33]

At the same time that Ervin was decrying how little "say" people had in the management of their own affairs, this secret employer alliance was determined to abolish an NLRB whose decisions were intended to promote organization and collective bargaining to enable workers to participate in the management of their own affairs at their workplaces. The secret and coordinated effort undertaken by the country's major employers, including those already organized and considered models of corporate propriety, to combat the NLRB on a series of fronts demonstrates the depth and breadth of this employer opposition. Their hidden campaign included the manipulation of both the media and public opinion and used means threatening to a democratic society. As the leaders of the organized employer resistance put it, they would never accept an industrial society in which a worker's voice was equal to management's or in which all management decisions were bargainable. For them, workplace democracy and free enterprise were fundamentally incompatible.

Even before *Fibreboard*,[34] one of the most hotly contested issues in U.S. labor law was whether the act entitled workers and their representatives to participate in the making of major business and investment decisions. The worth of the Act's protection of the freedom of association depends on the importance of collective bargaining, which in turn depends on where the line, if any, is drawn between exclusive management functions on one side and the subjects of joint union-management responsibilities on the other. Decisions that expanded employers' unilateral control over the most important entrepreneurial decisions undercut collective bargaining and, therefore, the freedom of association and the purpose and policies of the act. Collective bargaining at U.S. workplaces is the most significant collective act through which workers exercise their human right of freedom of association.

The line has been drawn by the choices of the Supreme Court and subsequent NLRB decision-makers. Those choices have serious human rights, moral, legal, and economic implications. The underlying question concerns the moral basis on which workers assert their right to participation in the business decisions that affect their lives. It also involves the moral basis on which management asserts its right to resist employee efforts to participate in those decisions.[35] We in the United States have declared a national labor policy that encourages collective bargaining and, therefore, worker participation in decisions that affect their workplace lives, but we reject it in practice. On paper, we have an impressive system of industrial democracy, but relatively few workers enjoy it.[36] The White House, Congress, and even organized labor can be held responsible for the rejection.

In many key ways, however, the Supreme Court and certain NLRBs took the lead in freeing management from the constraints of the law on the basis of value-laden dicta and speculation about the inviolability of management rights. As they did with common law judges, value judgments dictated the meaning of the law for those Supreme Court decision-makers. In the words of one labor law scholar, "assumptions and values about the economic system and the prerogatives of capital, and corollary assumptions about the rights and obligations of employees, underlie many labor law doctrines."[37] Even more significant is that in the Supreme Court decisions discussed here, the decisive values are not found in or inferred from the language of the statute concerning the subjects of bargaining or the legislative history of that language. As Justice Cardozo said, judges apply their own social and economic values when deciding cases. Many of these values, moreover, have remained unchanged since common law judges applied them long before the National Labor Relations Act.[38]

The Supreme Court's decision in *Fibreboard* is an excellent example even though the Court upheld the Kennedy-Johnson NLRB's ruling that the employer was obliged to bargain with its employees' union about its decision to subcontract bargaining-unit work. The Court, however, narrowed its ruling to the specific facts of the case, where the employer had replaced existing bargaining-unit employees with those of an independent contractor to do the same work on the employer's premises under similar conditions of employment. The Court went on, moreover, to emphasize that the employer's decision to subcontract "did not alter the company's basic operation" and that "no capital investment was contemplated" by the employer. What was most important to the Court, therefore, was that requiring the employee to bargain about subcontracting under those limited circumstances "would not significantly abridge his freedom to manage his business."[39]

The Supreme Court majority did not explain, or thought that it was unnecessary to explain, why the employer would not have to bargain with the union about subcontracting out the work of the employees the union represented even if it had involved the company's basic operation, or a capital investment, or if it might "abridge" the employer's freedom to manage the business. Joined by two other justices in a concurring opinion, Justice Potter Stewart felt constrained to give his reasons because the "Court's opinion radiates implications of such disturbing breadth."[40] Justice Stewart wanted it understood that the Court "most assuredly" did "not decide that every managerial decision which necessarily terminates an individual's employment is subject to the duty to bargain."[41] Stewart excluded from an employer's statutory duty to bargain managerial decisions concerning the volume and type of advertising expenditures, product design, and the manner of financing and sales even when those decisions affect the job security of employees. He asserted that it was "hardly conceivable" that those subjects would have to be negotiated with the employees' bargaining representative.[42]

In addition, Stewart asserted that even some management decisions that terminated employment entirely—such as investment in labor-saving machinery, liquidating assets, and going out of business—need not be bargained with the employees' representative. In a still-quoted statement that has become the controlling definition of labor policy in this area, Stewart also excluded from an employer's statutory obligation to bargain "managerial decisions, which lie at the core of entrepreneurial control."[43] The subcontracting involved in *Fibre-board* was different because it did not involve "larger entrepreneurial questions as to what shall be produced, how capital shall be invested in fixed assets, or what the basic scope of the enterprise shall be."[44]

Stewart's opinion, as evidenced by "surely" and "it is hardly conceivable," was based on nothing more than his own notions of what the extent of an employer's obligation to bargain should be. Stewart's classic phrase about the core of entrepreneurial control "tells us little more than that Justice Stewart knows a non-mandatory item when he sees one."[45] The values underlying Stewart's dicta and the Court's narrowing of the employer's duty to bargain were the same economic and property rights values held and applied by common law judges in pre–Wagner Act times. National labor policy was made according to Stewart's own visceral test and ideological commitment to a free enterprise economy. As he stated, "Congress may eventually decide to give organized labor or government a far heavier hand in controlling what until now have been considered the prerogatives of private business management. That path would mark a sharp departure from the traditional principles of a free enterprise economy."[46] Justice Stewart's interpretation of labor law demonstrates the staying power of common law rules and their underlying values.

The value judgment here is clear: Employees should be denied the right to bargain about a management decision that is of great importance to employees because of its effect on their terms and conditions of employment or even on the very existence of their jobs solely because that decision is also of great importance to management. Decisions at the core of entrepreneurial concern can also be at the core of workers' concern, but the Supreme Court in *Fibreboard* made it clear that employers' concerns mattered more.

This value choice not only freed employers from bargaining with unions about subjects "at the core of entrepreneurial control" but also gave judicial decision-makers in future cases the opportunity to apply that property rights concept—with dismal consequences for the right to bargain. This value choice also weakened workers' representatives and the freedom of association by limiting their involvement to bargaining over the *effects* of employer decisions already made. The great depth of the Court's desire to insulate employer decision-making from collective bargaining is revealed by the fact that under well-established law, then and now, an employer is free to act unilaterally on any subject after bargaining to an impasse with a union.

The Supreme Court used value judgments in making fundamental labor policy choices not only in *Fibreboard* but also in *Darlington Mills*.[47] In Darlington, the Supreme Court also found that some management decisions are "so peculiarly matters of management prerogative" that they must be free of government regulation; namely, the right to close the business completely even if for antiunion reasons. In dicta rivaling Justice Potter Stewart's, Justice Harlan wrote that a complete liquidation of a business "may be motivated more by spite against the union than by business reasons, but it is not the type of discrimination which is prohibited by the Act."[48]

The Court allowed that a partial closing would be an unfair labor practice only "if motivated by a purpose to chill unionism in any of the remaining plants of the single-employer."[49] Still, the purpose of the NLRA is to protect employees in the exercise of their rights, "not merely to preclude employers form profiting from destruction of those rights."[50] The Court's decision, however, ignored the rights and interests of those employees at the closed plant who lost their jobs because of the antiunion-inspired closing. The Court concluded that no effective remedy existed for the victims of a complete shutdown motivated by antiunion animus—including payment of those employees until they obtained equivalent employment elsewhere:

> The mischief in the Court's reasoning is that it ignores the rights of those who have been discriminatorily discharged. The essence of the Court's logic is that discharge for supporting the union is not itself an unfair labor practice, that it is no wrong as to the ones discharged and that the law is not concerned with their injury. Discrimination against them is an evil only when it intimidates others; any remedy given them is only to make others feel secure. This is to see in the execution of hostages nothing more that an intimidation of the living, it is to make murder a crime only when the killer's purpose is to instill fear.[51]

As one commentator noted: "The Court's holding is indeed inconsistent with the language and policies of the act, but it is surely explainable in light of the hidden values ["preordained conclusions"] courts wish to sustain."[52]

The Supreme Court's 1981 decision in *First National Maintenance Corporation v. NLRB*[53] expanded the list of employer decisions the Court chose to deem too important to be bargained with a union. In another dicta-filled decision riddled with value judgments unsubstantiated by legislative history or any other evidence, the Court decided that an employer's decision to close part of the business for economic reasons was "free from the constraints of the bargaining process to the extent essential for the running of a profitable business."[54] The

Court approached the case as a question of how to determine what management decisions were mandatory subjects of bargaining. It did this even though there was no statutory basis for classifying certain subjects as exclusive management prerogatives; indeed, Congress had explicitly rejected any such categorization when it passed the Taft-Hartley Act. (This fact was twisted in the Court's opinion into "Congress did not explicitly state what issues of mutual concern to unions and management it intended to exclude from mandatory bargaining.")[55]

Despite what it acknowledged was the open-endedness of the relevant statutory language and the absence of any basis in the legislative history of that language, the Court simply asserted that "Congress had no expectation that the elected union representative would become an equal partner in the running of the business enterprise."[56] The dominant influence of the personal value judgments of the majority of justices in the case is evidenced by their reliance on Justice Stewart's dicta concerning management rights.

The Court in *First National Maintenance* proceeded to fashion a cost-benefit test, not a rights test, to determine if there was an obligation to bargain: "In view of an employer's need for unencumbered decision-making, bargaining over management decisions that have a substantial impact on the continued availability of employment should be required only if the benefit, for labor-management relations and the collective bargaining process, outweighs the burden placed on the conduct of the business."[57] As one commentator put it, the test "turns the explicit purpose of the Wagner Act on its head" given that the act's purpose was to encourage industrial democracy through collective bargaining even when management decision-making might be "encumbered."[58] Not surprisingly, given the deciders' value preferences, the Court, after applying this test abstractly to the issue of partial closings, simply asserted that "the harm likely to be done to [First National Maintenance's] need to operate freely" in this matter "outweighs the incremental benefit that might be gained through the union's participation in making the decisions."[59]

Justices William Brennan and Thurgood Marshall, in dissent, criticized the majority for deciding an important question of industrial relations "on the basis of pure speculation." Brennan and Marshall also rejected the majority's cost-benefit test, not only because it, too, was based "solely on speculation" but also because it was a one-sided approach that took into account "only the interests of management" and failed "to consider the legitimate employment interests of the workers and their union."[60] The message was clear: The more important the entrepreneurial decision, the more excluded and protected it would be from the reach of the statutory duty to bargain. Despite the Court's cautionary words about the limited applicability of its decision, the Reagan-appointed NLRB majority not only adopted but extended the Supreme Court's value judgments favoring management prerogatives.

For example, that Board decided that a company's transfer of bargaining-unit work to non–bargaining-unit employees was a management right that could be limited only by a contractual provision explicitly prohibiting such transfers of work. Some sophistry lurked in the Board's contention that the wage provisions of the employer-union contract were not violated because there were no bargaining-unit employees left because their jobs were being performed elsewhere by nonunion workers not covered by the contract.[61] In another case, the Board ignored the Supreme Court's case-by-case cost-benefit analysis approach (whatever its demerits) and simply labeled in advance certain management decisions as not subject to mandatory bargaining: "Such decisions included, *inter alia,* decisions to sell a business or a plant thereof, to dispose of its assets, to restructure or to consolidate operations, to subcontract, to invest in labor-saving machinery, to change the methods of finance or of sales, advertising, product design, and all other decisions akin to the foregoing."[62]

All of this adds up to broken statutory promises and, more importantly, violations of the human right of freedom of association. The most fundamental aspiration of the human person is what philosopher Jacques Maritain called "the aspiration towards the liberty of expansion and autonomy."[63] He also called it a movement toward a liberation or emancipation from economic and political bondage. That liberation cannot occur without the exercise of the freedom of association. It downgrades this fundamental right to respect it only as a means or an instrument to bring about the exercise of other rights, such as the right to organize and bargain collectively or the right to strike. Rather, the right to strike, to organize, and to bargain collectively are species of the independent right of freedom of association.[64] The violation of the freedom to associate denies individuals what they need to live a fully human life. The freedom of association is also an essential component of democracy. It is, the "single human rights standard by which all regimes, all societies, all countries can be judged."[65]

A full human life requires the kind of participation in the economic, political, and social life of the human community that enables people to have an influence on the decisions that affect their lives. Yet, most people are subjugated to economic forces and economic power over which they are permitted to have little or no control. Rights and freedom are routinely left outside factory gates and office buildings with barely a murmur of protest. Consequently, far too many workers stand before their employer not as adult persons with rights but as powerless children or servants totally dependent on the will and interests of that employer.

What happened to the employees of *First National Maintenance Corporation* is a good example:

> The maintenance workers of a Brooklyn nursing home voted to be represented by a union. As a consequence, within four months they were on the streets. They had no union, no jobs, and no right to bump or transfer into another job. From this sad story, the United States Supreme Court would, four years later, fashion a narrative of rights and freedom. Not the rights and freedom of the workers, whose very names have been lost to history. Rather, the maintenance contractor who employed them turned out to be free, to have the right, not to meet at all with their union, nor any substantive obligation to them, and the same was true of the nursing home itself.[66]

Workers were promised that by exercising their fundamental human right of freedom of association by organizing and engaging in collective bargaining they would be able to gain some control over their workplace lives. They were told that democratic principles and human dignity "demanded that workers have a voice in the decisions that control their working lives."[67] They were also told that the "divine right of employers would give way to democratic industrial government"[68] and that the government of the United States would protect them and encourage them in this exercise of their freedom of association.

In a democracy, private power is a public trust. The very purpose of the United States, although too rarely realized, was to enable the powerless to restrain the powerful. Neither private nor government power would be permitted to control human lives, because both would be subject to the public will. Democracy is working only when it meets this test—and the right of people to participate in the decisions that affect their lives is one of the most fundamental principles of democracy and human rights. The right of workers to participate in decisions affecting their workplace lives, on which the Wagner Act was based, is the policy most consistent not only with democratic principles but also with the principles of human rights.

It is not possible to be morally neutral about these issues. It is also not possible to separate moral and ethical questions from economic and legal ones in fashioning a labor policy. At its most basic, for example, a national labor policy must determine the extent to which employers should be allowed to make decisions in isolation from the people affected by those decisions, particularly employees, and whether that decision-making power should be shared in some manner under some circumstances.

Labor never came close to achieving the system of workplace democracy envisioned by Senator Wagner. In 1984, a House Labor Committee concluded that the labor law had failed to achieve its purpose and, furthermore, was being used "as a weapon to obstruct collective bargaining" and to create only the illusion of protecting workers against discrimination.[69] My own study of Wagner-Taft-Hartley from 1947–1994, a book entitled *Broken Promise,* shows how a policy that encouraged the replacement of industrial autocracy with a democratic system of power sharing was turned into governmental protection of employers' unilateral decision-making authority over decisions that greatly affected wages, hours, and working conditions. More specifically, it demonstrates how the statute and NLRB case law have come to legitimize employer opposition to the organization of employees, collective bargaining, and workplace democracy—in other words, opposition to the exercise by employees of their human right of freedom of association.[70]

Since about 1970 the Taft-Hartley Act has primarily been interpreted and applied in ways that put federal government power in private employer hands by strengthening the managerial authority of employers who already had great power over their employees. That development, together with the decline of unionism, leaves unprotected the great majority of employees who do not have sufficient individual economic and political power to protect themselves. Almost seventy-five years after the Wagner Act, the overwhelming majority of employees are unorganized and unrepresented and work unprotected by collectively bargained grievance and arbitration systems in situations where they may be fired at will for almost any reason. A truly democratic government and a society that respected and promoted human rights would not be indifferent to the lack of democracy and freedom of association at the workplace.

It is foolish and deceitful to make a commitment to a national labor policy of encouraging collective bargaining and then allow employers to block the implementation of that policy by legitimizing their opposition to collective bargaining and increasing their ability to resist unionization. Workers' freedom of association is being violated in this country. Yet, as a Human Rights Watch report asserts, "Many Americans think of workers' organizing, collective bargaining, and strikes solely as union-versus management disputes that do not raise human rights concerns."[71] All people in this country, not only lawmakers and policy makers, need to understand the moral as well as legal issues involved in labor law and its implementation. Americans need to understand more than the rules of labor law; they need to understand the values underlying those rules. They need to understand, as well, that there are fundamental human rights at issue here and that their decisions about those rights will ultimately determine what kind of people they are and what kind of society they have.

The self-imposed legal isolation of U.S. courts, including the Supreme Court, however, diminishes the likelihood that international human rights principles and precedents will inform their decisions anytime in the near future. Consequently, the judiciary is likely to continue to perceive collective bargaining only as an economic instrument to give workers greater bargaining power and not as a manifestation of the human right of freedom of association. That explains why the judiciary continues to choose to apply the long-dominant values inherent in the market economic philosophy to worker-management relative power issues.

6

Violations of the Human Right to Life and Limb

Safety and Health at U.S. Workplaces

Whether understood as having divine, moral, or legal roots, the concept of human rights has at its core the sacredness of every human life. No aspect of human work is so directly and intimately associated with the sacredness of human life than the safety and health of men, women, and children who labor. There is no more basic or fundamental right: "It is in fact the right to life that we are talking about when we talk about worker safety."[1] Occupational disease and injury are not merely economic inefficiencies—they kill people.

In addition, the protection and promotion of human rights are intended to enable people to lead ever more fully human lives by expanding the range of their choices through access to the resources they need to make those choices realistic. Rather than being an expression of the sacredness of human life, however, the experiences of those who labor in this country express the sacrifice of human life to economic development. Although rarely expressed openly, only widespread acceptance of the conviction that certain lives are cheap can explain why this country has tolerated workplace-caused illnesses, injuries, disabilities, and death as well as the associated human suffering that continue to this day.

This same larger society recognizes that the right to physical security, particularly its own physical security, is indispensable to the enjoyment of all other rights. Although one is no less dead or maimed or assaulted by an on-the-job injury or an occupational disease than from a gunshot, U.S. society certainly treats the causes differently.

To the contrary, Emily Spieler asserts a "universal principle: that no worker should work in conditions that involve knowing exposure to preventable, predictable, serious risks"[2] to their health and safety. That so many working people in this country are exposed to such preventable, predictable, and serious risks is an injustice not merely a "misfortune." It is the consequence of deliberate choices concerning the role of government, economic philosophy, freedom of association and labor organization, employer power and authority, and moral values as well as greed, arrogance, and exploitation.

The enormous wealth and unprecedented prosperity that accompanied America's industrialization also came with horrendous human cost: "speed-ups, monotonous tasks and exposure to chemical toxins, metallic and organic dusts, and unprotected machinery"[3] that made U.S. workplaces among the most dangerous in the world. Long before attention was given to work-related illnesses, "thousands of wage earners, men, women and children [are] caught in the machinery of our record breaking production and turned out cripples. Other thousands [are] killed outright."[4] In 1907, when that comment was made, no one could say how many were killed, disabled, or otherwise seriously injured in this human carnage. But it was estimated that a "greater number of people are killed every year by so-called accidents than are killed in many wars of considerable magnitude."[5]

It is shameful that the United States still lacks accurate and comprehensive data on workplace injuries and workplace-caused illnesses. As late as 2000, Spieler, citing an estimate that 65,000 workers die each year from work-related injuries and illnesses, cautioned "that there are enormous difficulties (even in the United States where reporting is required) with determining the real number of occupational injuries, fatalities, and illnesses."[6]

Although workplaces are still dangerous for too many workers, researchers report that the U.S. public is "unaware that workers are in such peril."[7] Whether as a consequence of this ignorance or not, the public has made a greater commitment (weak as even that is) to protecting the environment than to protecting human beings at work. One of the tragic ironies here is that workers have been "silent canaries" or human guinea pigs, identifying through their suffering the toxic nature of many chemicals, for example, thereby "warning the rest of society of the problems."[8] As early as 1910, Alice Hamilton, one of the first U.S. specialists in the field of occupational disease, said that "knowledge about the health effects of new chemicals depended on the use of workers as 'guinea pigs.'"[9] In 1935, the *American Journal of Public Health* editorialized: "It seems the cart is always before the horse in industrial hygiene in this country" in that "the deleterious effects of new methods or new substances have been first discovered in the workers themselves (as the guinea pigs)...before scientific investigations were undertaken."[10] Almost forty years later, a group of prominent scientists issued the following statement:

> Workers have long served as unwitting "guinea pigs," providing useful toxicological data which helped to protect the public. The effects of most environmental pollutants, such as carbon monoxide, lead, mercury and also of most human carcinogens were first detected in workmen; the in-plant environment is a concentrated toxic microcosm of that outside....The demand of labor to participate actively in protecting the health and safety of workers is basic and inalienable and cannot be sacrificed to economic interests.[11]

The earliest efforts to rectify the injustice of preventable work accidents focused on lessening the economic burden on the victims and their dependents or survivors. Although necessary, this limited approach to workplace accidents and illness was a "body in the morgue approach"—as a union advocate would call it many years later—because no action would be taken until after a worker was injured or killed.[12]

As necessary and well-meaning as the financial compensation approach was and is, it also leaves untouched a most fundamental issue of distributive justice; namely, that only certain workers are exposed to the most severe risks to their bodies and lives. Production, mining, agricultural, and maintenance workers, for example, are more exposed to workplace hazards than managers or white-collar professional workers. As a result, many workers believe that "society considers them a marginal and expendable class" and that management "'couldn't care less if you died.'"[13]

Nothing much has changed in that regard. In the classic *Work-Accidents and the Law*[14] published in 1910, Russell Sage Foundation researchers focused on industrial accidents in Allegheny County, Pennsylvania, which encompassed most of the Pittsburgh steel district with approximately 250,000 wage earners, 70,000 in steel mills, 20,000 in mines, and 50,000 on the railroads. In one year, July 1, 1906, to June 30, 1907, 526 men were killed by work accidents, and hospitals in the county received another 509 injured. Of the injured for whom there were hospital records (researchers were able to locate hospital records for 294 of the 509 nonfatal accident cases), 25 percent suffered a "serious permanent injury," which was defined as "hopelessly crippled in one or both legs," a lost arm or hand or eye, partial paralysis, or a combination of such injuries. Almost 31 percent suffered "slight permanent injuries" such as "a lame leg, arm, foot, hand or back not serious enough to disable a man" or the loss of a finger or slight impairment of hearing.[15]

The lead author, Crystal Eastman, understood the social and economic class nature of the situation:

> In work accidents we have a peculiar kind of disaster, by which, roughly speaking, only wage-earners are affected, and which falls upon them in addition to all the disasters that are their common lot. A special cloud always threatens the home of the worker in dangerous trades, because his daily work involves physical risk to him, and on his life and strength depend the comfort and happiness of his family.[16]

Most revealing of the attitude that only certain people matter (or that some people matter more than others) is the author's need to inform the people of Pittsburgh, who took "moral comfort" in the belief that it was foreign laborers and not Americans that were being killed and injured, that 43 percent of the men killed in 1906–1907 were "American born."[17] Apparently, these people would care more about the workplace deaths, injuries, and illnesses of Americans than about those of Croatians, Poles, Russians, Slavs, Hungarians, Italians, Germans, Scots, Irish, and other immigrants working in the steel mills, railroads, and mines.

These were also working people who did "not have the luxury of grief" because the "tyranny of hard work in their lives" left little time for pondering what the author considered the "unanswerable 'why' of sorrow."[18] It was not "because they lacked feeling," Eastman observed, "but because they are so used to trouble that the thought of it has ceased to rouse them":

> That poor people are used to trouble is commonplace. I mean by "trouble," the less subtle disappointments of life, those which come with disease, injury, and premature death. Of all these rougher blows of fortune, the poor family gets more than an even share. This stands to reason, if experience has not already convinced one of it. To the ordinary causes of sickness,—unsanitary dwellings, overcrowding, undue exposure, overwork, lack of necessary vacation, work under poisonous conditions,—to all these, poor people are much more constantly

exposed than others. To injury and death caused by accident they are also more
exposed. Poor people's children play in dangerous places, on the street, near railroad tracks. The poor man's dwelling is not often fireproof. Poor people do most
of the hazardous work in the world, and the accidents connected with work
form the majority of all accidents.[19]

Eastman attributed an "unquestioning acceptance of misfortune" to a "what
can you do about it attitude."[20] Over eighty years later, Donna Bazemore, a former poultry plant worker in an industry whose workers were then predominantly African American females subject to racism and sexual harassment as
well as dangerous working conditions, explained to a House Subcommittee on
Labor-Management Relations that "it's natural to ask why they [these workers]
would take this kind of abuse." She said it was because "there is no other choice.
There aren't other jobs that are available. For almost all workers, the result
is that they keep their mouths shut and do what they're told."[21] Other workers in hazardous jobs echo the same resignation and futility expressed in the
Pittsburgh survey about who would listen; fear of being tagged a troublemaker
and losing one's job; nothing being done until someone gets hurt; being used
as guinea pigs; management being immune from the dangers they experience;
equipment being treated with more respect than workers; and an overall sense
of powerlessness and lack of control.[22] Human Rights Watch's 2004 report on
workers' rights in the U.S. beef, pork, and poultry slaughtering and processing
industry, aptly titled "Blood, Sweat and Fear," found that meatpacking work
"has extraordinarily high rates of injury" and that immigrant workers, "an increasing percentage of the workforce in the industry," are particularly at risk.[23]
Referring to the treatment and working conditions of the immigrants described
by Sinclair Lewis in his 1906 novel, *The Jungle,* Human Rights Watch concluded
that "a century later, abusive working conditions and treatment still torment a
mostly immigrant labor force in the American meatpacking industry."[24]

Byssinosis, or "brown lung" as Ralph Nader labeled it in the 1970s, is a disease of cotton mill workers caused by the inhalation of cotton dust. Its symptoms are chest tightness, shortness of breath, wheezing, and coughing. There
is still no cure for brown lung "once the disease has moved beyond the early
reversible stage."[25] Consistent with the evidence that only certain people matter, "Mill workers were considered to be the lowest class of whites and were
completely dependent on the good will of the mill owners for their economic
survival. Within such conditions, the mill workers lacked even rudimentary
social, political, or economic power."[26]

These are only examples of the long and lasting violations of the most basic human rights of workers in this country. The misuse of economic power and the widespread acceptance of the market economic philosophy and value judgments—what some call the "rules of the game"—cause this human suffering. Employers in the United States have had and continue to have the economic power to determine those rules. The prevalence of that power cannot be comprehended fully without understanding the dominance of the underlying values of market capitalism that give the free enterprise system of profit, efficiency, economic competition, and managerial control of the workplace priority over workers' rights to a safe and healthful workplace. The dominance of these values did not come about naturally or by accident. As in other areas, organized business, in regard to worker safety and health, used its great political power, wealth, and influence with the mass media to "teach Americans the virtues of profit making and free enterprise"[27] without making it appear that business was seeking special favors.

Business succeeded not only in dominating the prevailing political and intellectual climate but also in defining occupational safety and health issues in ways that made their protection through governmental regulation appear detrimental to economic progress. Employers blamed regulation of business for slow economic growth, diminished productivity, unemployment, inadequate savings and investment, and in every other way hamstringing the free enterprise system, including the ability to compete in international markets with firms not subject to such regulations.

Many academics, particularly economists of the free market persuasion, helped business make its case. This current episode of laissez-faire economics has its origins in Adam Smith's[28] basic philosophy and assumptions: that self-interest is what motivates people to act; that competition, not the state, is the regulator of self-interest; and that consequently, it was necessary that government leave the market alone and not meddle with it because "the invisible hand" as Smith called the "laws of market" would lead the self-interests of man in the direction of the best interest of the whole society. The rising industrialists of Smith's time found in his theory "the theoretical justification they needed to block the first government attempts to remedy the scandalous conditions of the times."[29] As Robert Heilbroner has written:

> But because any act of the government—even such laws as those requiring the whitewashing of factories or preventing the shackling of children to machines—could be interpreted as hampering the free operation of the market, [Smith's]

The Wealth of Nations was liberally quoted to oppose the first humanitarian legislation.[30]

In the early 1920s, Frank Knight, the founder of the free market School of Economics at the University of Chicago, remarked "that the distinction between laborers and the owners of companies is that laborers have freely elected to risk their health and safety, whereas owners have chosen instead to risk their capital."[31] Modern-day free market economists still maintain, as did Adam Smith, that workers freely accept employment that poses a higher risk to their health and safety. They do this mainly, Smith said, because they will receive higher wages to compensate them for the unusually hazardous conditions of work to which they will be exposed. Economic theory says that workers will bargain for these wage premiums, or hazard pay, as extra compensation for exposing themselves to workplace hazards and that employers will pay those wage premiums to attract those workers to hazardous jobs until the cost of removing or substantially reducing the hazards is less than the cost of premium pay. When workers' compensation benefits increased without injury reduction, economists blamed it on employee behavior. They concluded that when workers' compensation benefits increased, workers were less vigilant and, therefore, suffered more (and more serious) injuries because the higher benefits reduced the economic cost such injuries caused them.[32]

These hazard pay and workers' compensation theories betray arrogance as well as ignorance about the behavior of workers. Aside from the inadequacy of workers' compensation benefits, this is a "bizarre view of human nature under which the prospect of money in the future will persuade people to risk severe pain, hospitalization, dismemberment, and even death in the present."[33] As already discussed, moreover, the overwhelming number of workers in this country have no bargaining power to negotiate wage premiums—particularly when they can be fired at will. In addition, workers in many hazardous jobs can be replaced easily. Often these workers have no alternative jobs readily available. In reality, the pool of labor for many hazardous jobs consists of poorly educated and low-skilled workers who accept the risks for low pay. Workers also do not have adequate information about job hazards and what they are being exposed to, particularly given the uncertainty about the causes of many diseases. Contrary to economic theory:

> [M]anagement has sought to organize the process of production in many hazardous industries so as to reduce the need for highly skilled workers. To the

extent possible management replaces these workers with a combination of less skilled employees and increased supervision and control. Over time, managerial responses produce a pattern in which hazardous jobs require less education achievement, provide less on-the-job training, and offer fewer opportunities for worker autonomy, responsibility and creativity in the work process. These unskilled hazardous jobs pay lower wages than skilled safe jobs.[34]

Participants in Dorothy Nelkin's and Michael S. Brown's survey of chemical industry workers asked why they should be burdened "with the impossible choice between health and work."[35] In the words of one worker:

> Every worker has a choice. Any worker can quit his job. I mean when you come down to the brass tacks, anyone can quit. But the realities of life—family, the children, mortgage payment—impose certain limitations on the worker's right to just quit. I don't feel personally that people should have to quit to protect their health. I feel that the employer by obligation, by law, must provide a safe and healthy workplace. And if the employers live up to their obligations, then there would be no reason for a worker to make the choice.[36]

Another worker put it this way:

> You never balance the wage against the risk; you balance the wage against the alternative. And the alternative is starving when you're put in this situation. That's what so phony about this cost/benefit analysis. A worker in the plant doesn't say, "Well, I'm getting $6.50 an hour so I'm gonna take the risk." The worker in the plant says, "I'm getting $6.50 an hour. If I open my mouth I might get nothing an hour, or I might get minimum wage.... There's no difference for a person in that position. Either way they're trapped.[37]

John Stuart Mill over one hundred years earlier drew the same conclusion. In his *Principles of Political Economy,* Mill wrote that, contrary to Smith's notions, "The really exhausting and the really repulsive labours, instead of being better paid than others, are almost invariably paid the worst of all, because performed by those who have no choice."[38] In the late 1800s a British court echoed Mill: "If the plaintiff could have gone away from the dangerous place without incurring the risk of losing his means of livelihood, the case might have been different; but he was obliged to be there; his poverty, not his will, consented to incur the damage."[39] It would be an interesting study in values to try to determine why today's free market economists follow Smith and not Mill—at least concerning the hazard pay theory.

In sum, market economic theory would have a worker's health and safety bought and sold on the same basis as most commodities. Free market economic theory assumes that employers have the right to expose workers to toxic substances and other hazardous conditions of work. The hazard pay theory, in addition, affirms as proper a distribution of power that permits CEOs and skilled and educated employees to buy more safety than less educated and less skilled workers. Confronting a poor person with the choice of money rather than health and safety is on its face an indictment of the distribution of wealth in this society. Thomas McGarity and Sidney Shapiro observed sarcastically: "In a country that holds equality of opportunity as a primary value, perhaps the better measure for the value of a worker's life is how much it would take to induce the chairman of the board to leave his [or her] current job and undertake hazardous employment for a year."[40]

Many economists, however, maintain that issues of distributive justice are beyond their jurisdiction. As one put it:

> Those who die because society rejects inefficient lifesaving programs will not be around to benefit from the bigger pie. Does this fact require condemnation of any policy that stops short of maximum effort to prevent deaths? No. It is inevitable that public policy will create losers who are beyond the reach of compensation. But this fact should spur thinking about who the losers are and how we feel about their plight.[41]

The widows and orphans of those workers (losers?) whose deaths could have been prevented will surely be consoled to know that scholars will be thinking about their plight.

Employer control of the workplace was further legitimized when business went unchallenged in defining the nature of the workplace health and safety problem. For many years, the literature of occupational safety and health, for example, was focused on worker carelessness, worker failures to follow procedures or management's instructions, or poor personal habits outside of work such as drinking and smoking. The popular "accident proneness" explanation shifted the responsibility for accidents and illness from an employer to the victim. The concept was also used to justify the conclusion that voluntary education of workers to better safety practices and not government regulation was the way to prevent accidents.[42]

At the turn of the century, efforts to blame the workers were "built upon the general antipathy for immigrants,"[43] so accidents were presumed to be due to immigrants' ignorance. Later, fault would determine "who would have to pay for the suffering generated in the process of creating wealth."[44] Once again, not much has changed. Human Rights Watch found in 2004 that "Despite overwhelming scientific evidence of the hazards to workers in meat and poultry processing and other repetitive, stressed-based labor, corporations frequently dismiss MSD [musculoskeletal disorders] cases as 'anecdotes' and attribute the problem to workers' lifestyle and 'confounding factors' like housework, vitamin consumption, sports activities, and working on cars at home."[45]

Human Rights Watch also cited an "undercount of nonfatal occupational injuries across industrial sectors as high as 69 percent."[46] The report concluded that the design of the workers' compensation system in this country "encourages employers to attempt to prevent workers' compensation costs by reducing the filing of claims instead of the occurrence of injuries."[47]

The judicially enforced employment-at-will doctrine, moreover, not only sanctions employer domination of the workplace but also puts too many workers in the position of having to choose between their living in the form of a paycheck or their living in terms of their physical health and safety. This dilemma confronted and confronts the poor, unskilled, and uneducated workers in the most inhumane ways. In the textile industry before the 1970s, mill owners, particularly those in the South, had absolute power over their workers—"control over their bodies and minds, their living and dying" and used that power to suppress any union activity.[48] An NLRB representative holding hearings at the Hamrick Mills in Gaffney, South Carolina, a few years after passage of the Wagner Act, described these workers as "men, women, and young folks, who can neither read nor write—the fifth grade was the highest education any witness had gone—starving people and tired land. Girls with yellow teeth who chew snuff to keep lint from their lungs."[49] He understood that the violation of these workers' freedom of association left them powerless to prevent the violations of their human right to safety and health. He called their situation "tragic and revolting" and expressed the hope that their "few minutes say under the protection of the U.S. government" would "permit them to dare vision a time when they can demand social justice, for and by themselves."[50]

From the earliest days of the master-servant doctrine, however, the law made management's authority and freedom to operate the enterprise and direct the workforce superior to all other rights including workers' rights to a safe and healthful workplace. Under the common law, the master (employer) had an obligation to provide a reasonably safe place to work, reasonably competent employees, and instructions for employees when reasonably necessary. On the other hand, the servant (employee) had the burden of proving that the master had failed to fulfill any one of those duties. Given their market philosophy values, common law judges' notions of what constituted reasonable employer duties were difficult enough obstacles for any employee to surmount.

In addition to judicial support, however, employers had three powerful common law defenses against employee claims: (1) *assumption of risk* (i.e., the worker's injury "was caused by an ordinary danger of such work, or by a danger which the [employee] knew about, or should have known about, and that he continued working in spite of it"); (2) *negligence of a fellow servant* (i.e., that the injury was due to the negligence of a coworker, not the employer, and that, too, was a risk assumed by workers); and (3) *contributory negligence* (i.e., that the injury was caused at least in part by the injured worker's own negligence).[51]

These common law doctrines protected the strong from the weak:

> Almost every element of unfairness in this law arises, from one misconception; namely, that the two parties are on an equal footing. In the eyes of the law every working man, from the trained American locomotive engineer with a strong union behind him, to the newly-landed "Hunkie," tongue-tied and bewildered, is on an equal footing with the United States Steel Corporation in all its masterfully concentrated power. In the contract of hire, the law assumes that the workman is as free to accept or refuse a job as the employer is to take or drop him. In the matter of the release, the law assumes that the stricken and terrified widow of an ignorant laboring man is in a position of equal understanding and enlightenment in regard to the respective interests of the parties, with the hardened claim agent employed by the corporation.[52]

The two- or three-year delay in getting a decision from a court, moreover, meant little to a corporation but had a devastating effect on injured workers whose earning power was diminished or lost and on "the lives of the widow and children left helpless by the sudden death of their provider."[53]

Employers got off cheaply with low payments to victims of workplace accidents, which reflected the low value society placed on these workers and their families once their productivity was reduced or ended. In the first three decades of the 1900s, however, reformers in some states were able to get employer liability laws passed that weakened the common law defenses of employers. These laws also provided greater access to juries that were more likely to find employers at fault, which caused employers public embarrassment, and to arrive at verdicts that "began to raise the price of inflicting injuries upon workers to something above the level of poverty and destitution."[54]

As the price for limbs and eyes lost at the workplace rose, in part through higher premiums for employers' liability insurance, employers and their insurers sought a compensation system that eliminated uncertainty in the outlays for injury compensation and still allowed employers "to get off relatively cheaply with low payouts" to those who suffered workplace accidents.[55] The result was a series of state no-fault compensation systems under which employees gave up their right to sue employers for the medical expenses of disability, pain and suffering, and punitive damages in return for payment of limited compensation, according to a predetermined schedule of benefits, without showing a legal fault on the employer's part and with elimination of the employer defenses of assumption of risk, contributory negligence, and fellow servant responsibility.[56]

Although this workers' compensation system has benefited many workers injured on the job, employers have used the system not only to stabilize their compensation costs but also to transfer much of the financial burden of workplace accidents onto injured workers and the public that picks up much of the cost through taxation to pay welfare and social security benefits to those no longer able to work. Most compensation plans, moreover, ignore the problem of long-term disability and were structured in a way that made them unable to consider toxic illness claims that have lengthy latency periods from the date of exposure to the manifestation of an illness. The workers' compensation plans, moreover, have not lessened employers' control of safety and health matters. It is indicative of the dominance of the market economic philosophy that criticism of the workers' compensation system is directed at its allegedly detrimental effect on employers' ability to compete and at workers' allegedly malingering and bilking the system and not at well-documented incidences of malfeasance by employers within the system.[57]

In the politically turbulent and activist-driven late 1960s, occupational safety and health finally became widely acknowledged as a national problem. The Johnson administration drafted a bill that extended federal regulation to workplace safety and health, including empowering the Department of Labor through the use of injunctions to shut down any plant that posed an imminent threat to workers. President Johnson called the thousands of deaths and millions of injuries on the job the "shame of a modern industrial nation."[58] Secretary of Labor Willard Wirtz told Congress in 1968 that the proposed health and safety legislation was a victory for a new politics that "measure[d] progress in qualitative as well as quantitative terms"; rejected "human sacrifice for the development of progress"; placed "higher value...on a life, or a limb, or an eye"; and asserted "the absolute priority of individual over institutional interests and of human over economic values."[59] Although Wirtz never referred to human rights in his statement to Congress, he was expounding human rights standards.

The Johnson bill was killed by intense employer opposition that claimed most workplace accidents were caused by worker error and carelessness, that existing safety and health programs were sufficient, and that what was really needed was protection against an encroaching federal bureaucracy. However, the new Nixon administration, seeking to win blue-collar support away from the Democrats, proposed its own safety and health legislation. After some compromises—including deletion of provisions allowing the Secretary of Labor to close down a plant in situations of immediate danger and guaranteeing compensation for employees who walked off hazardous jobs—the Occupational Safety and Health Act (OSHA) was signed into law on December 29, 1970.[60]

The OSH Act has been called a radical piece of legislation because it promised workers a substantive right to safe and healthful workplaces and obligated the federal government to protect workers from occupational accidents and diseases. The Act empowered the Secretary of Labor to set and enforce safety and health standards covering all workers except those employed by the federal, state, and local government; it created the National Institute for Occupational Safety and Health (NIOSH) to develop and recommend safety and health standards, including for toxic substances; and it obliged employers to comply with those standards and "to furnish to each of his employees employment and a place of employment which were free from recognized standards that are causing or likely to cause death or serious physical harm to his employees." The Act also established civil and criminal penalties for violations of the Act; required the Secretary of Labor when issuing standards concerning toxic materials to set a standard that ensured "to the extent feasible on the basis of the best available evidence that no employee will suffer material impairment of health or functional capacity even if such employee has regular exposure to the hazard dealt with by such standard for the period of his working life"; and created a number of worker rights to be involved in the enforcement of the Act such as the right to information about hazards and to participate in workplace inspections.[61]

One senator predicted that OSHA "will mark the greatest single contribution to the health and welfare of American workers that has yet been made by Congress."[62] The congressman who sponsored the Republican version of the bill in the House considered the OSH Act an "unprecedented response by Congress to the need to help save the lives and protect the health of the working men and women throughout the nation."[63]

The promised right to health and safety in the Act is expansive and broadly defined: "to assure so far as possible every working man and woman in the Nation safe and healthful working conditions."[64] After almost forty years of the OSH Act, neither the Act nor OSHA, the agency created to administer the Act, has lived up to the noble intention of protecting workers from dangerous and disabling working conditions.[65] The promises of the OSH Act have been broken. Critics now call the promises "wishful thinking"[66] and lament that OSHA's sanctions reveal "an accommodation with human expendability."[67] They also charge that OSHA has shifted attention "from saving lives to saving money."[68] By 2005, OSHA had "virtually ceased issuing regulations that would limit potential exposure to causes of disease and other workplace hazards, even in the face of compelling scientific evidence."[69]

Whatever progress OSHA did make during its first ten years was dissipated during the Reagan administration. Despite the statute's promise of guaranteed substantive rights to occupational health and safety, OSHA and Republican and Democratic administrations alike left employers in control of the work process. Workers remained subordinate and shut out of decisions concerning their own health and safety. As in labor relations, employer competitiveness, efficiency, and profitability took precedence over occupational safety and health.

Although this is not the place to discuss in depth all the reasons the promises of the OSH Act have been broken, suffice it to say that those promises have been broken not by some uncontrollable impersonal forces but by deliberate political and economic policy choices.[70] The Reagan administration, for example, deliberately and systematically implemented an antiregulatory ideology that was most responsive to the needs of business. Reagan had promised to get what he called big government off the backs of business. In the opinion of a U.S. Chamber of Commerce official: "I don't think there's a regulatory agency in Washington that has delivered more on candidate Reagan's promises on regulatory reform—OSHA's way out in front in that respect."[71] Candidate Reagan's promises to businesses were kept but not the OSH Act's promises to working men and women. It is a classic example of how to repeal a statute without changing the law.[72]

No political administration has taken seriously the statutorily promised rights to occupational health and safety. Although the conservative Republican Reagan and Bush administrations displayed their hostility to OSHA, the Democratic Clinton administration's enforcement record was no better than its predecessor's on a number of measures. The Clinton record was the "worst in the history of the OSHA act" with the lowest number of annual inspections and the highest percentage of proposed serious, willful, repeat violations dismissed or downgraded and "worse than the Bush administration's" in regard to the number of serious, willful violations found and total penalties ultimately assessed."[73]

The story of OSHA's broken promises also includes weak and inadequate enforcement. OSHA can assess fines and seek criminal penalties. Many employers, in deciding whether to comply with the OSH Act, compare the costs of compliance with the costs of noncompliance: "Compliance costs include the expense of purchasing safety equipment or taking other preventive steps that OSHA requires. Noncompliance costs are related to the probability an employer will be inspected and the size of the penalties that will be assessed for any violations that are found."[74] The ability to target inspections on the most dangerous workplaces is the key to effective enforcement of the Act. There is not a substantial probability, however, that even dangerous workplaces will be inspected. There are only about four thousand federal and state OSHA compliance officers to inspect and ensure the safety of approximately 92 million employees in 6 million workplaces.[75] Although Congress in 1990 did increase the allowable fines, the fines imposed by OSHA are typically insufficient to induce employers to obtain new equipment or protective devices even in cases of death or serious injury. Larger fines and the nature of the citation, moreover, are often reduced in agency negotiations with employers.[76]

The OSH Act also provides that an employer can be sentenced to six months in jail for the willful violation of an occupational safety and health standard when that violation causes the death of an employee.[77] (The value judgments underlying that provision should be obvious.) OSHA has ignored the criminal prosecution option to enforce the law, and prosecutors are unlikely to pursue a criminal case with such weak penalties. Congress could increase the effectiveness of OSHA's enforcement powers by providing for longer sentences for employers whose willful violations cause employee deaths and extending criminal penalties to cases involving serious bodily injury.[78] But OSHA itself has not vigorously enforced the law by making full use of its existing enforcement powers.

Still following a policy conceived during the Reagan years, OSHA has rejected the role of aggressive enforcer desired by workers and assumed the role of cooperative consultant to employers. Instead, partnership agreements have become an integral part of forming alliances between OSHA and corporations, trade associations, and other organizations for the voluntary development and sharing of information concerning workers' safety and health. OSHA has put forth no requirements for employers to enter into such alliances, and the partnership agreements themselves have no enforcement provisions.[79]

People die or are maimed unnecessarily because of the failure to keep the promises made in the OSH Act. Stefen Golab, a sixty-one-year-old immigrant worker died in 1983 from inhaling cyanide fumes while working at the Film Recovery Systems plant in suburban Chicago. Two months before Mr. Golab's death, an OSHA inspector was at the company but did not venture past the plant's front office. The inspector who received the company's injury records concluded that the firm's injury rate was below the national average and left. A House of Representatives Committee on Government Operations reported that had the OSHA inspector "observed the conditions on the plant floor, he would have seen 70 boiling vats full of used film from which lethal cyanide vapors were being released, the floor covered with cyanide-contaminated solutions, warning labels on the cyanide containers painted over, and immigrant workers, many unable to speak English, unaware of the unsafe conditions." When OSHA, in the course of investigating Mr. Golab's death, discovered these health and safety violations it issued a citation and fined the company $4,855—which was later bargained down to less than $2,400.[80]

In January 1981, a worker at the Pymm Thermometer plant in New York wrote to OSHA:

> Mercury is being used, gas and ovens. Please, we don't know how to describe any more violations, but we are sure there are more. Please send an inspector down to see for himself. We only make the minimum wage so at least we will know our health is ok.[81]

OSHA did inspect the plant in 1981 and found serious violations including work surfaces covered with mercury and no protective gear such as respirator masks, aprons, or gloves for workers. OSHA issued a citation to the company and assessed a fine of $1,400. The agency also gave the company an October 1981 deadline by which to clean up the factory but then repeatedly extended that deadline. In 1985, after being informed by a former Pymm employee, OSHA discovered a hidden cellar where a mercury reclamation operation was being conducted—"a cellar virtually without ventilation, filled with broken thermometers, with pools of mercury on the floor, and noxious vapors in the air." Vidal Rodriguez worked in that cellar without a respirator for many months. He suffered brain damage due to long-term exposure to mercury. In 1986, OSHA fined Pymm over $100,000, which the company contested.[82]

On the other hand, no safety inspector had ever entered the Imperial Foods Processing Company in Hamlet, North Carolina, in the eleven years of its existence. In 1991, twenty-five workers died in fire and smoke and fifty-six others "were burned, maimed or suffered permanent respiratory or brain damage" when they could not exit doors locked due to suspicions that employees were stealing chicken nuggets. Even a cursory inspection could have prevented that human carnage.[83]

In 2003, the *New York Times* published a series of investigative articles about safety and health conditions at McWane, Inc., a privately held company based in Birmingham, Alabama. The company is one of the world's largest manufacturers of cast-iron sewer and water pipes and a regular on the Fortune 500 list. The first article in the series focused on the workplace at Tyler Pipe, a foundry owned by McWane, which was described as "part Dickens and part Darwin, a dim, dirty, hellishly hot place where many are regularly disfigured by amputations and burns, where turnover is so high that convicts are recruited from local prisons, where some workers urinate in their pants because their bosses refuse to let them step away from the manufacturing line for even a few minutes."[84]

Roland Hoskin had been employed at Tyler Pipe for two months when he descended alone into a pit to work on a balky conveyer belt. There were no safety guards on the conveyer belt, and it was running when he tried to fix it, both violations of federal safety rules. He was found on his knees with his arm crushed, his head pulled between the belt and rollers, and his skull split. Reporters David Barstow and Lowell Bergman's explanations of McWane's horrendous safety record of nine deaths and at least 4,600 injuries "many hundreds serious" in less than eight years echoed the explanations that have been given for the abuse of human life at the workplace throughout our economic history. They found that Mr. Hoskin was a victim of "a way of doing business that has produced vast profits" and "deliberate indifference" to the safety of workers. Foreign competitors of McWane's, particularly those in China and South America, with no regard for safety, were used as reasons for cutting costs, laying off workers, pressuring those who remain to work harder and more efficiently, and subordinating safety. to "production, to the commandment to keep the pipe rolling off the line."[85] One former McWane plant manager described the attitude toward workers: "they're nothing...they're just numbers. You move them in and out...if they don't do the job, you fire them. If they get hurt, or complain about safety, you put a bull's eye on them," meaning they are marked for dismissal. Supervisors were also urged to discipline injured workers by shifting the blame for an accident from the company to an employee: "If he steps in a hole, you know it's because he wasn't watching where he was going, not because there was a hole there that should have had a cover on it."[86] OSHA inspectors have found the company's injury reports to be suspect.[87] OSHA also found that three of the nine deaths at McWane plants were due to the company's "deliberate violations of federal safety standards." Others called it "reckless criminal conduct."[88] Yet, McWane has persisted largely unchecked because of a regulatory system that is incapable of stopping even flagrant and continual violations of worker's safety and health. Company officials acknowledged that the cost of regulatory fines was far less than the cost of complying with OSHA's standards. Only nine months before Mr. Hoskin's death, for example, OSHA had announced a fine of $160,500 against Tyler Pipe for "putting employees' lives at risk by allowing them to work on and around unguarded and moving conveyor belts."[89] At the time this series of articles was written in 2003, the Bush administration was proposing a cut in OSHA's budget.

There is no better human rights commentary on all of this than the questions asked by the friend of a seriously injured Tyler Pipe worker: "What does a life mean to them?" "How can the management or the owners go to sleep at night knowing that a family's dad is fighting for his life? That's all the family has. How can they sleep at night?"[90]

The history of the disregard by many U.S. businesses of their workers' occupational health is, if possible, even more scandalous and tragic than their disregard of workplace safety. Carcinogenic chemicals and dusts, as examples of health hazards, can be absorbed through the skin, the digestive tract, or by inhalation and can cause respiratory disease, heart disease, cancer, neurological disorder, systemic poisoning, or general physiological deterioration. Unlike safety hazards, the effects of health hazards might be long delayed and irreversible. Like safety hazards, however, blue-collar workers bear the major risk of occupational illnesses such as the following: lung diseases (asbestosis and byssinosis, silicosis, lung cancer, asthma); cancers other than lung (leukemia, mesothelioma, bladder, nose, and liver); cardiovascular diseases (hypertension, coronary artery disease, acute myocardial infarction); disorders of reproduction (infertility, spontaneous abortion); neurotic disorders (toxic encephalitis, psychosis, extreme personality changes); dermatological conditions (dermatosis, burns, scaldings); and psychological disorders (neurosis, alcoholism, drug dependency).[91]

The words *scandalous* and *tragic* are not adequate to describe employers' callous and deliberate disregard for human life in this country's asbestos, textile, and fuel industries, for example. Thousands of lives were lost and thousands others afflicted by asbestosis and byssinosis as a result of cover-ups decades long by irresponsible employers who knowingly hid from workers and the general public the hazards of their products and production methods.

In the 1920s, the petrochemical industry became key to the nation's economic development, particularly to the automobile industry. When tetraethyl lead was put into gasoline, it eliminated the "knock" in automobile engines and facilitated the development of today's automobile. Long before that discovery, lead had been identified as an industrial toxin. The industry's employers in the 1920s used the same arguments used today to give economic development priority over the health of workers and the general public. They argued that automobiles and oil and gasoline were "essential to the progress of the nation, if not the world" and that those preoccupied with health hazards were "reactionaries whose limited vision of the country's future could permanently retard progress and harm future generations."[92] One exuberant executive of the Ethyl Gasoline Corporation called tetraethyl lead an "apparent gift of God."[93] It is unlikely God had anything to do with the introduction of asbestos brake linings for the new high-speed lead gasoline-fueled cars in the 1920s—along with some other asbestos-containing products for home and workplace. As early as 1919, life insurance companies in the United States and Canada refused to sell policies to asbestos workers "because of the assumed health-injurious conditions of the industry."[94]

It would not be until five or six decades later, in the 1970s and 1980s, that the health hazards of asbestos would become widely known. That was because the lead and asbestos industries maintained tight control over the generation and dissemination of information, including hegemony over the scientific community. The industries' relationship with the scientific community has been described as an "incestuous relationship between private industrial health research institutes and industry."[95] The asbestos, lead, automobile, and gas industries funded these supposedly independent research centers and underwrote and controlled the use, if any, of their research findings about the effects of their products on the health of their workers and the public. Bought science and bought scientists were, therefore, an important part of what is nothing less than a criminal conspiracy. For a fee, they provided conclusions favorable to employers. As far as workers or the public knew, those conclusions were based on objective and independent scientific investigation.

That deceit produced a decades-long pattern of denial or minimization of the health hazards of whatever product or material these scientists were hired to exonerate. Their industry-financed studies were "more concerned with continued production and productivity than with worker health and safety."[96] Some of these scientists may have been more comfortable socially among management executives. Some were advocates of free enterprise and believed in the market philosophy. Others were part of the close economic ties between their universities and businesses. Still others were trying to advance their careers and reputations. Whatever their motivations, however, workers had no choice but to rely on the judgment of what they were misled to believe were neutral experts.

In the textile industry, moreover, workers and their representatives held heath science in what one author called "inordinate awe."[97] As a result, thousands of men and women were exposed to multiple health hazards about which information was not available to them or was systematically "misrepresented by the medical profession and researchers in the pay of corporate interests."[98] As if this was not enough, it was the policy at the Johns-Manville Company not to tell workers that the company had x-ray evidence of their asbestosis and to keep them working as long as they were not sick or disabled:

> The fibrosis of this disease is irreversible and permanent so that eventually compensation will be paid to each of these men. But as long as the man is not disabled it is felt that he should not be told of his condition so that he can live and work in peace and the Company can benefit by his many years of experience. Should the man be told of his condition today there is a very definite possibility that he would become mentally and physically ill, simply through the knowledge that he has asbestosis.[99]

At the center of workplace health and safety matters are employers because they control the workplace, the workers, safety and health hazards, as well as access to private property. Others—whether government agencies, universities, insurance companies, or health scientists—have accepted that private control of the workplace and have accommodated it in order to gain access to that workplace. The compromises that have been made to gain access in order to study or investigate these employer-controlled workplaces are in part the consequence of the dominant economic power of U.S. employers. Those compromises concerning such matters as who controls the nature and interpretations of a study, what questions can be pursued, and who has veto power over what can be published too often have resulted in a business-science community relationship "built on the misery of the exposed and endangered workers who are the subjects of those studies."[100] As the authors of the *Cotton Dust Papers* found,

"Business relations overrode the well-being of endangered workers and brown lung remained a secret." They also concluded that "the history of brown lung also shows that the keeping of such secrets caused diminished lives and agonizing deaths among generations of working people."[101]

Business relations—more specifically, maintenance of management control of the workplace, profits, property rights, efficiency, economic competition, and economic progress—still override the human rights of workers to physical security at the workplace. This determined opposition of U.S. employers taken as a whole and their allies in and out of government not only persists but exploits every new opportunity to stay free of health and safety regulations and to avoid financial liability for the detrimental effects of their products and methods on worker health. It is undisputed, for example, that the health risk posed by toxic agents cannot be proved with certainty or, as one writer put it, with "the compelling certainty that is reached through mathematical reasoning."[102] Because none of the available analytical processes can provide conclusive proof and because no single study is perfect (in that another piece of information could have been gathered and another factor considered), agencies conducting risk assessment have used a weight-of-the-evidence approach in determining the need for protective action and in establishing health standards to reduce hazardous exposures.

In 1993, the U.S. Supreme Court in *Daubert v. Merrill Dow Pharmaceuticals*[103] decided that "general acceptance" was no longer a sufficient precondition for the admissibility during trials of expert testimony concerning scientific evidence. The Court held that the trial judges when faced with an offer of expert scientific evidence must determine at the outset, before a jury can hear that testimony, "whether the reasoning or methodology underlying the testimony is scientifically valid."[104]

In the post *Daubert* years, courts have been aggressive in excluding the testimony of plaintiffs' experts, thereby blocking many tort litigations through what one writer characterizes as "a politically invisible interpretation of the words 'scientific' and 'knowledge.'"[105] In part causing this and in part a consequence, an entire industry has emerged with its own experts whose job it is to raise doubts about each scientific study to be used. In contrast to the weight-of-the-evidence approach, these experts argue that regulation cannot proceed (or expert scientific evidence be heard by juries) until more conclusive evidence is presented.

The tobacco industry has perfected this strategy: "For nearly fifty years, tobacco companies hired scientists to disprove that smokers were at greater risk of dying of lung cancer, heart disease, and other tobacco-related illnesses than were non-smokers. The industry also hired scientists to refute evidence that environmental tobacco smoke increased disease risk in nonsmokers."[106] It was a campaign that delayed regulation and compensation for decades. As one tobacco executive characterized the strategy, "Doubt is our product."[107]

Opponents of workplace safety and health regulation, including the U.S. Chamber of Commerce, are working to extend this approach to federal agencies such as OSHA.[108] It is a legalistic antiscientific approach that would prevent OSHA from relying on the holistic weight-of-the-evidence standard. The piecemeal scrutiny of each individual study ignores the strength of the entire body of scientific evidence considered as a whole. No single study provides conclusive proof.

There have always been judges who mask their ideological opposition to government regulation in "hard look" jargon that covers up their judicial policymaking. What the post-*Dauber* experience reveals, however, is the implementation of a systematic strategy designed once again "to bend science to the will of regulated industry" and to persuade scientifically uninformed (some say "scientifically illiterate") judge-gatekeepers to help business avoid regulation.[109]

Among other antiregulatory actions, the buying of scientists will continue to be part of the plan. Employers

will devote greater resources to sponsoring diversionary research. When adverse scientific studies are published, regulatees will hire consultants to fill the scientific literature with critical and contrary commentary that these regulatees will later cite to support claims that the adverse studies are "fatally flawed." Regulatees will attempt to pack advisory committees with sympathetic scientists in the hope of slipping qualifying language into advisory committee reports, and they will send industry scientific consultants to advisory committee meetings to campaign for such qualifying language. In the end, lawyers for the regulatees will bring all of this regulatee-generated information to the attention of credulous judges applying the corpuscular approach required by stringent regulatory–*Daubert* review to discredit each study relied upon by the agency. The end result will be fewer rules to impede the regulated community and fewer protections for the beneficiaries of congressionally mandated programs.[110]

In 1980, the Supreme Court in a 5–4 decision rejected a standard promulgated by the U.S. Secretary of Labor to regulate occupational exposure to benzene, a toxic substance shown to cause cancer at high exposure levels.[111] That was thirteen years before *Daubert,* yet Justice Thurgood Marshall, writing for the dissent, understood that the "critical problem" in such cases was "scientific uncertainty." He was concerned that because scientific knowledge is imperfect and a precise quantification of risks is impossible, the majority's high threshold for the evidence needed to prove the existence of significant risk would "subject American workers to a continuing risk of cancer and other fatal diseases" and would "render the Federal Government powerless to take protective action on their behalf." Marshall added, "Such an approach would place the burden of medical uncertainty squarely on the shoulders of the American worker, the intended beneficiary of the Occupation Safety and Health Act."[112]

These beneficiaries of congressionally mandated programs are human beings, real people who work. When scientific proof is demanded rather than precaution in the protection of workers' health, unnecessary and avoidable workplace deaths and debilitating workplace illnesses will continue. Again, this will be the result of deliberate choice, not of some misfortune beyond anyone's control. This is not speculation. Industry-hired scientists, for example, "have challenged the designation of various substances as 'cancer-causing' and have disputed the evidence underlying the assignment of this designation to alcoholic beverages, beryllium, crystalline, silica, ethylene oxide, nickel compounds, and certain wood dusts"—all after each of these substances had been examined by the International Agency for Research on Cancer and been found to be "carcinogenic to humans."[113]

Employers, abetted in many cases by "science" purchased in academe and elsewhere, denied for decades and, too often, continue to deny responsibility for work-caused human suffering. Employer resistance to the promotion and protection of the fundamental human right to safety and health continues unabated at workplaces across this country. It is a deplorable violation of the human right to life. For too many employers, economic costs are clearly more important than human life. That is a crime against humanity.

7

The Value Choices of Courts, OSHA, and Labor Arbitrators

Management Rights over Workers' Human Rights

Callous disregard for human life at work has persisted in this country from its earliest days to the present time. It amounts to gross immorality and violation of fundamental human rights. Human life has been used merely as another resource and commodity in the marketplace. This gross immorality is a crime. Over thirty years ago, during an OSHA hearing to set standards for fourteen carcinogens, a union representative deplored the toleration of unnecessary deaths and suffering caused by exposure to those chemical agents:

> Sir, in a truly civilized society we would hold personally responsible those who participate in this crime, both the callous creatures and the cancer peddlers who bartered moral and statutory obligations. In a just society they would now be undergoing rehabilitation in a penal institution. Instead, they walk freely—some of them are or have been in this room—as if evil is its own reward.[1]

When employers willfully violate workplace safety laws or intentionally disregard preventable and predictable workplace hazards that any reasonable person would know could cause death or serious injury to their workers, the deaths and human suffering that result are not accidents or misfortunes. They are murders committed at the workplace. Film Recovery Systems, Pymm Thermometer, Imperial Foods, and employers in the asbestos, lead, and textile industries, for example, not only intentionally disregarded and were indifferent to death-causing preventable hazards but actually exploited those hazards for their own financial gain. The House committee that discussed Film Recovery and Pymm entitled its hearing, "Getting Away with Murder in the Workplace."[2]

As strange as it might seem from a common sense perspective, willfully killing people this way at the workplace is not considered the same, however, as willfully killing them away from the workplace. Under the OSH Act, for example, a willful violation of an OSHA standard that results in an employee's death carries a maximum penalty of six months in prison and a $10,000 fine. Such willful acts are considered misdemeanors not felonies. These criminal sanctions, moreover, apply only to willful violations that result in death *not* to willful violations that result in serious injuries—such as the permanent brain damage suffered by Vidal Rodriguez at Pymm Thermometer.

OSHA rarely seeks criminal prosecution in cases where the agency itself concludes that workers have died because their employers willfully violated safety standards. Congress has repeatedly rejected bills to increase fines and prison sentences for employers whose willful violations of the Act result in worker deaths and to expand criminal prosecution to include serious bodily injury as well as death. Congress, on the other hand, has passed a federal law "that provides for one year in jail for maliciously harassing a wild ass"—as Ralph Nader emphasized—"not for killing the wild burro, harassing."[3] The Environmental Protection Agency (EPA) is, putting it mildly, far more aggressive than OSHA in obtaining prison sentences.[4]

Why are wild burros regarded more highly than U.S. workers? There is more to this than political power, public ignorance, callousness, or disregard. Related to the well-defined and widely accepted values of market philosophy, there has been a less well-defined but widely accepted belief in this country that employers operate in a separate commercial world with its own accepted morality, approved behavior, and agreed-on objectives. Acceptance of that presumed separateness has meant acceptance of dual and often conflicting standards of judgment, one for the commercial world and one for the larger society.

The larger society's acceptance or toleration of commercial world conduct simply because that conduct is accepted in the commercial world helps explain the absence of outrage and protest in the larger society against even the worst abuses of workers' health and safety. Most people in the larger society are unable even to conceive of employers or their managers as murderers or of them being prosecuted and imprisoned for maintaining hazardous workplaces.

It is also commonly accepted in and outside the commercial world that all forms of business and the managers of those businesses are supposed to act in ways that maximize profits. Employers' profit maximization within the commercial world, however, can conflict with the larger society's goals such as (as least as written in the OSH Act) protecting workers' health and safety. The influence of the dual standard of judgment is obvious in the observation of one commentator: "Whether and under what circumstances the corporation and its decision makers lawfully can or ethically should pursue these societal goals despite a conflict with profit maximization remains unclear."[5]

Some maintain that in large corporations, individual anonymity in the bureaucracy obscures moral blame in ways that discourage corporate social responsibility. Policy-making corporate executives, moreover, are so far removed from the workplace consequences of their decisions that they are not held responsible for what happens there. Even when they admit blame, "corporate officials do not see themselves in the same light as strict criminals, particularly those responsible for murder or manslaughter."[6]

Ralph Nader responded to that claim in a 1994 address to a safety and health conference: "Human beings, when they have a lot of power and plans are abstractly implemented down the hierarchy, can become horribly desensitized. Their worst and cruelest natures can come out in this manner."[7] The solution he recommended would move these people "down the abstraction ladder" by requiring top executives to "go down to the area of the disaster and work." For example, "the head of a steel company where fifteen workers died in a company mine and the evidence shows that the company knowingly and recklessly violated OSHA standards, should have to go down into that coal mine and work with the surviving miners." Nader said that this "behavioral sanction" would have the greatest deterrent effect on high-level executives "short of going to prison."[8]

The moral choice that has to be made is whether employers' duty in human rights and in law is so important, so essential to a decent society that the sanctions on employers who knowingly and willfully fail to fulfill that duty to the serious detriment of their employees' health and safety should be the most severe society can impose.[9] When asked if it was a criminal act when an employer willfully violates a safety and health standard and, consequently, kills or seriously injures a worker, a witness testifying before a House subcommittee replied in a way most consistent with human rights:

> This is a particular species of white collar crime, and if the person willfully undertakes to violate, to jeopardize life, to the person who dies whether they are shot by a bullet on the street or whether they go off a roof and fall 55 feet and die, the death is the same.
>
> Because we are sometimes more educated and feel somewhat deferential towards white collar criminals, the corporations that we have prosecuted come out with things like. "I shouldn't be charged or my corporation shouldn't be charged." And yet, the injury was there, the deaths were there.... The death is the same, and it could be far more preventable [than street crime] and many of the white collar criminals don't come from a deprived background, they don't come out of the ghetto where they had no chance....
>
> These are white collar criminals, they are sophisticated, in many cases. They are operating businesses. They have resources to address the problem. They are not deprived. They don't address the problem and the difficulty and the tragedy ensues. They should be criminally prosecuted.[10]

At the sentencing hearing of a small businessman who admitted violating the Pennsylvania criminal law by, among other things, falsifying reports to the government about the elevated levels of lead in his employees' blood, the businessman defended his actions as necessary to keep his business alive, thereby maintaining jobs for his thirty or forty employees. He was described by his attorney as a law-abiding businessman who went down the wrong path "under immense economic pressure."[11] The Assistant U.S. Attorney emphasized that neither the employer nor his attorney mentioned "the tragedy and the trauma to numerous [company] employees whose health was jeopardized, and in at least one case, seriously compromised by [the businessman's] false statements to OSHA and to the way he ran his company." She added that "in greed" the employer was "hiding from his employees the fact that they were being lead poisoned and exposed, that the lead that they were being exposed to was poisoning them."[12]

The judge in that case concluded that incarceration was justified because the employer's "lies were about the blood levels of the employees. You were engaged in hazardous employment. This isn't a moment of weakness, this is weeks of deliberate disregard of your fellow human beings."[13] This court's application of the long-preached principle that no person is above the law raises to employers the prospect of additional court action of this sort to protect employees' health and safety. It also raises the larger question, however, of whether employees' health and safety should be dependent solely on a top-down regulatory system of government agencies, expert professionals, court decisions, and the decisions of employers—particularly employers who have used their political power to persuade the state not to impede too seriously on their decision-making freedom.

It is most consistent with human rights that the people whose health and safety are at risk be able to participate in the workplace decisions that affect their physical and mental well-being. Workers are the best qualified to recognize workplace problems not only because they are on the job every day but because their best safeguard is to be in control of their circumstances on the job. It has been argued, moreover, that worker participation in workplace health and safety "is necessary to keep alive the OSH Act promise of safe employment and places of employment"[14] in part because OSHA's inspection staff will never be sufficient to inspect any more than a relatively small fraction of U.S. workplaces. Many years ago, the then Federal Coal Mines Administrator testified that "Federal inspectors could never achieve continuous mine safety without the day-to-day participation of the miners themselves.... Without minute-by-minute vigilance by these men, each was a safety expert in his own right, the mine is bound to revert to unsafe conditions or practices."[15]

Employers often do encourage worker participation when it is designed to increase productivity or to improve worker morale and deepen commitment to an employer's objectives. That is not the power-sharing kind of participation that workers need to promote and protect their workplace safety and health. That power-sharing form of participation would require rejection of the common law–rooted notion of the boss as master and "acceptance of the concept of the workplace as a field of common endeavor where both employer and employee have rights and responsibilities."[16]

In the United States, Congress and the courts as well as employers have rejected anything but minimal and marginal involvement by workers in the determination of workplace conditions. Employers prevailed on Congress in the early 1990s to reject legislative proposals to require joint safety and health workplace committees, for example, because employers feared that such committees would encourage unionization. In contrast, Canada and Sweden rely heavily on worker participation in the regulation of workplace safety and health. In each country, workplace safety committees oversee the workplace, alert inspectors, provide employees with information, establish training programs, inspect workplaces, keep safety and health records, and participate in the planning and execution of safety and health programs. In Canada and Sweden, worker participation combined with regulatory agency enforcement constitute an integrated top-down, bottom-up enforcement system. In the United States, however, "weak enforcement is followed by even weaker mechanisms for worker participation."[17] Cooperative enforcement programs between OSHA and employers in the United States, for example, "have curtailed government inspections without increasing employee participation."[18] Value choices as much as, if not more than, economic and political power are responsible for the U.S. attitudes toward workers' safety and health.

Among the powers of the labor-management safety committees in Sweden is the ability to veto, for safety and health reasons, plans for new machinery, materials, or work methods as well as the ability to shut down dangerous operations until the hazard is corrected. In the Canadian and Swedish systems, moreover, workers have a "strong and enforceable right to refuse unsafe work."[19]

The legal right to refuse hazardous work without retaliation is essential if employees are going to take control over their own lives in regard to workplace health and safety. The right to refuse unsafe work is also an important moral right because without it workers' lives matter less than management authority, efficiency, productivity, or profit margins. The right to refuse to perform hazardous work is, moreover, a necessary part of the morally superior preventive approach to occupational health and safety. If the workers the OSH Act was supposed to protect could protect themselves, enforcement of the Act's promises would not depend solely on the political interests of elected officials or the changing fortunes of one political party or another.

In the United States, however, independent collective action by workers is effectively discouraged not only in regard to the enforcement of the promises of the OSH Act but also in regard to the promises of the National Labor Relations Act (NLRA). Because the dominant corporate values in this country are the maintenance of employer control and authority at the workplace and a fear and distrust of workers' motives, courts, administrative agencies, and labor arbitrators have defined permissible work refusal circumstances so narrowly that few employees can or do refuse unsafe work.

The right to refuse unsafe and unhealthful work is indispensable to respect for workers' rights as human rights. The United States violates human rights "by forcing employees to work in dangerous situations and perhaps complain about it afterwards" and by enforcing an underlying value choice that "would rather have employees die than have a few employees stop work unnecessarily."[20]

As a Reagan-appointed OSHA official warned, recognizing workers' right to refuse hazardous work without retaliation would bring about a "fundamental rearranging of our entire American business."[21] How revealing it is that an

OSHA official is primarily concerned with the consequences of a safety and health strategy for U.S. business rather than with the consequences for workers' safety and health. If human rights principles are to be applied in U.S. labor-management relations and U.S. labor law and policy, there will be many such clashes of rights and values. The crucial question is what standard of judgment will be used to resolve these conflicts.

In U.S. workplaces, worker participation to protect and promote their safety and health is not considered a human right or much of a right of any sort. As the Supreme Court said in *Whirlpool v. Marshall*[22] in regard to the OSH Act, "as a general matter, there is no right afforded by the Act which would entitle employees to walk off the job because of potential unsafe conditions at the workplace."[23] The Court also emphasized that Congress had rejected a derisively referred to "strike with pay" provision during legislative debates "to avoid giving employees a unilateral authority to walk off the job which they might abuse in order to intimidate or harass their employer." The Supreme Court also cited congressional rejection of the shutdown provisions in other bills that would have given federal officials the authority "drastically to impair the operation of an employer's business."[24]

The Court, in *Whirlpool*, allowed, however, that "the Act does not wait for an employee to die or become injured"[25] and proceeded to uphold a Secretary of Labor's regulation that protected the "right of an employee to choose not to perform his assigned task because of a reasonable apprehension of death or serious injury coupled with a reasonable belief that no less drastic alternative is available."[26] The Court concluded that such instances would be few because they would have to involve "highly perilous and fast-moving situations."[27]

In the Court's opinion, there was also the reassurance that the Secretary of Labor's regulation did not require employers to pay workers who refused to work when faced with imminent danger, did not empower OSHA to shut down an unsafe operation, and did not give employees the power to require their employers to correct the hazardous conditions at issue or to clear the workplace of any hazards.[28] The ultimate protection for employers, as the Court pointed out, was that "any employee who acts in reliance on the regulation runs the risk of discharge or reprimand in the event a court subsequently finds that he acted unreasonably or in bad faith."[29] Fear of employee dictation is a bugaboo that runs through this and other Supreme Court decisions involving employee self-protection of their own safety and health at the workplace.

Key cases decided under the National Labor Relations Act regarding refusals to work for reasons of health and safety identify standards of proof to be used under that statute. The Supreme Court held in *NLRB v. Washington Aluminum Co.*[30] that Section 7 of the NLRA, which gives workers the right to engage in concerted activities for the purposes of collective bargaining and other mutual aid or protection, includes concerted refusals to work in unsafe conditions. The company had discharged seven employees who left work because their work area was bitterly cold. The Court found that the workers' actions were intended to "correct conditions which modern labor-management legislation treats as too bad to have to be tolerated in a humane and civilized society like ours."[31] The employees involved in that case were not unionized. Such a refusal by unionized employees could be barred by a no-strike clause in a collective bargaining agreement or by an implied no-strike agreement where grievance and binding arbitration are contractually agreed upon dispute resolution procedures. In addition, this decision provides no protection to workers acting individually.

The Supreme Court said in *Washington Aluminum* that the reasonableness of the workers' decision to engage in concerted activity was irrelevant to the determination of whether a labor dispute existed under the NLRA. The Court proceeded, however, to cite National Labor Relations Board (NLRB) findings in this case of a workplace "so cold" that the workers' concerted action in leaving their jobs was a "perfectly natural and reasonable thing to do."[32] In the same decision, therefore, the reasonableness of the employees' concerted action seemed to matter or not matter.

Section 502 of the NLRA on its face appears to provide protection for all workers covered by the Act who refuse work assignments for health or safety reasons and to justify that action if taken in good faith: "the quitting of labor by an employee or employees in good faith because of abnormally dangerous working conditions for work" shall not "be deemed a strike."[33] The Supreme Court's interpretation of Section 502 in *Gateway Coal Co. V. United Mineworkers of America,*[34] however, established a most stringent standard far more restrictive than good faith. In that case, miners walked off the job to protest the alleged safety hazard caused by the reinstatement of two company foremen who had falsified records to show no reduction in air flow after the collapse of a ventilation structure had reduced airflow in the mine substantially. When the United Mine Workers of America that represented the workers refused to arbitrate, Gateway Coal Company brought an action in court to compel arbitration of the dispute.

The Supreme Court rejected the union's contention that a good faith belief that an immediate danger existed ("no matter how unfounded that view") was all that was required.[35] The Court also rejected the Third Circuit Court of

Appeals' interpretation that an honest belief, even if in error, that abnormally dangerous conditions for work existed necessarily involved the protection of Section 502.[36] Instead, the Supreme Court chose to adopt the unsubstantiated value judgment of the dissenting Third Circuit judge who merely asserted his belief that when a union raises Section 502 as a justification for a work stoppage, the union must provide "ascertainable, objective evidence, supporting its conclusion that an abnormally dangerous condition for work exists."[37]

The tests chosen by judicial decision-makers reveal their values. The Third Circuit's decision in that regard "is noteworthy for its broad reading of Section 502 and the sympathy shown for the plight of workers facing unsafe conditions."[38] Given the absence of legislative history, the language of Section 502 permits employees to refuse work when they perceive abnormally hazardous conditions. That reading is most consistent with humanitarian or, more precisely, human rights considerations. It is a test that requires only a good faith belief on a worker's part. This subjective test, moreover, protects an employee who stops work because of a good faith belief that abnormally dangerous working conditions exist from the risk of subsequently being proved wrong.

The inhumanity of the objective test adopted by the Supreme Court is inherent in the test itself. It places the heaviest burden possible on workers who must act immediately when confronted with what they believe are urgent and serious threats to their health and safety. That action must be taken when no experts or possibly only an employer's experts are available. The objective test, therefore, punishes workers "for a lack of knowledge about industrial disease and safety which they cannot realistically be expected to possess."[39] Yet, it is the worker who assumes the risk not only of being wrong but also of being right but unable to meet the high standard of objective proof to some decision maker's satisfaction—decision makers not personally endangered by the peril.

The risk workers assume under the objective test also creates a Hobson's choice of working thereby risking life or limb or stopping work thereby risking loss of employment because a later trier of fact finds that the physical facts do not support the employees' belief. No decent or enlightened society would require workers to make that choice. That is particularly true when economic necessity pressures many employees to choose a job and wages over their own health and safety. In other words, "the fear of job loss will motivate them to continue to work in danger."[40] Either choice, however, disrespects workers' humanity and their human rights to a safe and healthful workplace.

These decisions demonstrate not only the value judgments of the Supreme Court but also "the inescapable truth" that judges "safely ensconced in their

chambers do not feel threatened" by what goes on at less secure and less insu-
lated workplaces such as those in mills and foundries, mines, and farms.[41] In
great part, the Third Circuit Court of Appeals in *Gateway* opposed the submission to labor arbitrators of cases involving refusals to work for reasons of health
and safety for the same reason:

> Considerations of economic peace that favor arbitration of ordinary disputes
> have little weight here. Men are not wont to submit matters of life or death to ar-
> bitration and no enlightened society encourages, much less requires, them to do
> so. If employees believe that correctible circumstances are unnecessarily adding
> to the normal dangers of their hazardous employment, there is no sound reason
> for requiring them to subordinate their judgment to that of an arbitrator how-
> ever impartial he may be. The arbitrator is not staking his life on his impartial
> decision. It should not be the policy of the law to force the employees to stake
> theirs on his judgment.[42]

As the Supreme Court decided in *Gateway,* however, it is the "policy of the
law" to require workers to use whatever labor arbitration procedures are available to them even in safety and health cases. The Supreme Court said that there
was little justification for the Circuit Court's fear that an arbitrator "might be
too grudging in his appreciation of the workers' interest in their own safety."[43]
The Supreme Court decided that, rather than have safety and health "depend
on the relative strength of the parties," it was better to have safety and health depend "on an informed and impartial assessment of the facts" by an arbitrator.[44]

Impartiality means the absence of bias, but realistically it cannot mean the absence of personal beliefs and values. As former Supreme Court Justice Benjamin
Cardozo said, "We may try to see things as objectively as we please. None the less,
we can never see them with any eyes except our own." The "process of justice," as
Cardozo called it, is not "coldly objective and impersonal."[45] That is no less true
of labor arbitrators than for judges or any other quasi-judicial decision makers.

In a fundamental way, what distinguishes unionized employees from at-will
employees is that unions have negotiated contractual protection against unjust
discipline through "just cause" limitations on employers' authority to discharge
workers. Labor arbitrators in the United States have adopted and developed
standards for what constitutes just cause for discipline and through their decisions have created an arbitral common law of unjust dismissal.

In their decisions, however, labor arbitrators create and apply rules that,
among other things, embody presumptions about the nature of the power and
rights relationship of employer-employee as well as the sources of employee

and employer rights. In doing so, they, as do judges, choose among applicable sets of principles. Although the basic foundation of law (whether made by legislators or judges or negotiators of contracts) is moral choice, little attention has been given to the values and conceptions of rights and justice underlying these laws and contractual provisions. These value choices not only condition the thinking of decision makers but also provide them with ultimate standards for judgment. These value judgments also pre-position a decision maker's approach to particular case situations, thereby exerting a powerful influence on the outcome of these cases.[46]

In the United States, labor arbitrators function in the context of a dominant theory of industrial and labor relations known as *industrial pluralism.* Industrial pluralists deny that the interests of labor and management are inherently incompatible and believe that the conflicts of interest that do arise are susceptible to adjustment. Collective Bargaining is the central labor relations problem solving device and "establishes an industrial citizenship for workers, enforced by the union-management contract."[47] The collective bargaining contract is considered the constitution of the workplace upon which a body of industrial law is to be built. The overwhelming number of the constitution-contracts contain grievance procedures that workers and their union representatives could use to protest alleged violations and provisions for final and binding arbitration of unsettled claims. The development of an industrial common law comes about to a great extent through the interpretation of the constitution-contract by these labor arbitrators. It is a private system of self-government that decries government intervention including judicial intervention. Labor arbitrators in the industrial pluralist conception of labor-management relations, therefore, are private judges in a private system of justice.

This theory was the basis, at least in part, of arbitral views of the sources and nature of worker and employer rights. Although the industrial pluralists advocated joint labor-management determination in a system of self-governance, a sphere for management rights needed to be defined. In one obvious sense, determination of the scope of the joint determination would determine what rights each side had. In a deeper and more revealing sense, however, the determination of the scope of joint determination was itself the result of preconceptions about what worker and employer rights ought to be.[48]

The War Labor Board (WLB), established in 1942, had the most powerful influence on the nature of modern labor arbitration. The WLB's mission was to prevent interruptions of any work that contributed to the prosecution of the war and to resolve all labor disputes by peaceful means. The Board considered the final and binding resolution by an arbitrator of all workplace grievances essential to the accomplishment of its mission. In pursuing its objectives, the WLB applied industrial pluralist doctrines to achieve the maintenance of maximum production, not the establishment of workers' rights. WLB alumni constituted the most influential arbitrators, who shaped the field of labor arbitration by forging what one distinguished arbitrator called "a body of principles that has withstood the test of time."[49]

In its Termination Report after the war, the WLB emphasized that "proper" grievance-arbitration procedures in labor-management contracts had "removed obstacles to high morale and maximum production."[50] Consistent with the industrial pluralist theory of union involvement only in areas of enterprise policy that the theory deemed susceptible to joint determination, the WLB established a protective "zone of managerial prerogative" within which it gave total deference to the unilateral exercise of employer discretion.[51]

The presumption that there were certain rights inherent in management expanded employers' rights and drastically limited workers' rights. The presumption legitimized employers' hierarchical systems of workplace control. Despite theoretical talk of joint constitutions and joint sovereignty, this presumption denied workers and their union representatives any participation in those most important matters at the core of entrepreneurial control on which not only their wages, hours, and working conditions, but also the existence of their jobs, depended.[52]

Take as an example, the hallowed and long-standing "work now, grieve later" rule under which an employee is expected to perform an assignment and then file a grievance. First, this rule is extracontractual, originated not by employers and unions but by the WLB and an influential arbitrator, Harry Shulman. Second, this rule is value-laden. It favors management control and the need for efficiency, maintenance of discipline, and order at the workplace, and private property ownership prerogatives over union and worker protests about working conditions. The rule permits employees to complain about their treatment, but only in a way (and at a later time) that does not interfere with any of management's functions.

The notion that management acts and union reacts gives employers the right of initiation as well as broad discretion in deciding how to assert its own interpretation of the contract. Workers (and a union), however, may not use self-help when they seek to assert their own interpretation of their contract. Doing so is impugned as "self-help" and is cause for discipline. In addition, the employee, who may not exercise self-help at the workplace, has recourse only to the grievance-arbitration process, where the same doctrines that underlie the "work now, grieve later" rule will guide the arbitrator—if the dispute gets that far.

The "work now, grieve later" rule favors management authority and objectives. This rule, like the objective evidence test, confronts employees with an unfair dilemma in safety and health cases: to work and risk their health and safety or to refuse to work and risk their jobs. The rule condemns self-help in those workplace situations involving worker safety and health where self-help is essential. As already discussed, giving workers the right to refuse hazardous work without retaliation would empower them to take control over and protect their own lives when confronted with threats to their safety and health—without facing the unfair dilemma. As things stand now, however, this extracontractual rule results in the contractual rights of unions being treated differently from the assertion of such rights by employers.[53]

In addition, the presumption that certain rights are inherent in management was fashioned into the arbitral principle of reserved management rights. After the advent of unionization and collective bargaining, management reserved to itself all those inherent powers that were not expressly given up in a collective bargaining agreement with a union. Consequently, collective bargaining contracts became the exclusive source of workers' rights whereas employers' most important rights had sources outside the contract, mainly in the values of those who presumed the "oughtness" of the reserved rights theory. This conception of the sources of rights at the workplace is a *value choice* consistent with the value choices concerning employer rights made throughout U.S. labor history. The values underlying common law employment doctrines are embedded in U.S. beliefs about economic and workplace relations. The inherent management rights presumption was a direct descendent of those values and, as such, exposes an inherent contradiction in the industrial pluralists' joint determination theory: that the parties who were supposed to engage in mutual self-governance under a jointly negotiated "constitution" had not only unequal power but also unequal rights.

The industrial pluralist conception of labor-management relations also defined the role and authority of labor arbitrators as limited:

> He [the arbitrator] is rather part of a system of self-government created by and confined to the parties. He serves their pleasure only, to administer the rule of law established by their collective agreement. They are entitled to demand that, at least on balance, his performance be satisfactory to them, and they can readily dispense with him if it is not.[54]

When implemented along with the value judgments favoring inherent management rights, the widespread acceptance of Shulman's assertions about the role of labor arbitrators in this country further limited the recognition and exercise of workers' rights. It became standard arbitral doctrine that arbitrators:

- were restricted to the interpretation and application of contract provisions;
- had no authority to add to or in any other way change the parties' contract;
- were "creatures of the parties," serving only them and the standards they establish;
- were committed to acceptance of the will of the contracting parties; and
- must uphold a contractual mandate even when it violates the arbitrator's sense of fairness.

The term *parties,* moreover, referred only to the employer and the union that negotiated the contract, who agreed to submit an issue to arbitration, and selected and paid the arbitrator. This approach, therefore, considered only collective interests and rights but not the rights of workers as individuals.[55]

As servants of the parties, arbitrators are not employed to make the plant a better place to work; their job is to protect the principles and values, good or bad, set forth in the contract. Their overriding responsibility "is to preserve the parties' bargain, not to change it." This, in turn, led to the conclusion that arbitration "is not a search for truth and justice" or "some abstract ideal of justness and fairness" but rather a search for the "mutual intent of the parties." As one arbitrator put it, management and unions had every right to create "their own private worlds."[56]

The industrial pluralist doctrines continue to have a powerful influence on U.S. labor arbitration. Over the years, arbitrators, absent clear contractual limitations, have conceded broad authority to management. This includes what is to be produced and when and how it is to be produced; what work is to be done; the freedom to make technological change and to set and enforce production standards; to establish new jobs and job classifications; to eliminate jobs; to assign duties to employees; to hire or not to hire (except as limited by statute); to determine the size of crews; to schedule work; to require overtime work; to subcontract bargaining-unit work if done in good faith; to establish and enforce plant rules; to lay off employees; to transfer, promote, and demote employees; and to require job applicants to submit to a physical examination.[57]

At a 1989 meeting of the National Academy of Arbitrators (NAA), two distinguished arbitrators asserted that the reserved rights theory—what they described as "the employer has all rights other than those it has contracted away"—"is so fundamental to bargaining relationships that it is seldom challenged." They added, "Indeed, the management rights clause becomes irrelevant, once the arbitrator accepts the 'reserved rights' theory." They maintained that arbitrators choose to apply the reserved rights presumption because it preserves the parties' bargain.[58]

At that same meeting, a union attorney objected to "the exaggerated concern with management operational prerogative." He argued that the reserved rights doctrine could not be defined as an attempt to preserve the parties' bargain because it "has nothing to do with what the parties said, intended, or agreed to at the bargaining table." He correctly described the doctrine as an assumption that arbitrators make without any proof—an assumption "founded in the world view of arbitrators that the economy operates best when management makes the operational decisions."[59] A management attorney countered that employers do not need arbitrators to bestow reserved rights upon them because those rights are "simply a reality, a fact of life in our capitalist society—a right stemming from controlling the purse strings."[60]

Many arbitrators acknowledge the existence of values and value judgments in the industrial pluralist scheme but contend that the only values in the arbitration decision-making process are those of the employer and unions involved. To the contrary, disputes are not readily resolvable by reference to some fundamental purpose of a collective bargaining agreement because labor and management have conflicting objectives and an arbitrator's decision depends on which objective is chosen. In other words, in the real world the labor arbitrator must choose "among several potentially applicable sets of principles."[61] This decision-making requirement of choosing from among alternatives and often conflicting principles is the essence of the creative function of the labor arbitrator.

My research into the body of common law principles and rules applied by labor arbitrators has demonstrated an arbitral commitment to extracontractual doctrines of private property rights; employer hierarchical authority and control; management freedom to operate the enterprise most efficiently; and the need to discipline employees whose actions were considered challenges to management's order. These are extracontractual doctrines that have as their aim the maintenance of managerial control over all aspects of an enterprise. They embody value judgments that, as Robert Rabin has put it, "reflect the interests of the dominant power in the work relationship."[62]

These values also pre-position a decision maker's approach to particular issues, thereby exerting a powerful influence on the outcomes of these cases.

Arbitrators, in exercising this prerogative of choice, are making judgments that reflect, among other things, their own political, social, and economic philosophies. The standards for judgment that arbitrators use when they decide cases determine whether they see the workplace through the eyes of employees on the shop floor, in offices, or in classrooms or from the perspective of those who manage those enterprises. Shulman's statement that an arbitrator does not "sit to dispense his [or her] own brand of industrial justice" was, as distinguished arbitrator Sylvester Garrett put it, a "pleasing euphemism" but "not entirely accurate."[63]

Decisions, including labor arbitration decisions, are human choices. Consequently, there is an important subjective element to the nature of the decision-making process. Because human choice is involved, every decision by a judge, an agency's administrative law judge, or an arbitrator is in varying degrees a value judgment. As previously mentioned, *neutrality* means an absence of bias; it does not mean that each arbitrator or judge has no assumptions about the nature of the enterprise and the place of employees in that enterprise.

My research has focused on cases that involved conflicting value choices and allowed the decider maximum freedom to exercise personal discretion in choosing from alternative values and outcomes. The two projects most relevant to this book addressed subcontracting[64] (now euphemistically called "outsourcing") because those cases not only raise issues of management rights and worker job security, and workplace health and safety[65] but also involve the fundamental clash between management's rights to operate the enterprise and workers' rights to a safe and healthful workplace. Those cases are most likely to evoke arbitral value judgments. The dominant value themes in the subcontracting cases were that management rights are necessary for the continued existence of the free enterprise system, and the pursuit of efficiency is one of the most important and fundamental rights of management. The reasoning was based on the value judgment that free competition is worth more to society than it costs—a philosophy of progress wherein efficiency is the dominant concern.

In law professor–arbitrator James Atleson's studies of values in the decisions of judges in labor law cases, he found a set of values that included the following:

1. Continuity of production must be maintained and should be limited only when statutory language clearly protects employee interference.
2. Employees, unless controlled, will act irresponsibly.
3. Employees possess only limited status in the workplace, and, correspondingly, they owe a substantial measure of respect and deference to their employers.

4. The enterprise is under management's control, and great stress is placed upon the employer's property rights in directing the workplace.

5. Despite the participatory goals of the NLRA, employees cannot be full partners in the enterprise because such an arrangement would interfere with inherent and exclusive managerial rights.[66]

In Atleson's study of arbitral values in cases in which employers disciplined employees for swearing at their supervisors, he found that "arbitrators...uncritically accept hierarchical notions of order and control in what is traditionally championed as a joint, and contractual, endeavor."[67] The cases he examined raised questions about the status relationship between employers and employees that arbitrators answered by applying master-servant notions to the supervisor-worker relationship—a value judgment that the employer-employee relationship must necessarily be the unequal relationship of superior and subordinate. Even without evidence that production would be affected, Atleson found that arbitrators' "immediate concern is always the avoidance of overt signs of militancy, expressions of equality, or a rejection of hierarchy." Because none of these cases involved a refusal to follow management's orders, Atleson also concluded that the underlying arbitral value was that "disrespect for 'authority' is undesirable and also punishable."[68]

Law professor Robert Rabin, commenting on these studies of arbitral values, deplored the hierarchical and autocratic vision that treats workers "as children, or worse, as prisoners." He summed up the core of the difference between the traditional and nontraditional arbitral conceptions of the sources or workers' and employers' rights by emphasizing the "need to develop a model that gives due recognition to individual worth, yet harmonizes individualism with the basic need to get the work done."[69]

In worker safety and health cases, once again the dominant arbitral theme was management's rights to operate the enterprise and direct the workforce—rights deemed superior to all other rights including workers' right to a safe and healthful workplace. Almost twenty years ago, my study of the decisions of U.S. labor arbitrators in cases involving safety and health disputes revealed a fundamental clash between management's right to operate the enterprise and workers' rights to a safe and healthful workplace.[70] Although that study identified four major categories of safety and health cases, (refusal to work, safety rule, crew size, and disease and disability) the focus here will be on worker refusals to work for reasons of health and safety. An analysis of arbitral decisions in these refusal-to-work cases over the twenty years since that study confirms the findings of the original research.

The basic rule in these cases is the "work now, grieve later" principle. As discussed above, that rule reflects the underlying value judgment that management has the right to direct and control the workforce. Equally axiomatic in U.S. labor relations is that a threat to worker health and safety is an exception to the rule of work now, grieve later.[71] My original and updated studies found, however, that arbitrators do not except health and safety from this rule. They instead perceived these refusal-to-work cases as insubordination cases. Management's right to direct and control the workplace, therefore, becomes the starting point for arbitral decision-makers, and challenges to that right—that is, refusals to work—are considered insubordination. This approach downgrades workers' fears and concerns about their safety and health to the level of an excuse for not obeying an order to work. As far as an employer is concerned, there is nothing that distinguishes a refusal to work for reasons of health and safety from any other type of refusal to work.

This arbitral value judgment that an employer's authority should be dominant at the workplace has powerful detrimental consequences for workers' ability to protect their own lives, limbs, and health at the workplace. Although technically, an employer carries the burden of proof in all discipline cases, treating these cases as insubordination cases puts the burden on the already discharged or otherwise disciplined workers and their representatives to prove to an arbitrator's satisfaction that the work assignment, equipment, or work environment was sufficiently hazardous to health and bodily integrity to justify the refusal to perform the work. The point that must be underscored is that arbitrators in allocating the burden of proof in these refusal-to-work cases rely on accepted value judgments concerning reserved management rights, *not* upon specific contractual provisions.

Arbitrators make this burden even more onerous for employees by imposing on them the most difficult standard of proof to meet; namely, *objective proof.* That standard requires workers to produce what arbitrators call "objective evidence of a dangerous condition," "demonstrative, objective or factual evidence," or "scientific evidence."[72] It is a standard of proof most difficult for workers to meet because they must act "without the benefit of any safety engineering or medical evidence as to the severity of the situation" or adequate information concerning workplace safety and health.[73]

Arbitrators also impose on employees a *reasonable belief* standard of proof defined as "more than a mere presumption" or "some colorable basis in the facts of the work situation confronting [them]"[74] that justifies a belief that it would be unsafe. Although by definition reasonable belief would seem to require a lighter burden of proof than the objective proof standard, most often there is only a slight difference, if any, between what arbitrators require of workers under the two standards. Arbitrators emphasize the factual basis, if any, for the perceived danger under both standards, and the facts required to substantiate a reasonable belief are often identical to those needed to demonstrate objective proof.[75]

The least applied standard of proof is *good faith belief*, defined by arbitrators as a fear that is "genuine," "sincere," "honest and not a subterfuge."[76] The actual use of this standard by arbitrators is so rare that there have been only two reported cases from 1945 through 2003 where an employee's good faith belief was the sole or even primary basis for justifying a refusal to obey a work order for reasons of health and safety.[77] A good faith belief is used more often as a basis for mitigating penalties imposed for insubordination.

The insubordination mode of analysis used in these refusal to work cases, with its associated heavy burden of proof on workers, is the result of arbitrators' value judgments that employers' freedom to operate the enterprise and direct the workforce are superior to all other rights including workers' right to a safe and healthful workplace. By their acceptance of this conception of the relative importance of employer and worker rights—even when the health and safety of human beings is involved—labor arbitrators in the United States become part of and help enforce an industrial relations system that maximizes employers' control of employee discipline and minimizes employee interference with management's freedom to operate the enterprise.

The restraining effect on worker conduct is obvious, particularly to workers, because the risk of failing to meet their heavy burden of proof is high and the consequences potentially disastrous since insubordination is commonly considered just cause for discharge. More specifically, it confronts workers with the dilemma they face under previously discussed Supreme Court decisions: to work and risk life, limb, or health or to refuse to work and risk their jobs. Their human rights are disrespected whichever choice they make.

Other arbitral considerations also demonstrate the preeminence of the management control value judgment in arbitrators' thinking. Arbitrators cite favorably, for example, the fact that an employee had always carried out management's orders "without question" and that the employee's objections to performing the work at issue were not presented in an "arrogant" or "combative" way or with "aggressive animosity" but in a "respectful manner [that] did not subject the foreman to ridicule or embarrassment."[78] Despite the fact that a worker's safety or health could be jeopardized, compliant, dutiful, and ever subservient behavior is rewarded. It is also important to arbitrators that the refusal not be a planned test of managerial authority. Arbitrators generally condemn any concerted refusal to obey management's orders even for reasons of health and safety whether or not that refusal is justified. The seriousness of individual threats to management authority is compounded when those individuals join together in protest.[79]

Management control is also reinforced by arbitrators who approach safety and health cases with the presumption that employee negligence and failure to follow instructions, not employers, are responsible for accidents. Many arbitrators also apply another presumption from the common law; namely, the *assumption of risk*. Despite state and federal rejection of this theory, through workers' compensation acts and the OSH Act, respectively, its continued use by arbitrators also augments employer control and adds to employees' burden of proof.

An analysis of arbitration cases concerning the refusal to work for reasons of health and safety published since the original study in 1985 revealed that nothing had changed. The burden of proof remains on workers and their union representatives "to demonstrate where work assignments are refused that the work, indeed, is unlawful or unsafe, or detrimental to life, limb and health."[80] As one arbitrator put it, "They [employees] must follow instructions and grieve later, unless they are willing to take the chance that they can prove they had a reasonable belief that complying with the instructions would endanger their safety and health." In that case, the "grievant gambled and lost."[81]

The standard of proof, moreover, remains the onerous objective proof or reasonable belief, with little difference between the two. Workers can win these cases despite heavy burdens and stringent standards of proof. In one case, for example, the arbitrator found that a broken plug could "cause death or serious physical harm" that was "beyond the normal hazards inherent in the operation."[82] Other employees were able to satisfy the objective proof standard by producing medical evidence of a "weakened back";[83] persuading an arbitrator that an injured wrist that deprived a worker of the use of his right arm justified his refusal to climb ladders and crawl in areas subject to "dust outs," which darkened one area "either to zero or inadequate visibility";[84] and presenting evidence (discovered after the suspensions) that the sludge workers were ordered to clean up contained traces of polychlorinated biphenyls (PCBs), and three "deadly toxic solvents."[85]

Other workers, however, could not prove that their assignments were actually unsafe "in an objective sense"; for example, the employee who despite "genuine fears and anxieties about working underground" had his discharge upheld because his union produced "no medical evidence to support that the Grievant's health might be impaired by so doing."[86] In other cases where employees could not meet the required standard of proof, arbitrators claimed to be applying a "reasonable belief" standard but defined and applied that standard as if it were a synonym for objective proof. In the words of one arbitrator, "A 'reasonable' belief is not merely a subjective feeling. It is a demonstrably objective conclusion based upon some tangible evidence or hazard." A worker must produce "adequate support" for his or her belief or "objective, ascertainable evidence" or a "showing by appropriate evidence" or "the employee's belief must be factually supported according to an objective standard and such support must take the form of specific conditions and not vague, irrelevant, or general statements."[87]

Even when workers were able to meet this reasonable belief standard, it was clear that the circumstances involved constituted objective proof. In one case where "6700 pounds of material had fallen from the ceiling including the suspended ceiling, light fixtures, wiring, ductwork, and the old mesh-interlined plaster ceiling," walls had collapsed in the building only a year before, and building inspectors "could not guarantee the safety of the building," the arbitrator found that the employees "had reason to be frightened."[88] Apparently the roof has to fall in before workers' refusals to work are justified. In another case where employees were required to "Spiderman" their way into hoppers containing enough ash to bury them and where footing was slippery, an arbitrator found that an employee met a reasonable belief standard of proof because a slab of ash fell on him inside a hopper; he had "heard that a man had once been buried in ash in a plant hopper"; and he had "never previously been inside a hopper."[89]

Arbitrators, in placing the burden of proof on workers in these cases, are relying on value judgments concerning reserved management rights, not upon specific contractual provisions. In making the burden of proof on workers as heavy as possible, these arbitrators confirm not only their choice of employers' rights over workers' rights but also their desire to discourage challenges to the exercise of managerial authority at the workplace. They have persisted, therefore, in treating these cases as insubordination cases.[90] One arbitrator, for example, told a grievant, who had to work where asbestos particles would more than likely be in the air because of asbestos removal work, that "nothing in the contract provided that the job [asbestos removal] should be halted while all employee doubts about safety are resolved." The arbitrator concluded that the worker's refusal to perform his assigned job was insubordination.[91]

In another case, the arbitrator implored the union to "recognize the peril to the Company and to the security of all the other employees if any employee at any time could refuse a work assignment and expect to be excused because he claimed he feared an injury or re-injury." He stressed that because the company's ability to remain competitive is "just as important to the Bargaining Unit employees as it is to the Company," the grievant "was doing a disservice to his fellow employees in refusing to operate in the manner in which he was directed."[92] The arbitrator left no doubt about whose interests he considered paramount:

> If the Arbitrator were to sustain the Grievance, he would be directing the Company to reduce the 28 pound requirement to the 18 pounds the Grievant argued was the amount he could handle safely and without fear of injury or re-injury. This, in effect, would then become the standard for all other operators of the Stevens Plater. This would mean production of over 37 percent fewer parts coming off the Stevens Plater and would mean the Company would have to try to get an increase in the price charged [to] the customer or lose the business.[93]

Although common law values of property rights, contract, and free enterprise have dominated U.S. labor relations, U.S. courts, and U.S. labor arbitration, contrary nontraditional values have also had an influence. In the early 1960s, for example, Arthur Goldberg, then Secretary of Labor and later Supreme Court Justice, commented in a speech to the American Law Institute that he had "often wondered why the genius which produced a law of property rights or of commercial instruments failed utterly to produce a law of job rights."[94] When he was general counsel of the United Steelworkers of America in 1956, Goldberg identified worker rights that existed independently of a contract and were as entitled to fulfillment as management's reserved rights. Goldberg however, did not identify the sources of those rights. He referred to the right to strike, to organize, to safe and healthful working conditions, and "to a fair share of the Company's income" as "Labor's Reserved Rights" and called them "inherent rights."[95] It was historical fiction, he argued, to maintain that "management's reserved rights were all embracing to the exclusion of any labor right," and he denied that the contract was the grant of certain rights to workers who otherwise would have no rights.[96]

Two years later, at a 1958 meeting of the National Academy of Arbitrators (NAA), Willard Wirtz, who would become Secretary of Labor during the Kennedy administration, asserted that neither institutional security, nor operative efficiency, nor the will of the majority was a sufficient reason "for disregarding certain independent individual interests."[97] That was a rejection of the commonly held arbitral understanding that "parties" meant only employer and union. Wirtz's emphasis was on *due process,* which he defined as the exercise of any authority with a due regard to balancing individual and group interests. Wirtz advocated a role for the arbitrator that included a necessary element of independence. He maintained that whereas acceptability to the employer and union is a legitimate consideration, it is "no ultimate standard."[98] Labor arbitrators, Wirtz contended, had an obligation and the authority to protect individual rights and interests and, in doing so, "to look ... to standards that are unaffected by the individual's election of representatives and by the actions of those representatives."[99] Wirtz's speech was a breakthrough call for the recognition of individual rights of workers in the grievance-arbitration process even when that meant "piercing the institutional, representative veil."[100]

In another speech to the NAA thirteen years later, Wirtz was even more definite about both individual rights in labor arbitration, asserting that "only the individual matters," and about the sources of the rights of individual workers:

> But a good deal more than procedures comes from the uncommon law of arbitration that only the individual matters. Nothing else. Not the individual as a remote and uncertain beneficiary of something called progress or the gross national product. Not the individual as a sparrow to be fed by gorging the horses. No. The individual as the owner of rights and interests—job rights, personal rights, human rights—at least as much entitled to protection as a piece of real estate or machinery. The individual as somebody the system is designed for instead of the other way around.[101]

Wirtz's ideas were radical in that they struck at the fundamentals of the traditional arbitral view of the sources of worker rights, the role of the labor arbitrator, and the preeminence of collective rights and interests. He identified a source of rights in each individual worker rather than only in the provisions of collective bargaining agreements. He told arbitrators they had an obligation to uphold those individual rights even when they conflicted with the institutional interests of the employers and unions that selected them and might not select them again. In the exercise of their decision making, therefore, arbitrators could no longer be merely "creatures of the parties." The idea that the grievance-arbitration process was designed for individual workers, moreover, clashed with the traditional notion that the process was created and controlled by employers and unions and was intended to serve their collective interests. Finally, no one before Wirtz, at least within the confines of U.S. labor arbitration, had spoken of workers possessing human rights that were entitled to protection.

By 1971, when Wirtz addressed the NAA, Congress had passed several laws extending statutory protection for individuals at the workplace: Laws such as the Equal Pay Act of 1963,[102] Title VII of the Civil Rights Act of 1964,[103] the Age Discrimination in Employment Act of 1967,[104] and the Occupational Safety and Health Act of 1970[105] emphasized individual rather than collective rights. The 1971 meeting of the NAA was devoted to the topic "Arbitration and the Public Interest"; that is, whether arbitrators should consider these and other laws "external" to the grievance-arbitration process in deciding their cases.

The proliferation of so-called external laws protecting employees' workplace rights, moreover, blurred the distinction (if there ever was a realistic distinction at the workplace) between public rights and private rights. Despite the industrial pluralists' conviction that the obligations of public law were not to be worked into the arbitration process, federal and state law providing for the enforcement of labor arbitrators' awards meant that labor arbitrators also participate in the coercive power of the state. As one nonarbitrator speaker told the NAA meeting in 1963, if labor arbitration insisted on operating as "a separate solar system unattached to the national labor policy" as set forth in court decisions, the exercise of arbitral power would amount to a "usurpation of judicial authority [and] a major step toward industrial anarchy."[106] In 1967, a state judge told the NAA that "the worlds of public adjudication and private arbitration cannot live in isolation; no iron curtain separates them."[107]

Jean T. McKelvey, the first woman president of the NAA, in her 1971 presidential address, "Sex and the Single Arbitrator," explored how labor arbitrators decided contract grievances that involved alleged sex discrimination. She reported a "general arbitral reluctance to resolve questions of law which are intermingled with questions of contract interpretation." She called this negative attitude toward administering the public policy against discrimination "alarming," "outmoded and irresponsible." McKelvey warned that if arbitration "is to survive and to be 'relevant' to the emerging needs of a new social and economic order, it cannot simply remain as part of 'the Establishment.'"[108]

At the same time that most arbitrators were using the collective bargaining contract as a shield against public policy, some arbitrators recognized that private institutions had an obligation to honor and uphold rights recognized by statute as well as by contract. At that same 1971 NAA meeting, for example,

Wirtz urged arbitrators to shake free of "tired habits" and "rusty precedent" and to make suspect every hard and fast rule. Only then could arbitration realize its potential "for meeting infinitely greater needs than those we have spent most of our professional lives putting it to."[109]

What was at stake in these fundamentally different conceptions of the labor arbitration process were the civil rights, constitutional rights, and human rights of workers, particularly workers who do not have the financial resources to pursue long and costly legal action and whose life experiences convinced them that such efforts would be futile anyway. It was unrealistic, therefore, for pluralist arbitrators to propose that when statutory issues are intertwined with contractual issues, arbitrators should consider only the contractual aspects, leaving it to the aggrieved worker or his or her union to pursue the statutory aspects in the judicial system.

The debate over the relevance of so-called external law, moreover, was conducted in a way that obscured the central issue: the conflict between individual worker rights, regardless of the sources of those rights, and the dominant conceptions concerning employer rights. As Arthur Goldberg pointed out, unlike management rights concepts, there has not been a developed coherent concept of the fundamental rights of employees at their workplaces despite that people's work has the most direct affect on their lives. Julius Getman, at an NAA meeting almost thirty years ago, stated: "Just as we recognize that the possession of certain rights is crucial to political freedom, it should seem obvious that they or similar rights are also vital to industrial dignity and self-respect."[110] Although arbitrators readily adopted and applied extracontractual common law principles in their contract language interpretation and discipline cases, most claimed that other extracontractual sources of rights, such as the Constitution and statutes governing the workplace, were beyond their authority to consider. One arbitrator told Getman that "to ask arbitrators even in the Bicentennial year, increasingly to incorporate fundamental freedoms and individual rights into an expanding concept of 'just cause' [for discipline] is to ask them...to swallow a constitutional camel when they have been unable to agree upon ingesting the statutory gnat."[111]

That statement accurately summed up the prevailing attitude of labor arbitrators toward sources of workers' rights not set forth in collective bargaining agreements or implied from provisions in those agreements. The only community that mattered in the arbitration process, in this view, was the industrial relations community not the larger society. Justice, therefore, is whatever produces the results that are in accord with the expectations of that industrial relations community; more specifically, the parties (employers and union) that establish the laws governing that community.[112]

For traditional labor arbitrators, the "Golden Age of Arbitration" is the era of industrial self-government.[113] The nontraditional conception of workers' rights in regard to their employers and their unions, however, required a very different kind of arbitrator and arbitration process. As arbitrator Clyde Summers put it in 1974, to enforce these workers' rights:

> Arbitrators cannot conceive of themselves as being fundamentally servants of union and management, that union and management are their customers and their clientele, and that they are to serve the interests of those institutions...[A] rbitrators must take upon themselves a quite different role and responsibility. They must assume a responsibility beyond the union and the management.[114]

The broader responsibility Summers had in mind included a responsibility to workers, which is rarely found in arbitral safety and health decisions. A worker was discharged for refusing to work under a furnace that had several leaks and electrode cooling problems. The arbitrator, recognizing that the employee was afraid, stated that "humanitarian considerations would validate the argument made by the Union [that] the psychological as well as the physical well-being of the individual must be considered and neither can be ignored."[115] "Nonetheless," the arbitrator decided, "the Company has a business it must run in an efficient and productive manner [and] recognizing the dangers associated with any kind of maintenance work in a large facility of this nature,... the Company must be able to assign employees to such work."[116]

The long-standing dominance in U.S. economic history of the proposition that management rights must take precedence over all else should not obscure a more humane value judgment; namely, that nothing is more important at the workplace than human life and health. That is a human rights standard, not a management rights standard. One of the purposes of human rights is to eliminate or minimize the vulnerability that leaves people at the mercy of others who have the power to harm them.

Human beings do not become something less than human beings when they enter the workplace, and, therefore, they have a right to protection of their physical security from those who can harm them there. Safety and health while at work are requisite component parts of most people's physical security. The right to safety and health has long been included in national and international human rights declarations, treaties, and laws. Emily Spieler puts it powerfully: "It is in fact the right to life that we are talking about when we talk about work safety," and "the right to life is deeply embedded in every human rights declaration, and it is presumed in these declarations that individuals' lives must be protected from those who wield unequal power."[117]

The principle aim of human rights, therefore, is to challenge and change existing institutions, rules, practices, and dominant values. If arbitrators used a human rights standard rather than a management rights standard to decide cases involving refusal to work for reasons of health and safety, several important changes would result.[118] A necessary and fundamental change would be to make worker health and safety truly an exception to the "work now, grieve later" rule in the literal sense that the rule would not apply at all to refusals to work for reasons of health and safety. It has become an arbitral mantra that health and safety are exceptions to the rule. In practice, however, arbitrators treat safety and health as affirmative defenses to insubordination charges in the context of disobedience to the rule. The management rights value judgment underlying that insubordination mode of decision making is contrary to the human rights value affirming the sacredness of human life as more important to promote and protect than property rights or other interests such as profits, efficiency, cost-benefit analysis, management authority, and economic progress.

At the workplace, therefore, when the basic human right to physical security collides with management rights, the resolution of that conflict of rights must occur outside the context of the insubordination-oriented work-now, grieve-later rule. If arbitrators (or other decision makers) resolve that conflict of rights in a human rights context, other fundamental changes must be made in the arbitral approach to these cases. One of the most important would be to place on employers, rather than on employees, the burden of proving that workplaces were safe or that work assignments did not endanger the health or safety of their employees.

It is revealing that, given the traditional arbitral justifications for management rights, including property rights, these same arbitrators find no duty on those exercising those property rights to prove that their workplaces are safe. Placing the burden on employees to prove a workplace unsafe or, more precisely, that a workplace is abnormally hazardous, presumes that employers' workplaces are as safe as can be expected, given the nature of the work. That reasoning releases employers from any obligation to eliminate long-standing safety or health-threatening problems and expresses an acceptance or toleration of those hazards to worker health and safety. (In other words, the standard of safety applied is whether the job is as safe, or unsafe, as it usually is). As Emily

Spieler has pointed out, "the toleration of higher levels of workplace risk permits a continuation of abusive conditions."[119] This presumption of safe workplaces also means that workers who refuse to work, alleging reasons of health and safety, "will be viewed as unreasonable, unless they can prove otherwise."[120] This is only a slight variation on the common law *assumption of risk* notion. The more dangerous the work, according to this value scheme, the less likely it is that workers will be able to convince a court or an arbitrator that any situation is abnormally hazardous. Unsafe working conditions, therefore, threaten employees in more than one way. The arbitral requirement that employees prove that threats to their health and safety are abnormal, imminent, and serious, moreover, requires workers to delay refusing to work until they risk serious injury or even death.[121]

Placing the burden of proof on employers in these cases would shift the focus from employee behavior to employer responsibility. Adoption of the human rights value judgment would mean that decision makers would perceive these refusal-to-work cases in their essence as employee safety and health matters, not as matters of insubordination and management rights. The burden of proof would be on the employers, who not only have legal obligation to provide a workplace free from recognized hazards but also have possession of and control over the property, machines, and processes that constitute the workplace. Requiring employers to meet the highest standard of proof (namely, that their workplaces are, in fact, safe and their work assignments, in fact, did not endanger worker health or safety) would confirm the sacredness and dignity of human life and its paramount importance—even at the workplace.

Workers have a human rights claim on their employers to do the best they can with available risk-reduction technologies and methods to protect human life and limb at the workplace. Employers subject to a human rights standard would be required to install risk-reduction technologies even though the cost of such technologies might exceed the benefits according to a purely economic analysis. This approach incorporates the moral and ethical superiority of preventing workplace death, injury, and illness, rather than requiring workers to prove they faced imminent serious and abnormal risks to their health and safety before their refusals to risk their physical security will be considered justified.

Obviously, it would be unrealistic to require employers to provide an absolutely risk-free workplace. Workers do have a human right, however, "to work in an environment that is free of predictable, preventable and serious hazards."[122] That human right at its most basic requires employers not to "create dangerous conditions, knowing that workers are likely to be seriously injured

[when] the employer does so without regard for the serious and life threatening risks to workers."[123] It is no accident when injuries or death result from this deliberate disrespect for human life.

A human rights standard would also hold employers responsible for allowing dangerous conditions to exist (even if an employer did not intend to create those dangers) when those employers are aware of those dangers but choose not to eliminate or minimize them. Employers would not be held responsible where workplace hazards are unknown or unpreventable due to the current state of technology and information. Employers would be responsible, however, for providing employees (and potential employees) with complete and up-to-date information concerning any known workplace and job risks to health and safety.

If an employer successfully carried its burden of proof, then the worker or workers involved would be required to demonstrate a good faith belief that the workplace or work assignment was a threat to safety or health. If the employee successfully carries that burden, the grievance would be sustained. If not, the insubordination question could then be considered. This approach would give maximum respect to the human right to physical security. It would also prevent workers from being confronted with the unfair dilemma—to work and risk their health or safety or to refuse to work and risk their jobs. Another way to avoid this dilemma would be to have employers propose discipline for workers who refuse a work assignment for reasons of health and safety but to permit those workers to remain on the job, performing other work until the issue of the proposed discipline is resolved in arbitration or otherwise.

The use of a human rights standard of judgment would also require fundamental changes in the current superior-subordinate conception of labor-management relations at the workplace. Whereas it would be preferable to have people's human rights respected and enforced at the workplace by all involved, workers have those human rights "whether the law is violated or not, whether the bargain is kept or not, [and] whether others comply with the demands of morality or not."[124] Consequently, if those rights are not respected and enforced otherwise, enforcement through self-help is necessary and justified.

All of this—applying a human rights standard rather than a management rights standard to refusal to work for reasons of health and safety cases; making these cases health and safety cases rather than insubordination cases; shifting to employers the burden of proof on the key safety or health issues and making that burden a heavy one; lightening the workers' burden to a good faith belief; and protecting workers' right to refuse hazardous work without employer retaliation—is antithetical to the authoritarian vision of the U.S. employment relationship and the values underlying it. It is also antithetical to the rules and values that arbitrators with the traditional view of the sources of worker and employer rights bring to these cases. Yet, only arbitral adoption of the value judgment that nothing is more important at the workplace than human life and health will satisfy the human rights standard.

U.S. labor arbitration is historically rooted in pluralist values of inherent management rights, hierarchical systems of workplace control, rules such as work now, grieve later, and common law employment doctrines of property rights, contract, and free enterprise. The U.S. Supreme Court, moreover, in the *Steelworkers* trilogy established in law the principles of the pluralist theory.[125] It will require a momentous change in these values and conceptions to have human rights principles become sources of worker and employer rights in U.S. labor arbitration. Yet, only arbitral adoption of the value judgment that nothing is more important at the workplace than human life will satisfy the human rights standard.

How will it come about? The quick answer, given U.S. labor history in general and the history of U.S. labor arbitration in particular, is that it will never happen, and it is futile to try to make it happen. There are many good reasons to be pessimistic, but the ability of challengers to redefine a policy issue by presenting new perspectives on old issues and by questioning the values on which the prior resolution of those issues was based can help initiate change.

Ultimately, arbitrators will determine whether change occurs because their decision-making function requires them to choose from among alternative and often conflicting principles and to create and appropriate standards for making those choices. Arbitrators, however, are unlikely initiators of change, particularly since the sine qua non for being an arbitrator is acceptability to the employers and unions that choose arbitrators. This institutional connection and the need to retain acceptability "exerts a gravitational pull" toward decisions that meet the expectations of the parties (employers and unions).[126] Put another way, "those arbitrators who are too far out of line in their images will find that the marketplace will take care of them in due course."[127]

Arbitrators have not acknowledged candidly or investigated thoroughly the ramifications of the fact that their acceptability or expendability is determined by the same parties whose disputes they decide. Change, therefore, most likely must be initiated elsewhere. Change from within the process is still a possibility. At the same time that arbitrators are sensitive to the intentions and desires of employers and unions, advocates for labor and management have full knowledge of the approaches and arguments that have been successful or unsuccessful with arbitrators. Justice Oliver Wendell Holmes, for example, advised lawyers that they would "need to know how judges behave."[128] If arbitrators are giving the parties what they want while the parties are trying to get what they want by conforming to the traditional practices and values of arbitrators, then the circle of unbroken conformity is complete.

Union advocates are most likely to break out of this circle. Although unions in the United States have a long history of commitment to the protection and advancement of workers' rights, it is only recently that many union leaders and members have come to understand workers' rights as human rights. As unions come to perceive themselves as human rights organizations promoting and protecting such fundamental human rights as the right to freedom of association and collective bargaining, safe and healthful workplaces, and discrimination-free treatment, there will be a necessary carry-over to the grievance-arbitration process.

Raising human rights issues in the arbitration process will likely produce a response from the employer side, thereby ensuring that the issue will be on the record of the case. That is an important first step given the reluctance of arbitrators to consider any matter not raised by the parties at the hearing of a case. It will enable arbitrators to include human rights issues in their decision making without going beyond the confines of the record established by the parties.

Unions can also pursue human rights clauses in contract negotiations with employers. Human rights clauses in collective bargaining agreements could become as common as management rights clauses. Since traditional labor arbitrators limit workers' rights to those set forth in collective bargaining agreements, they will have to consider workers' human rights if those rights are written into contracts. Contract language, for example, could constrain arbitrators in ways that enable workers to exercise their right to refuse hazardous assignments. Such language could define the circumstances in which refusal is justified, thereby setting forth explicit exceptions to which the work now, grieve later rule would not apply. Contracts could establish a good faith belief standard for workers to meet, rather than objective proof or reasonable doubt, and clearly place on employers the burden of providing a workplace free from recognized hazards as well as the burden of proving that its property, machines, and processes are safe. Contracts could also guarantee (1) that workers not be required to perform work they believe in good faith would threaten their life or health and (2) that workers in those situations could be reassigned (without loss of pay, benefits, or seniority) to another job and would be returned to their original job following abatement of the hazard.

There is also much that can be done from outside the labor arbitration process to bring about change, particularly to introduce the human rights standard into arbitral decision-making. Sustained investigation of the common law of labor arbitration and its underlying values is essential. Every hard and fast rule must be suspect. The reluctance to investigate and discuss these rules may be because most of those who write about labor arbitration are labor arbitrators who might be reluctant to jeopardize their institutional connections. Whatever the reasons, this reluctance has led to the acceptance and repeated application of rules without questioning, or knowing, or caring about a rule's origin, about what the rule assumes about the oughtness of the power and rights relationship of employer and worker, or about whether a rule needs to be reexamined, reevaluated, modified, or rejected. This has serious consequences for workers' rights because those unexamined rules and their underlying values are at the foundation of the grievance-arbitration system of dispute resolution.

U.S. labor arbitration rules and values need to be reconsidered using human rights principles as standards of judgment. The amount of research that remains to be done in this area is enormous. Many subject areas that involve sources of rights come readily to mind such as: privacy at the workplace (including drug testing and surveillance); employee loyalty (or disloyalty); subcontracting ("outsourcing"); personal appearance; off-duty conduct; sexual harassment; gender, racial, religious, and age discrimination; alcohol- and drug-related matters; strike and picket line conduct; just cause; just cause and wrongful dismissal in nonunion employment situations (the ultimate in reserved management rights); differences in the arbitration of private- and public-sector employment disputes; and the arbitration of statutory issues in nonunion settings. The addition of an international comparative analysis would add another vital dimension to this research.

Almost forty years ago, an attorney addressing the NAA doubted that any member of the Academy "would approve the firing of a Negro employee in the deep South for drinking at a racially segregated water foundation...regardless of the strength of the employer's defense grounded on an asserted need to maintain order and discipline." He took the position that "plant norms" and "business needs" must yield to "more compelling considerations."[129] At a later meeting of the NAA, those "more compelling considerations" were defined as constitutional and civil rights that affected the "basic human quality" of a person.[130] These employment discrimination cases involved fundamental rights that, some argued, were in such a different category that arbitrators needed to be "responsible to someone other than the parties."[131]

There are still orders of rights in society, and there is still an unmet need for workplace justice. The right not to be discriminated against is a fundamental human right, as is the right to physical security. These and other human rights are the "more compelling considerations" to which other rights and interest must yield.

Several years ago, Lewis Maltby told the NAA that "the tragic shortcoming of American constitutional law is its failure to protect human rights in the workplace."[132] This chapter has demonstrated that neither U.S. courts nor labor arbitrators understand workers' rights to workplace safety and health as a human right. There can be no true workplace justice, however, without recognizing and respecting those rights of human beings that are more compelling than any other rights or interests at the workplace. That will occur only when courts and arbitrators utilize human rights standards in their decision making.

8

SURREPTITIOUS VIOLATIONS

Human Resources and Workplace Human Rights

To achieve their business objectives, employers always have needed to control their employees. That control, whatever form it took, was intended to get workers to conform "with management's stereotype of the ideal employee: efficient, disciplined, willing, cheerfully obedient and loyal."[1] Although every period in U.S. history had its own "best practices" form of control, it is clear from a historical perspective that the form of control considered best by any employer in any period was the one that increased productivity and profits. Some employers found the use of coercive power applied through a military-like hierarchy of authority (with workers at the bottom) to be most effective. Other employers found that understanding and manipulating human behavior was more likely not only to control the men and women they employed but also to get them to work harder willingly and to generate their loyalty to the employer and the employer's efforts. In either case (or in the many variations and combination of these two approaches), workers were subordinated to the decision-making power of employers.

Special thanks go to former Cornell Presidential Scholar Aaron Graff Gingrande for his expert assistance in preparing this chapter.

Although command, subordination, and discipline are indispensable in economic enterprises, those who command have always sought and propounded ideologies of management, other than employer power, to justify subordinating workers to their authority.[2] These justifications—whether called ideologies, theories, or values—are beliefs about how the employer-worker relationships ought to be conducted. These beliefs underlie the rules that govern workplaces. These rules define the status, rights, duties, and relative power (or relative powerlessness) of those at work, including what standard of treatment they deserve.[3]

Reinhard Bendix, an expert on work and authority, has written that "Ideals of management are attempts by leaders of enterprises to justify the privileges of voluntary action and association for themselves, while imposing upon all subordinates the duty of obedience and the obligation to serve their employers to the best of their ability."[4] The indoctrination of beliefs justifying management authority rather than their coerced imposition can induce workers to submit voluntarily and willingly to employer control. Bendix also pointed out, for example, that even individuals whose ideas and interests differed before being employed were subject "to the universal tendency of men who are employed in hierarchical organizations to obey directives and to identify their own interests and ideas with the organization and with all those persons who share this identification."[5]

When employers exercise overtly coercive power, workers know that their freedoms are being restricted and their rights violated, if they even know what their rights are. But when psychology and an array of other so-called social sciences are used to control human behavior, employer power "shifts from the visible to the invisible, from the known to the anonymous"[6] and from the open to the hidden. Because manipulation "blinds the victim to the fact of manipulation,"[7] it is among the "most seductive levers of social control."[8] It is also one of the most insidious and dangerous because it can blind workers to violations of their human rights.

The fundamental human right of freedom of association, particularly the right of employees to organize a union, engage in collective bargaining with their employers, and participate in making the decisions that affect their workplace lives, has always been a contentious employer-worker issue in the United States. Early on, this understanding of the freedom of association was called *industrial democracy* and its proponents contended that "political freedom can exist only where there is industrial freedom; political democracy only where there is industrial democracy."[9] Employers and government can provide fair employment standards such as wages and conditions of work, but worker participation can be provided only by workers themselves and their labor organizations.

Employers, however, used their behavior-influencing techniques for workplace control, particularly a then-emerging social science called *human relations* to define workplace democracy in psychological terms rather than in political and economic terms. The emphasis was on individuality: the promotion of a democratic ideal based on innate ability and individual expression and development. By that definition of industrial democracy, "individuals were to be freed to achieve their own potential."[10] Many employers also sponsored non-union employee representation plans at their workplaces. It was a workplace democracy that used pseudo-democratic forms, methods, and language to secure worker commitment to managerial objectives without requiring any significant changes in management authority and control of the decision-making process.

The language of workplace democracy and human rights is used with equal facility, therefore, by various people, groups, and organizations with conflicting views and values. If freedom of association comes to mean all things to all people, then it could end up meaning nothing at all—to workers' great detriment.

The forms of these employer practices have changed over the years as have their names—employment management, personnel management, scientific management, welfare capitalism, human relations, human resource management, strategic human resource management—but their central objectives of increased productivity and profitability have remained the same. Frederick Taylor's version of *scientific management* was in its time an employer "best practice," claiming to increase productivity, lower costs, increase wages, reduce waste, and promote industrial peace. The best way of performing a task was determined by subdividing a job into its smallest units of time and motion and then recombining those elements into "methods of least waste" and standardizing the production process. It has been described as employers taking labor skills from employees for "analysis" and handing them back piecemeal to workers "with the result that they [workers] could no longer be masters of a craft."[11]

In important ways, scientific management increased employers' power over workers and the production process and strengthened the hierarchical system–subordinate authority structure. Yet, Taylor claimed that scientific management would "achieve a 'mental revolution' which set the employer and worker pulling together rather than apart."[12] The mental revolution was that employers and workers would "take their eyes off the division of the surplus" and "turn their attention toward increasing the size of the surplus" until "there is ample room for a large increase in wages for workmen and an equally large increase in profits for the manufacturer."[13] The mutual economic self-interest of workers and employers (the "economic man" philosophy) meant that they had a shared interest in increasing production motivated by incentive pay, which meant higher profits and wages.

Proponents of scientific management also maintained that it would bring democracy to the workplace by replacing the arbitrary, dictatorial, and often prejudicial authority of foremen with the neutral scientific authority of scientific management. Describing this practice as scientific, moreover, implied a neutral objectivity and a disinterested and impartial expertise that would discover and apply the "immutable, unarguable facts of any given situation." Consequently, arbitrary dictation (and every other personal exercise of authority) would cease because every issue was subject to scientific investigation and resolution on the basis of ascertainable fact. This, too, would make the workplace more democratic.[14]

Scientific management was a struggle for control of workers and their work. High wages, workplace democracy, restraints on the exercise of arbitrary power, neutral dispute resolution based only on facts, and worker-employer harmony also meant that all the reasons to organize unions and to bargain collectively were removed. As Taylor put it, "collective bargaining becomes a matter of trifling importance."[15]

It should come as no surprise to anyone who has worked that workers, including management executives, regulate their output. Management-oriented social scientists called it restriction of output. Taylor knew this was true of "virtually every factory in the country"[16] and that explains why he wanted to take control of the rates of production away from workers and give it to management. Scientific management was a "resolute attack on all methods of output restriction."[17] Taylor believed that by linking pay to individual productivity, management could separate the individual worker from a work group that deliberately slowed down the pace of work.

Workers, on the other hand, knew that improved performance under an incentive rate meant the job would be retimed resulting in a cut in their pay. They experimented within work groups "to see just how high they could go without exposing themselves to a rate cut."[18] A comprehensive independent study in the late 1920s found rate cutting, alienated foremen, and restrictive practices:

> Foremen working at cross purposes with time-study men and showing workers how to make time studies inaccurate; workmen billing time by the hour because

the day's "limit" had been reached; men afraid to let the management learn of improved methods which they had discovered by themselves; older workers teaching youngsters to keep secret from the management the amount they could comfortably produce in a day; managements trying first one "wage incentive" plan, then another, in an effort to induce men to do what we believe they really wanted to do in the first place.[19]

The report concluded that "For every worker...who appeared overtaxed, we encountered dozens who were successful matching wits with management in self-protective resistance against wage incentive plans, piece rate cuts and prospective layoffs."[20] Workers were protecting their jobs by working slower thereby, they believed, making their jobs last longer. It was a powerful defensive weapon against employers bent on increasing output.

Employers themselves resisted Taylorism. Relatively few U.S. employers accepted all of it, rather choosing among scientific management's "arsenal of devices" to improve their management of labor.[21] (One researcher has estimated that over 90 percent of U.S. industry had adopted the wage incentive aspects of scientific management by 1940.[22]) Yet, the "social philosophy rather than the techniques of scientific management became a part of prevailing management ideology."[23] Employers who rejected the "mental revolution," however, recognized the limits of treating workers as human machines and the need to deal with the "human element" as it was called.[24]

More in tune with the humane approach to capturing the allegiance of their employees, many employers from even before scientific management's popularity had instituted employee welfare programs. The programs were paternalistic whether inspired by philanthropy, humanitarianism, religion, commercial shrewdness, or a combination of those motives. They looked to reverse the impersonality and mutual indifference and distrust that characterized the employer-worker relationship.[25]

Early reformers, particularly in the Social Gospel Movement in the late 1800s, called for the application of Christian principles to govern the management of workers. They were concerned about the growing working class, the majority of whom were immigrants. They wanted to make "foreign-born workers more like middle-class native-born Americans by improving their moral condition through 'uplift.'"[26] George Pullman created an entire company town to control and influence his workers' lives. Henry Ford had classes taught by company volunteers and developed English and Americanization classes on company premises. As one writer commented, "The main expenses borne by the company were lesson sheets and electricity. The loyalty engendered must have seemed cheap at the price."[27]

A welfare secretary, most often a woman, administered social programs including, as they developed over time, lunch rooms, safety campaigns, beautified workplaces, plant doctors and nurses, employee representation plans, home-ownership plans, occasionally pension and stock ownership plans, and sports teams and other forms of recreation. These programs and activities were intended to integrate not only workers but also workers' families into the company "to enhance the corporate message and tighten employee identification with the firm" and win the loyalty of workers.[28]

That tightened identification with the employer, the core objective of all management of labor plans, was intended to blunt the appeal of unionism by demonstrating to employees that their employers could provide employees with all they could want or need.[29] Paternalistic firms "boasted that picnics, parties, and clubs helped create a 'nice friendly attitude' that kept out union organizers."[30] Concern for employees expressed through company welfare benefits for employees also "gave lie to the claim of union leaders that employers were the enemies of the workingman."[31]

Company welfarism did not change the hierarchical power relationship between employers, who determined worker success or failure by their own unilaterally developed standards, and workers who were subject to that employer control. Despite the moral, humanitarian, and religious dimensions of some employer welfare plans, moreover, employee welfare plans had to be good business and result in increased production, lower costs, loyal and contented employees, reduced conflict, and increased profits in order to be continued. The ultimate measure of success was economic performance, not the uplift of workers.

Early in the twentieth century, a new field of employment management challenged welfare secretaries for jurisdiction over the "human element" of the workplace. These employment managers charged that welfare work was based on sentimental and charitable impulses, whereas employment management "was driven by the bottom line." Female welfare workers were "emotional," whereas male employment managers were "rational," "scientific," and comfortable with hiring and firing workers ("inherently a man's job"). Employment managers wanted to assume the welfare function and include it with other functions such as hiring, job placement, and firing in a centralized employment department headed by an executive with a professional status equal to that of financial management, sales management, or production management.[32]

The percentage of employers that adopted welfare policies was probably small, although such policies were used extensively by large companies.[33] Various aspects are still utilized at workplaces today. Employment management did become dominant, however, and laid the foundation for what became known as personnel management and, later, human relations, human resource management, and strategic human resource management.

This new profession of employment management was deeply divided between the psychological approach and the political and economic approach to what was called the labor problem. This different understanding of the workplace continues today in the separation between human resource management and industrial and labor relations not only in academe but also at the workplace. In the United States, that separation still reflects drastically different conceptions of workers' rights, particularly workers' rights as human rights.

Because history has not been considered important by most industrial relations and human resource scholars in the United States,[34] it is not commonly known that employment managers who were known as reformists advocated a concept of social change and corporate social responsibility whereby business could and should be made an instrument of public interest. Their role, as they saw it, was to regulate labor relations in the public interest. Some thought they could be agents of the public at workplaces by acting as mediators between workers and employers. This would require, they argued, more authority inside the companies in the form of executive status and a centralized employment department as well as independence to enable them to be representatives of the public interest.[35] Others advocated for powerful government agencies to investigate pressing economic problems and to "compel the corporations to operate in the public interest and to promote distributive justice by enforcing labor laws based on social investigation."[36]

Whatever their approach, these reformists in the field of employment management agreed that the existing hierarchical authority structure at the workplace needed to be changed to enable workers to participate in the business decisions that affected their lives on and off their jobs. They advocated the development of worker representation systems to make that participation effective. They also rejected the laissez-faire market philosophy, supported unions, believed there was an inherent conflict of interest between employers and workers, and promoted collective bargaining and collective bargaining agreements as the most effective and democratic way of resolving employer-worker conflicts.

The influence that these reformists had did not survive World War I. The triumph of "managerialism" was evident as early as the 1920s and was completed in the 1930s. During the New Deal years, human relations experts in psychology and sociology used their newly acquired body of expertise to support employers' efforts to keep control of their workplaces. They accomplished that in part, as already noted, by weaving their version of personnel science into an ideology of American business that portrayed employers as preservers of rather than threats to American democracy.[37]

Managerialists in the employment management field, moreover, professed a harmony of interest between employers and workers. They denied that there was any inherent conflict between labor and management or that the hierarchical authority structure was in any way the cause of whatever unrest that did exist. Rather, labor unrest, they maintained, was caused by maladjustments between workers and their jobs and could be resolved by fitting workers to existing jobs through various psychologically and sociologically based techniques and methods that would result in increased productivity and "increased contentment of the working force."[38] There was no need, therefore, for fundamental reform of the system, government regulation, or unions or for employment managers to be more then staff advisors to managers. By the end of the 1920s, employment management was known as *personnel management*, a term that reflected more precisely the new profession's "narrowing focus on the management of individuals in industry."[39]

The core values of that personnel management remain unchanged. Those values need to be probed carefully and thoroughly because they constitute and influence every vital aspect of labor relations, including the nature and sources of worker and employer rights, which rights get priority when they conflict, and the nature of the relationship between employer and worker.

Personnel management developed its methods and ethos in the 1920s, but "personnel men found it easier to preach and write about how useful they could be and how important they should be, than actually to win authority and status."[40] Outside of large firms, personnel management was anemic, being thought of as a costly frill that produced few tangible economic benefits.[41] At the same time, although many universities had schools of business, education in business was scorned by the intellectual community. Consequently, there was a movement to "build an intellectual foundation for business education."[42]

Some in the personnel management field saw and exploited the mutual advantages of cooperation between academe and business. Academics offered a "presumably objective, outside perspective, as well as specialized knowledge not available inside the corporation,"[43] and business offered private-sector customers for academic psychologists who themselves were seeking university recognition and status for their discipline. Personnel managers also offered the opportunity to demonstrate psychology's practical applications, thereby advancing their own professional agenda. Universities ultimately solidified their ties with personnel managers by establishing specialized academic programs in personnel administration that became a de facto requirement for a job in personnel.[44]

One major objective of this academe–business collaboration was to create a science of workplace human relations. What became known as *industrial psychology* was the basis for this new science. The social sciences emerging in universities were disciplines manned by professionals (not reformers) who were dedicated to objective research and use of the scientific method. Psychology, moreover, promised an understanding of human behavior based on the application of the techniques of a quantitative social science. This was, purportedly, scientific, not what was disparaged as the politically inspired and subjective approaches to issues such as distribution of power between employers and workers. Psychological experiments and test results could be expressed in numbers, which gave the appearance of objectivity. Because intelligence, aptitude, attitude, and physical and mental health could be measured, the research method determined the subjects to be researched. Consequently, individual workers, rather than organizations and economic or social conditions were studied.[45]

Despite the claims of neutrality, the decision to concentrate on the psychological study of individual workers was "profoundly political."[46] It was a choice not to address the imbalance of power at the workplace or workers' rights but, instead, how employers can select the best worker for a job, fit that worker to the job in an existing hierarchical workplace, and motivate that worker to be most productive. Industrial psychologists concentrated on the construction of tests that could be used by employers in the selection, placement, and performance monitoring of each employee and, in the process, would demonstrate the psychologists own usefulness. In essence, they were developing tools for employers to use to understand, control, motivate, and manipulate human behavior.

This collaboration between academe and business had the power and resources to define what the labor problems were and to control the choice of subjects to be studied as well as the approach to be used in those studies. Academics in this collaboration also had the power and the prestige to define what were rational and irrational behaviors at the workplace, and productive and nonproductive solutions to workplace issues. In today's human resources terminology, they determined the best practices for the achievement of management objectives. These academic researchers, moreover, worked on problems of concern to employers with the objective of solving those problems in a way useful to employers.

Many academics sold their services to employers for career advancement and funding for their research. Employers provided not only funds but also indispensable access to workplace sites and subjects. Employer-funded foundations also supported selected research projects and identified areas and subjects for future research.[47] Management controlled these social scientists not only because it funded them but also because "industrial social scientists, without prodding from anyone, have accepted the norms of America's managers."[48] As Loren Baritz has written, "most managers have had no trouble in getting social scientists to grant managerial premises because such premises have also been assumed by the social scientists."[49] Despite these social scientists' assertions of scientific objectivity, the evidence supports Baritz's conclusion that "this commitment to management's goals, as opposed to other groups and classes in American society, did color their research and recommendations."[50] These were not neutral scientists. By providing to employers techniques, values, and ideas concerning worker control and manipulation, these social scientists were doing what they professed they would not do—namely, become accessories to the reinforcement of employer power not only at the workplace but in the larger society as well. In sum:

> What in fact did happen is obvious. Social scientists busied themselves in industrial research questions, hired themselves out as industrial consultants, made recommendations to management. Management gratefully accepted the practical contribution of social scientists and went about its business of repressing unionism, controlling the attitudes and thinking of its workers, driving output up, driving costs down, and regaining a firm grip on American social, intellectual, political and economic life.[51]

What some consider the most important industrial social science research project ever conducted, and what all agree was a pioneering work, was carried out between 1927 and 1932 at the Hawthorne Works of the Western Electric Company. Western Electric was an exponent and user of scientific management not only to increase productivity but as part of its effort to avoid unionization. Before the Hawthorne study began, industrial psychologists had assumed that physical conditions of work were directly related to worker productivity. Consequently, the study began as illumination experiments; that is, as an attempt to determine the relationship between illumination at the workplace and worker productivity.

The results were perplexing because the production of every group of workers studied increased regardless of whether they worked with greater illumination, no change in illumination, or even when illumination was progressively decreased. This was the starting point for the experiments for which Elton Mayo, then a professor at the Harvard Business School, had overall responsibility.[52] Mayo's career was devoted to finding ways to improve human relations, particularly in industry.

Mayo's group continued to emphasize the physical rather than the psychological determinants of productivity. They altered various physical factors such as rest breaks, work hours, and temperature as well as methods of pay. The result, once again, was an increase in productivity regardless of the changes made—even when the work day was lengthened. Eventually, the researchers concluded that "changes in the total psychological climate in the test room" was a possible explanation.[53] More specifically, the researchers discovered that the women studied had formed a small group and that "within the whole group there were several subgroups, cliques, and isolated individuals."[54] Mayo pointed to the fact that members of the group had a positive attitude toward the company's intentions because the group was consulted, their comments "listened to and discussed," and their objections were "allowed to negative a suggestion." In other words, the group had developed what Mayo called a "sense of participation" and had become a "social unit."[55]

The downside, as the researchers also concluded, was that the group was regulating or restricting (as the researchers termed it) its output, adjusting reports of daily production, and deciding how much work would be done. It was the small group and not the management that controlled the level of production and set the standards to which individual members of the group were pressured to adhere.[56] Supervisors, moreover, were part of the work regulation process: "placed as they [supervisors] were in a compromising position by being observers of breaches of rules, dependent on the good will of the men and not really powerful enough to control them, they tended to side with them."[57] This regulation of production was explained, revealingly enough, not as any hostility toward management or as the workers' desire to protect their jobs or wages but as being an "'integrating mechanism' which enhanced the solidarity of the group."[58] Later the research group believed what they had discovered was "an attitude of resistance to change." Regulating output, in other words, was a challenge to management's authority.[59]

Under Mayo's influence, however, the researchers' report suggested initially that the workers simply had no incentive to work harder. Mayo promised that a management elite, trained in the methods of human relations, would change workers' attitudes so they would identify with management's goals. The challenge was how to enable management to reestablish (or establish) control at the workplace by getting the informal worker groups and their individual members to accept the goals of formal management groups: "Either the thinking of the [informal] group would have to be changed or the power of the [informal] group would have to be canceled."[60] No other options were considered. Mayo wanted to bring about what he termed "effective collaboration" between workers and managers.[61] The human relations theories that the Hawthorne experiments generated and Mayo popularized armed personnel managers with new methods and tools with which to create relations at the workplace that would result in that worker-management collaboration.[62] Workers' human desire for cooperative group activity needed to be redirected from being used for workers' self-interests and goals of job and income preservation to worker commitment to management's self-interested goals of productivity and profits.

By the late 1940s, *human relations,* with its promise of winning worker loyalty to the employer, had become and would remain for decades the dominant managerial method.[63] In great part, it meant managing workers' emotions and attitudes as the way to influence and manage their behavior at work. Despite the cover of scientific jargon, it was a clever and sophisticated process of manipulation and exploitation for management ends.[64]

The psychological devices of manipulation included the use of nondirective interviews in which workers determined the flow of the conversation bounded only by a series of open-ended questions about work and management. Mayo considered the interview to be a key, although indirect, method for management to gain the cooperation of workers. As Mayo put it, "Someone, the interviewer, representing (for the worker) the plant organization outside his own group, has aided him to work better within his own group." The interview, Mayo said, was the means to bring about "inner change" in work groups and individual workers. It was "the beginning of the necessary double loyalty—to his own group and to the larger organization."[65]

The Hawthorne researchers had found that the interview provided workers not only a cathartic release of what Mayo called "useless emotional complications"[66] but also a feeling of recognition and importance and a sense of participating in management decisions. This sense or feeling of participation led workers to view their own work situation as well as management more favorably, improved morale and reduced grievances, and increased their productivity.

The manipulation and deceit was in creating the perception of participation without any reality of participation. The goal was "to get the workers to accept what management wants them to accept *but* to make them feel *they* made or helped to make the decision"[67] without any changes in the superior-subordinate authority relationship at the workplace. Worse yet, workers could be led to believe "that they were members of a work community best managed by the authoritarian framework of modern industry."[68]

The interviewing process subsequently developed into a personal counseling program that had many of the same characteristics and objectives. As one former counselor recalled, she and her colleagues were told to deal "with attitudes toward problems, not the problems themselves."[69] Again, the message was: Change workers' perceptions without any intention of changing workers' reality. By adjusting workers to their situations, thereby making them happier in their work, employers, through their therapist-counselors, expected to reduce conflict, absenteeism, and turnover and to increase production. They also hoped that by detecting signs of worker dissatisfaction and assuaging those workers involved, counseling could help avoid unionism. Interviewing and counseling were management's counter to the informal work groups' regulation of output.[70] They were also part of the growing science of human behavior—which later put workers "in the picture" with other devices such as consultative committees, graphic displays, and employer in-house magazines.[71]

Mayo abhorred conflict. He considered it a "social disease" and, at the workplace, the result of mental disorders.[72] In other words, conflict was in the worker's head; more precisely, in the worker's "negative revery." These negative reveries, Mayo believed, were often caused by a feeling of economic insecurity. Mayo also believed that these emotional discontents could be directed at employers in the form of resistance to authority. Mayo's concept laid the foundation for personnel work "that treated strikes and workers' grievances as symptoms of deeper psychological and psychiatric problems of individuals rather than a response to legitimate economic grievances." (Mayo wanted to go further. He proposed that the application of his theory be under the direction of psychiatrists at each workplace.)[73] Careful recruitment and selection techniques as well as attitude surveys, interviewing, individual counseling, and two-way communication of information would enable management to discover and treat the causes of worker dissatisfaction.

Mayo denied the inevitability of worker-employer conflict and asserted, instead, the unitarist position that company and workers formed a community.[74] Critics have charged the Mayo group with ignoring unions thereby promoting their belief that managerial action alone would resolve problems. When unions were not ignored, they were considered "symptoms of trouble."[75] Consistent with his views on conflict, Mayo labeled workers who joined unions psychotics who were maladjusted to their work. According to industrial social scientists who shared Mayo's attitudes, a union joiner was "stupid, overly emotional, class conscious, without recreational or aesthetic interests, insecure, and afraid of responsibility"[76]—in sum, mentally abnormal.

At the workplace, employers undermined unions through the use of human relations techniques to win worker loyalty and to identify workers' economic well-being with their employer's economic well-being and by demonstrating to workers that unions were unnecessary because management could and would give them what they needed. In effect, workers would be too satisfied to want a union. Textile Workers Union research director Solomon Barkin considered the combination of employers' human relations and welfare practices the most important reason for union membership decline by encouraging "loyalty to the enterprise and weav[ing] the worker into the employer's social and economic fabric."[77]

In 1978 Gordon Jackson, a labor relations attorney who specialized in combating union organizing campaigns and developing programs of "union prevention," wrote what became a classic book entitled, *How to Stay Union Free.*[78] It is a handbook of human relations doctrines and techniques. The basic premise of the book is that unions are the result of bad management, or, in the author's words, "unions do not unionize employers—employers organize themselves."[79] He described unions as the uninvited partner that intruded on management's prerogative, created a "we-they" division between workers and management, and attempted to ruin the "traditional '*esprit de corps*,' teamwork and camaraderie enjoyed by the *union free* employer" and "rank and file employees."[80] Human relations doctrine abounds in the author's advice to supervisors (in addition to pledging commitment to the union-free policy of his or her employer):

a) motivate employees; b) sell employees on the organization's favorable qualities and positive benefits; c) recognize employee unrest; d) be accessible and responsive to employees' concerns, grievances, frustrations and complaints; e) eliminate sources of employee dissatisfaction; f) take interest in employees' needs and personal problems; g) reflect an engaging personality; h) instruct clearly; i) make sure the employee understands his [or her] work duties and responsibilities; j) constructively counsel and discipline employees for improper work or violations of the rules of conduct; k) sincerely (and lavishly) praise and compliment employees for their good efforts; and l) gain the love and respect of the employees under his [or her] supervision.[81]

Another key to remaining union-free was the "selection of employees who will neither feel the need for a union…nor be attracted to a union at a later date because of their latent behavioral characteristics and behavioral patterns."[82] An employer-controlled "participative management" was recommended; one that does not turn over business operations to the workers. That controlled participation included a communication program, described as the lifeblood of participative management, which "gives employers recognition that they so much desire by making them feel part of the organization";[83] individual periodic interviews to allow employees an opportunity to get problems off their chests as a way of discovering employee discontent and addressing it promptly;[84] interviews at the workplace using open-ended questions that "force the responding employees to make some kind of statement" revealing his or her feelings;[85] the use of employee attitude surveys "to monitor employee discontent and frustration";[86] and employer newspapers and newsletters that "lavishly report on events surrounding employees."[87]

Employee programs rooted in company welfarism were also recommended to recognize the employee, involve the employee "in friendly interaction with management outside of working hours," and demonstrate an employer's desire "to share a spirit of brotherhood with management" away from the workplace. These programs included picnics with employees' children in attendance with managers doing the physical work "to show employees they are working for them as well as with them"; open houses so that employees could show their families "with pride" his or her role in the overall operation of the company; and sporting events, which were touted as unparalleled in creating esprit de corps.[88] The author also urged "the prompt elimination of employees and supervisors who do not meet the standards of the union free employer."[89]

Human relations posed and its surviving principles continue to pose a powerful and effective counter to the unionization of workers. Yet, unions during the peak days of human relations mounted only a hollow response limited in essence to characterizing human relations as cow psychology; that is, "contented workers will give more 'milk.'"[90] By the time of Mayo's human relations, conservative, job-control, business unionism had long accepted the private property values on which the concept of inherent management prerogatives was based. When these unions renounced any intentions to seek codetermination at the workplace or any substantive variation of codetermination, the way was free of any obstacles to management's unilateral decision-making power. Unions bargained about the effect of those management decisions on wages, hours, and working conditions but did not fight to change the existing hierarchical power structure at the workplace. (The courts, as we have seen, prohibited codetermination when unions did seek it.)

Employers in the United States were hostile even to this conservative unionism, however, because union attempts at job control and improved wages and working conditions impinged on what employers asserted were their court-backed sacrosanct prerogatives.[91] In sum, employers wanted and obtained full and unchallenged authority. They also want that authority legitimized voluntarily and enthusiastically by all members of the enterprise. Unions still mount a challenge to management in the industrial relations (or labor relations) aspects of the worker-management relationship. Some of those challenges, particularly the contractual just-cause limitation on management's authority to discipline and discharge through recourse to binding neutral arbitration, constitute important inroads into management's human resources authority. As unions decline, however, so do these limitations on employer control. Workers themselves, organized or unorganized, have resisted management authority and, in their own ways, have fought for control over their own jobs. Human resources has been a seductive lever of employer control, however, that has violated workers' human rights, especially workers' freedom of association rights.

A job redesign movement that began in the 1970s was hailed by many, particularly some academics, as a new Golden Era of Work that was a sharp and distinct break with the past. Work would now be safer and cleaner, would require less physical effort, would involve more interesting and intellectually challenging tasks, and would free workers from machine- and assembly line–set pace of labor.[92] This new method of production purportedly rejected the principles and values of scientific management ("Taylorism") as well as "Fordism"—the assembly line "concept [that] tends to exclude the creative and managerial skills of the people who work on the line."[93]

This new way has many names: lean production, the Japanese model, synchronous manufacturing, flexible specialization, innovation-mediated production, high-performance work systems, even world-class production systems. Whatever the name, this new production system promised far less hierarchical organization, employer participation, and a work team structure. The new system was portrayed as the opposite of the old system that was exploitive and dehumanizing. Self-directed teams of workers, also called autonomous work groups, self-managed teams, or high-performance teams, would set work schedules and performance targets, design jobs and job layout, determine material flow, tools to be used, the method and pace of production, and control the work environment. Some characterized this as a "fundamental shift in work from an emphasis on manual to mental labor."[94]

Under Fordism, the pace of the assembly line dictated the pace of work for assembly-line workers. A worker in the automotive industry under that system did not stop the line "unless someone was dying." The fact that only a foreman had the authority to stop the assembly line "represented the boundary between the judgment of workers and the judgment of superiors."[95] The claim that under the new production system workers could stop the line without punishment meant that workers could control the pace of their own work. Given the history of assembly-line worker subservience in the automobile industry, this worker power to stop the line seemed "nothing less than revolutionary," because it "would turn Fordism inside out" and would be a "radical break from the entire history of automobile shop floor practice."[96]

After this trumpeting—particularly by academic researchers in industrial and labor relations whose constant preoccupation with change lacks the tempering or moderating effects of a knowledge of history—there is no new Golden Era of Work, no revolutionary break with the past, and nothing like the worker control that was heralded. There has been far more continuity than change. Employers have always sought increased productivity and profitability through ever-higher performing work systems. Human resources, by whatever name, has always sought to facilitate increased productivity and profitability by securing not only workers' acceptance of changes in method and organization of work but also workers' cooperation with and, ultimately, identification with their employers' objectives.

There is also persuasive evidence that the new best practices associated with the new world-class production systems are merely variations on the ever-constant theme of management control of the workplace and not a workplace transformation. Some researchers, particularly those who, before drawing conclusions, worked in plants with the new production system, describe it as "team Taylorism."[97] Laurie Graham, for example, found "continued reliance on Taylorist principles of production." Rather than a factory utopia, she experienced a work process that not only incorporated Taylorism but also went beyond Fordist principles to control even the social aspects of work.[98] Other research has concluded that the alleged management by commitment was actually a process of "seduction (by corporate values), and [peer group] self discipline."[99]

Human resources still seeks to win the "hearts and minds" of workers,[100] to improve firms' performance, thereby justifying human resources' existence. Employers' goals are still of overriding importance, managerial prerogatives still prevail, and unions remain undesirable and unnecessary. The substance of management control has remained unchanged; it is the form of management control that has changed in ways often detrimental to workers.

This latest post–scientific management, post-Fordism version of high-performance systems has evoked calls for what is purportedly a new role for human resources. That new role involves human resources as an elite strategic corps of business partners enhancing employers' competitive advantage[101] and "maximum organizational performance" by conforming human resources strategy to corporate strategy.[102] As one highly respected expert put it, "The new agenda would mean that every one of HR's [human resources'] activities would in some concrete way help the company better serve its customers or otherwise increase shareholder value."[103] In this view, workers have value and become what are called "organizational assets" when they improve the efficiency and effectiveness of the company. It is human resources' responsibility to deliver and develop this so-called human capital so that the enterprise can become more competitive and execute its business strategy successfully.

As a partner with senior and line managers in moving "planning from the conference room to the marketplace," human resources would be an agent of change, "an agent of continuous transformation"[104] at a time when the pace of change is "dizzying and dazzling."[105] Among other things, human resources would replace resistance to change with resolve and "fear of change with excitement about its possibilities."[106] Competition requires change, and change and other competition-driven events require an "increasing commitment from employees who are being asked to give their emotional, intellectual and physical energy to ensure firm success."[107] As explained by one pair of experts, "it is the difference between hiring out as a mercenary and becoming a Marine."[108]

Because an employer's narrow self-interest (such as a target return on investment) alone rarely inspires Marine-like workplace effort, the recommended way to get workers "to put out the extraordinary effort required to realize company targets" is to get them to identify with and commit to their employer's "vision" and philosophy; that is, to what their employer "stands for."[109] Experts in this area explain that an employer's core ideology is comprised of core values and a core purpose. *Core values* are the "timeless guiding principles" of an organization. (One might not be surprised to discover, for example, that the Philip Morris Company's core value is the "right to freedom of choice" or that the

Walt Disney Corporation's is the "nurturing and promulgation of 'wholesome American values.'"[110]

Core purpose is an organization's reason for being. That reason for being is always deeper and truer than simply making money.[111] Wal-Mart says that the real reason it is in business is "to give ordinary folk the chance to buy the same things as rich people," the Walt Disney Corporation exists "to make people happy," and the NIKE corporation, perhaps more frank, says its purpose is to enable people "to experience the emotion of competition, winning and crushing competitors."[112]

Getting employees to commit to their employer's values and purpose requires human resources staff "to put a great deal of effort into communication"[113] because "shaping organizational values" depends "less on analysis and logic and more on emotion and intuition."[114] Other experts who doubt that core values and purposes can be imposed or bought into recommend to employers that they hire only people who are predisposed to share the company's core values and purpose. Attract and retain those people, these experts advise, and let those who do not share an employer's core values "go elsewhere."[115] Whatever the method, some experts believe that companies can replace churches, communities, and even families in giving meaning to employees' lives and that the workplaces can become "primary means for personal fulfillment."[116]

Calls for human resources to achieve this highest trust commitment from employees, however, occur simultaneously with calls for human resources to abandon or downgrade what some experts claim was its former role as "people persons," employee advocates, "management conscience," and "in-house Socialists focused on feel-good events."[117] Regardless of the historical inaccuracy of these perceptions, they are contrary to the "radical departure from the status quo"[118] in which human resources is now a "value added player" whose primary responsibility is delivering the behavior needed to realize the business strategy and whose performance "must now be judged on whether it enhances the firm's competitive advantage by adding real measurable economic value."[119]

There are still calls in the relevant literature for human resource professionals to be advocates for employees.[120] As a respected academic, Thomas Kochan, warned, however, "tilting too far in the direction of becoming an advocate for employee concerns would do little other than re-marginalize the function within the management structure."[121] That is because human resources, after all these years, still has a credibility problem so serious that there is public discussion about whether it should be abolished or outsourced unless it can demonstrate its positive contributions to employers' financial performance.[122] (Those workers who have been downsized, rightsized, reengineered, or outsourced or in some other euphemistic way disposed of will appreciate the irony in that.) Human resources always has needed and still needs to justify its existence by showing its contribution to employee productivity and employer profits. That need dictates the nature of the balance it must strike between employer and employee rights and interests. Human resources has always been a partisan of employers whatever the best practices of the time.

At the same time human resources professionals and academics talk abut generating worker loyalty they talk in jargonese about a "career-resilient workforce," meaning workers "now hardened by downsizing, delayerings, rightsizings, layoffs, and restructuring." They assert openly that the "traditional definition of loyalty must go."[123] That traditional loyalty was supposedly part of a mythological (certainly not enforceable) social contract pursuant to which hourly workers received eight hours of pay for eight hours of work and white-collar workers received long-term employment in return for good and loyal service.[124]

For workers this is the real meaning of change management. Today's best practice models are silent about whose goals are being served when a practice is good for an employer (such as layoffs) but bad for workers.[125] Instead, there are proposals for a new "psychological contract," ill-defined regarding content, that would get new shorter-term employees to work "with the care and interest of people who expect to be there for the duration of their careers."[126] More precisely, "employees must feel like valued, trusted, and respected members of the corporate community *while they are a part of it.*"[127] Bluntly put, workers are required to be both dependable *and* disposable.

The overwhelming number of workers have no advocates at their workplaces. When reading of workers as human capital or as a company's human assets, one cannot help but be reminded of times when labor was treated as a commodity. Loyalty and commitment, moreover, run only in one direction. Layoffs are not a new phenomenon but they have become essential in today's cutthroat competition. It has become standard business practice to lay off or terminate employees regardless of how well a company is doing in order to improve its bottom line even further, particularly when the stock market looks favorably on such cost cutting.[128] A leading textbook, granting that many see employee "separations" negatively, points out several benefits including the possibility that "a persistently low turnover rate may have a negative effect on performance if the workplace becomes complacent and fails to generate innovative ideas."[129] One prominent authority refers to "downsizing" as "cleaning debris" and "yard work."[130]

There is nothing but worker insecurity in the midst of all the talk about worker empowerment and control. A popular human resources textbook, for example, describes precisely how managers and employee relations specialists perceive employees in this decision-making process. The authors extol a company they say is known for its excellent employee relations and commitment to a philosophy of respect for the individual. They then state that managers must "keep them [employees] informed about what management plans to do with the business, and tell them how those plans may affect their jobs." Managers "should also give employees the freedom" to grieve the employer's decisions and should listen to the grievances but, the authors concluded, management could have good reasons not to change the decisions.[131] Where is the worker empowerment and control?

In countries other than the United States, the value underlying employer-employee relations "is that employees are members or partners in the enterprise and are thereby entitled to a voice in the decisions of the enterprise which affect them."[132] In the United States, the assumption is that employees are only suppliers of labor and have no stake in the enterprise other than to be paid for labor performed. This fundamental difference in values results in significantly different legal rules and labor relations systems.[133] In the United States, one of those legal rules is the common law rule of employment-at-will, which states that employers are free to discharge (or retain) employees at will for good cause, or no cause, or even for bad cause. Labor law professor Clyde Summers has written that this distinctive feature of U.S. labor law "by giving total dominance to the employer, endows the employer with the divine right to rule the working lives of its subject employees."[134] The employer has sovereignty except to the extent that it has granted rights to its employees contractually by negotiating limitations of its sovereignty with a union or its unrepresented employees or had its sovereignty limited by legislation such as the National Labor Relations and the Occupational Safety and Health Acts or by judicial decision creating exceptions to the rule. (Summers concluded that these judicial exceptions "have been so grudgingly applied by most courts that they are little more than paper shields against arbitrary employer actions.")[135]

The underlying value in the U.S. employment relationship of employer dominance and employee subservience continues to be the prevailing force in U.S. labor law:

> The employer as owner of the enterprise, is viewed as owning the job with a property right to control the job and the worker who fills it. That property right

gives the employer the right to impose any requirement on the employee, give any order and insist on obedience, change any term of employment and discard the employee at any time. The employer is sovereign over his or her employee subjects.[136]

The employment-at-will rule has precluded employees from asserting any realistic claim of being partners in the enterprise with a right to participate in decision making. Employers have also used it as a tool in running the business and controlling employees.[137] Human resources textbooks, however, justify the rule because it acknowledges an alleged symmetrical relationship between employer and employee whereby employees are free to terminate their relationship with their employer as well.[138] (It would seem that this apparent symmetry understates a worker's need for job security and overstates an employer's need to fire a worker without cause.)[139] One textbook, to the authors' credit, pointed out that it was "apparent that employment at will has stacked the deck in favor of employers," estimating that approximately 150,000 workers were wrongfully discharged each year without legal remedies or recourse.[140]

There is no persuasive evidence that employers want it any other way. For example, a handbook rule exception to employment-at-will was established when courts considered employee handbooks or policy manuals distributed to employees by employers to be implied contracts of employment if they contained procedures for discharging employees or assurances that employees would not be dismissed without cause. Employers' reaction was not to welcome due process and fairness to the workplace but rather to eliminate employers' vulnerability to implied contract lawsuits by "including employment-at-will statements in all employment documents [such as] employee handbooks, employment applications, and letters of employment"; "training supervisors and managers not to imply contract benefits in conversations with new or present employees"; "having written proof that employees have read and understood the employment-at-will disclaimers"; and the inclusion in all employee handbooks of a "disclaimer that expressly provides that all employment policies and benefits contained in the handbook are subject to change or removal at the sole and exclusive discretion of the employer."[141] The objective is to avoid any restrictions on an employer's power to discharge a worker without cause, while human resources departments can continue to use employee handbooks as important sources of information about such issues as employee benefits, dress codes, smoking, drug-testing procedures, family leave policies, sexual harassment, and attendance rules.[142]

Employers and their human resources staffs continue their "perennial purpose"[143] of getting workers to identify with employer goals, thereby creating a "cooperative workforce willing to conform to company demands."[144] They also continue to use a careful selection process that weeds out those who do not accept an employer's philosophy or do not believe that what is good for the company is always good for them. With methods that combine coercion with consent, employers using the world-class production process want workers' complete cooperation in the firm's competitive struggle.[145] (Labor-management conflict is replaced with other types of conflict beneficial to employers such as individual worker competition with peers and the competition of "our company" against its competitor companies.)[146]

Rather than liberating workers by giving them control over their work and participation in the decisions that affect their workplace lives, Graham found that the components of the world-class production system—pre-employment selection, orientation and training for new workers, the team concept, a philosophy of Kaizen (i.e., continuous improvement),[147] shaping shop floor culture from the top down, a computerized assembly line, and just-in-time production—created an "invisible 'iron cage' of control over individual workers."[148] The methods of control are new to some extent, but there is still no democratic workplace.

Teamwork in itself does not necessarily liberate workers from coercion or from others' control or promote and protect their rights. Announcing that there are no more bosses and workers at a workplace but only "associates" and "advisors"[149] does not change anything but labels. The new production systems have been called "management by stress"—physical and psychological—in which "a kind of worker empowerment takes place, but only insofar as it conforms to an even more carefully regimented shop-floor regime."[150] Work under lean production, moreover, "far from providing a replacement to the mind-numbing stress of mass production, systemically intensifies work by specifically and comprehensively removing any obstacles to the extraction of effort."[151]

The computerized assembly line does differ from the traditional Fordist line, but mainly because "it provides additional means of scrutiny and discipline over the workforce."[152] Graham found that workers can stop the line, but signals in the form of lights or sound focused departmentwide attention on the team with a problem. A computer system also recorded how often each team stopped the line—a "blaming process."[153] Management exploited this social pressure, in turn, "to put tremendous pressure on specific teams."[154] In another location, all green lights on a line means workers are not working as hard as they could. The line speed is then increased to locate the weakest points so that managers can "constantly readjust and rebalance to make production ever more efficient."[155]

The computerized assembly line is ever-higher performance at the expense of pressured, stressed, and controlled workers:

> To summarize, the intent of this multidimensional, web-like structure is to create an inescapable, highly rationalized system of worker compliance. Compliance is gained indirectly as a worker identifies with teammates and internalizes the responsibilities of team membership. In turn, team membership creates a form of discipline that is either self-imposed or exerted by peers. If indirect measures fail, compliance can be directly enforced through the authority structure. Technical discipline reinforces social control with the computerized assembly line and just-in-time production setting the pace of work. Technical controls interconnect with indirect, social controls via the team structure where workers find themselves isolated within their independent teams from the rest of the plant. Ideologically, teams are unified through the company's common goal of profit making.[156]

Even before Mayo, employers and human resources professionals, knowing the resistance power of small informal work groups, sought ways to control them or break them up. The world-class production system makes it much more difficult for workers to protect themselves by gaining control over the pace of work because it dominates the social aspects of work. Traditionally workers have turned to each other for self-defense, for example, by finding ways to create some free time for themselves on the job while still meeting production quotas.

Workers in automobile plants told Graham that "there was absolutely no chance to work ahead and create any spare time or relieve the tension. The line was simply too fast."[157] The concept of Kaizening, "always searching for a better way," forces workers constantly to shave seconds from their tasks. Increases in efficiency on one job, moreover, frequently has the domino effect of intensifying some other worker's job.[158] Kaizen means continual rebalancing of the work to eliminate idle time and underused workers. At one location, a worker with idle time stood apart, so "everyone will be able to see that he has free time and there will be less resistance if he is assigned one or two more jobs."[159] Management has used the Kaizen approach not only "to capture a worker's secrets for gaining spare time" but also, as scientific management, "to gain control over workers' creative knowledge and use of it to its own advantage."[160]

In addition, organizing work around teams in these circumstances creates a situation where workers are pressured to assume the responsibilities of team membership. Consequently, if self-discipline does not get a worker to cooperate, peer pressure will be exercised. Instead of groups of workers regulating their own production, these groups of workers pressure each other to enforce high productivity standards.[161] That is the "ideological dimension, necessary to the proper working of a team concept factory."[162] This coercive control, exercised by team members over themselves, could be employers' most powerful means of securing worker compliance with management's objectives and methods.

Whether the production schemes are new or old, the vast majority of employees in the United States remain powerless and vulnerable at their workplaces. Despite the claims of worker empowerment in the plant, researchers reported that the new shop floor was not "a hotbed of worker autonomy and knowledge creation."[163] There was "little or no evidence of systemic and regular job rotation, multiskilling, small group problem solving, decentralized decision making and employee participation." Workers, one researcher said, were merely "a pair of hands" to management.[164] Managers did not encourage or value worker participation or input, workers followed detailed procedures, jobs were kept simple to reduce training time, and decisions conformed to management's desires.[165]

In the automobile companies where the new world-class production is centered, the companies outsource a large percentage of parts and components to low-wage, often offshore suppliers. An army of temporary workers with lower wages and no benefits and other contingent workers constitute what Graham has called the "other face" of the Japanese model.[166] Through the use of subcontractors and temporary workers, workers are rendered "disposable rather than adaptable" and the pressure of constant insecurity becomes a motivator. Graham asks, "What could provide a company with greater flexibility or control than institutionalizing a throwaway workforce?"[167]

In the end, workers, as they have always, face the same stark choice: "to keep their jobs they must conform to management expectations," and they do what they have to do to keep their jobs.[168] Where there is no union representation, human resources fills the gaps. Even where there is union representation, in the automobile sector, for example, some union leaders welcomed the new production methods in part because they hoped the promised participatory schemes would democratize the workplace. Team leaders, who are union members, "are often effectively incorporated into management"[169] as evidence of another form of enterprise unionism where the union has a drastically reduced role except in cooperation with management in increasing productivity.

For many such unions in the United States, their powerlessness as worker advocates has come to the point where it is the management that decides if union representatives "should be invited to the party" or be bypassed by management that imposes change unilaterally.[170] Unions could receive an invitation to the party if they renounced their old reactionary, adversarial ways and cooperated with management in restructuring the business, cutting costs, making workplaces more productive, and loosening restrictions on employers.

The thrust of the academic industrial relations literature, for example, is that unions have to adopt a new partnership with management and a mutual gains approach or face "marginalization and decline."[171] In sum, the justification for union representation "becomes contributing to efficiency and effectiveness at the enterprise level," not worker representation and advocacy.[172] As the late Clark Kerr pointed out over forty years ago, however, "the union that is in constant and complete agreement with management has ceased to be a union."[173]

In the larger labor relations–human resources world, beyond the reach of the new world-class production schemes, however, employers' views of unions remain unchanged. Human resource management still treats unions negatively as outsiders, adversarial conflict causers, and impediments to managerial flexible and efficiency. The employee selection process attempts to identify and reject union sympathizers. It is still maintained that unions are the result of bad management and, therefore, unnecessary if management treats workers "fairly."[174] During a human rights conference held in 2002, Thomas B. Moorhead, a former vice-president of human resources then a Labor Department official, stated that it would "hurt" managers' advancement "if employees they managed formed a union":

> If I have learned one thing in over thirty years of dealing with unions, it is that managements, not unions, organize a workplace. More precisely, bad management causes workers to organize, so, of course, it will reflect badly on those managers. In hundreds of conversations I have had with local union leaders over the years, it was never wages or benefits that got employees interested in a union; it was their treatment by management.[175]

Leading human resources textbooks acknowledge that managers in all types of companies want a union-free workplace. These books also detail the strategies human resource management recommends to remain union-free, and the list is only a slightly more sophisticated version of Gordon Jackson's book, *How to Stay Union Free,* of thirty years ago.[176]

There has never been nor is there now any production scheme, or human resources best practice, or market imperative that would lead employers voluntarily to offer workers human rights and democracy at their workplaces. Workers who want human rights, dignity, and participation in the decisions that affect their lives, off as well as on their jobs, "still need a union that can organize and fight for them."[177]

Most workers, even without a union, know management's intentions, however, and have the resources and some power to resist in various ways, some more effective than others.[178] Even in the Japanese model that "creates a highly controlled atmosphere aimed at preventing workers from expressing their inherent resentment of authority and domination," U.S. auto workers are aware of the gap between shop floor reality and the team concept's promise of workplace democracy.[179] One researcher found that in the two new production systems factories where he worked, workers did not identify their interests with those of the organizations, did not make management's goal their own, and did not contest management's asserted prerogatives.[180]

Worker resistance took different forms. "Surviving the system" generally involved individual actions such as avoiding overtime, not participating in discretionary activity or company rituals, withholding true feelings on application forms, and avoiding confrontations with team leaders. These actions did not require management to make any substantive changes at the workplace. Actions characterized as "moderating the system" included attempts to gain control over the speed of work, break time, overtime, and uses of seniority. Finally, "beating the system" occurred when workers achieved change by actively and directly challenging management, usually through collective action such as plantwide opposition to management's shift rotation decisions and working unscheduled overtime and a refusal to work off the clock.[181] According to Graham, "only when workers stood their ground, in solidarity, were they able to force management to capitulate—or in some cases simply adhere to formal preexisting company policies."[182] In one historic form of resistance that management has never been able to eliminate, workers informally decided among themselves what was "legitimate of managers to expect of them" and then enforced that standard against rate busters or slackers through peer pressure to conform.[183]

Ben Hamper began his book, *Rivethead: Tales from the Assembly Line,*[184] with a description of "family night" at the Fisher Body plant where his father worked—one of those human resources–inspired family nights intended to solidify the relationship of workers, spouses, and children with an employer. Hamper called it the "annual peepshow" where intolerable noise and heat gave credence to his father's "daily grumble" and explained why "the old man's socks always smelled like liverwurst bleached for a week in the desert sun." His father installed windshields "with a goofy apparatus with large suction cups that resembled an octopus being crucified":

> We stood there for forty minutes or so, a miniature lifetime, and the pattern never changed. Car, windshield. Car, windshield. Drudgery piled atop drudgery. Cigarette to cigarette. Decades rolling through rafters, bones turning to dust, stubborn clocks gagging down flesh, another windshield, another cigarette, war's blinking on and off, thunderstorms muttering the alphabet, crows on powerlines asleep or dead, that mechanical octopus squirming against nothing, nothing. NOTHINGNESS.[185]

Hamper said he wanted to shout at his father, "DO SOMETHING ELSE!"[186] No amount of psychological manipulation can change the reality of jobs that destroy self-worth, dehumanize, deny individuality or personhood, and, ultimately, reduce people to "a heap of defeat with limbs attached."[187] Hamper called the products of such jobs "numbed-out cyborgs willing to swap cerebellum loaf for patio furniture, a second jalopy and a tragic carpet ride deboarding curbside in front of some pseudo-Tudor dollhouse on the outskirts of town."[188] A meaningless job, but only the prospect of not having that job was more "dreadful."[189] As Hamper put it, "We weren't going anywhere. That pay stub was like a concrete pair of loafers."[190]

Where is the research detailing worker perceptions of and reactions to human resources schemes? Hamper called one such "game plan" laughable, "if it weren't for the fact that it was *your brain* that these follies were being foisted upon."[191] The plan was to improve quality by dressing up a mascot as a large cat to be known as Quality Cat and later, after a company-initiated contest, as Howie Makem. Hamper describes Howie as having a "head the size of a Datsun" and wearing a "long red cape emblazoned with the letter Q for Quality." One coworker was angered because "what they are tellin' us is that we are so retarded growth-wise that all we can relate to are characters along the lines of Saturday morning cartoon figures." Eventually Howie's appearances would be greeted with a barrage of hurled rivets tossed at his "generous skull" and "heckled unmercifully."[192]

Further research could reveal if workers generally think of supervisors as "weasel[s] in a short-sleeve shirt, deputized to protect the status quo"[193]—or would describe the human resources department as "an alien frontier full of neckties, wingtips, belt beepers, bright lights, serious cologne and high command. Well-groomed fly-boys sucking on silver pens with pictures of children propped like tombstones on their desks"[194]—or would ask rhetorically, "Why would any of us give a shit about the specifics of the [employer's] great master plan?"[195]

Hamper and his coworkers on the assembly line "became comrades in the battle to destroy the monotony"[196] and drudgery of the system by working up the line (completing work ahead of schedule) or doubling up in order to get some free time—used for card playing, going to the cafeteria, or horseplay such as Dumpster Ball or Rivet Hockey.[197] In Hamper's words, "Sometimes the power-gods had to be reminded that it was we, the workers, who kept the place runnin.'" If pushed too hard, "the forty greasy serfs you thought you had conquered would be lined up for last call with grins on their kissers and shrugs on their shoulders."[198]

Meaningless and dehumanizing jobs abound. They are not only for those in subordinate nonmanagerial positions. The truest description of managerial office work is Joseph Heller's "The Office in Which I Work," a chapter in his novel *Something Happened*.[199] In that office, everyone is afraid of somebody else in the company who might say or do something that could get them fired.[200] The narrator of the story, who significantly has no name, acknowledges that he has "lost the power to upset things" that he had as a child; "I can no longer change my environment or even disturb it seriously. They would simply fire and forget me as soon as I tried."[201]

Other than selling something, it is unclear what the company does. (As for that deeper, truer purpose for the company's existence, the narrator says, "the company exists to sell.")[202] Despite the fear, the narrator says most people like working there because they "make money and have fun" and "somehow the time passes."[203] The systematic wasting of human life on the assembly line is essentially the same as the waste of human life evident in the narrator's description of the office workday:

> We wise grownups here at the company go gliding in and out all day long, scaring each other at our desks and cubicles and water coolers and trying to evade the people who frighten us. We come to work, have lunch, go home. We goose-step in and goose-step out, change our partners and wander all about, sashay around for a pat on the head, and promenade home till we all drop dead.[204]

When a comanager asks the narrator for job advancement advice, the narrator advises him to play golf and buy a blue blazer and better suits. When the manager replies that he has a good sales record, the narrator tells him that a good sports jacket matters more. The narrator concludes, however, that it was too late for the manager "to change himself to everyone's satisfaction."[205]

The narrator asks himself, "Is this really the most I can get from the few years left in this one life of mine?" He answers his own question with a "Yes!" The reasons for that "yes" are essentially no different from Hamper's: "Because I have my job, draw my pay, get my laughs."[206] He is "continually astonished," however, by the number of his coworkers who "fall victim to their own (our own) propaganda" and "actually believe what we do is really important":

> When salesmen and company spokesmen begin believing their own arguments, the result is not always bad, for they develop an outlook of loyalty, zeal, and conviction that is often remarkably persuasive in itself. It produces that kind of dedication and fanaticism that makes good citizens and good employees.[207]

No human resources department could have said it better—of course, the word "fanaticism" would be deleted.

The real-world accuracy of Heller's fictional office is confirmed by both too many people's real work experiences and comparing his story with the six "Advancement Suggestions" contained in a leading human resources textbook. The first suggestion for rising in the employment world is that, although job performance is important, "interpersonal performance is critical." People are advised, moreover, to "set the right values and priorities" but, of course, that means discovering the organization's values and aligning or realigning oneself with those values. That is brainwashing—in a more objective sense. Related suggestions include "provide solutions not problems" ("Nobody likes to hear complaints"), and be a team player. It is also important to be "customer oriented" in the broadest sense, meaning that anyone with whom you have an exchange is your "customer." (In other words, be a never-off-duty pitchman or in the words of the sales maxim: "Always be Closing.") Most revealing of the critical nature of the facade of this advice—and Heller's office—is the final suggestion to "Act as if what you are doing makes a difference."[208]

Concluding Comments: Human Resources, Human Beings and Human Rights

As other essays in this book have demonstrated, it is not only the state that has the power to violate people's rights; employers in many ways have even more direct power over workers' lives. Worse yet, much of this employer power is aided and abetted by the government. Judged against a human rights standard, it is an injustice that human beings are treated as things or resources for others to use. A human being has the right to be free from domination and manipulation regardless of the source of that domination and manipulation. Every human being is sacred in the human rights tradition, and the source of their rights and dignity is their humanity. Their rights and dignity do not depend on their contributions to employer profitability or business competitiveness.

Respect for those human rights and workers' exercise of them at their workplaces should not depend on an employer's decisions to grant that respect or on some human resources best practice or employer production scheme that indicates that it would be good for the business to do so. The economic profitability standard or cost-benefit standard cannot be the ultimate determinant of whether human rights will be respected, promoted, and exercised at the workplace. Human rights are end values in themselves; they are not merely means to an end. They are not some new best production or human resource practice of the day, trumpeted by academics, that will be in place only until the next best practice or fad comes along—maybe to be hailed as a new Golden Era of Work.

As Henry Shue has written, "to enjoy something only at the discretion of someone else, especially someone powerful enough to deprive you of it at will is precisely not to enjoy a right to it."[209] If the Boss giveth, then the Boss can taketh away, and victims will have no defense without established forms of participation.

Ever since employment, employers have needed to control workers and to have acceptable legal, economic, political, religious, and social justifications for exercising that control. Ever since the managerialists triumphed over the reformists, human resources has been (and has sought to be) an important instrument of management in implementing, facilitating, and justifying employer control at the workplace. The objective of human resources by whatever name has always been to get employees to believe that their employer's goals and interests and their goals and interests are one in order to increase production and profit and to keep management free of unions.

Judged by a human rights standard, human resources personnel and other managers in business organizations would be held accountable for manipulating human beings and helping to subordinate workers' human rights to the interests of the organization. It has been and continues to be a manipulation that is an affront to human dignity and human rights, particularly when workers perform life-stifling, dangerous, dirty, onerous, and meaningless jobs. It is also a manipulation that introduces workers to see the world through their employer's frame of reference in order to maintain and legitimize employer control at the workplace without changing the power relationship of superior employer and subordinate employee. It is a manipulation that seeks to induce maximum effort, dedication, and loyalty from workers that employers treat as disposable and to whom they pledge no loyalty. It truly is a manipulation that uses people as resources for economic ends.

This manipulation, or what human resources people prefer to call "motivational management," exploits workers' desire and need for approval and acceptance on the job as well as their fear of job loss, especially in an employment- (read termination-) at-will power relationship. Workplace manipulation violates workers' human right to act and make personal choices in an autonomous, self-determining manner without being subjected to seductive behavior-influencing techniques often so subtle that they blind workers not only to the fact that their behavior is being manipulated but also to violations at the workplace of their human rights.

This critique of human resources values, methods, and objectives using a human rights standard of judgment echoes the critics of the Mayo human relations school of a half-century ago, the principles of which still underlie much of human resources. These critics, although not using the language of human rights, rejected the claim that workers needed to submerge self in a business organization and to accept their employer's goals to find freedom. They, too, objected to the manipulation of workers to bring about acceptance of management's purposes. They charged, moreover, that the basic conflict of interest between labor and management had been ignored (disparaged today as outdated "adversarial" labor relations) as had the associated issues of conflict resolution, which had been reduced to ways for employees to blow off steam without changing the hierarchical power structure or permitting employees to share power.

Finally, these critics accused human relations practitioners and academics of an active antiunionism, demonstrated in part by excluding unions as sources of worker power and participation and considering them either as external intrusions on management authority and flexibility or as symptoms of deficiencies in internal management.[210] It is still human resources doctrine, for example, that unionization is caused by bad management; that unionization is the misfortune that befalls an employer with flawed human resources policies and procedures; and that unionism is, among other things, unnecessary.

This active antiunionism of human resources, euphemistically termed "union-avoidance" or "staying union-free," is in violation of one of the most fundamental human rights: the right of all people (which includes workers) to participate in the decisions that affect their lives, including their workplace lives. Regardless of the quality of management or an employer's good or bad employee relations, exercise of the freedom of association at the workplace is necessary so that workers can secure their own rights and interests through participation in workplace decision making and eliminate the vulnerabilities that leave them at the mercy of others. As stated in Chapter 4 on freedom of association, servility, or what some call powerlessness, leaves human beings dependent on the benevolence, pity, charity, or arbitrary power of others—or on the allegedly impersonal forces and fortunes of the market.

Clyde Summers has called the U.S. employment relationship one of employer dominance and employee subservience. Subservience and servility are incompatible with human rights. That is why the promotion and protection of workers' freedom of association is a pivotal right under international law that enables so many other human rights to be realized. It enables people to participate in the workplace decisions that most directly affect their lives and the lives of those dependent on them; it protects workers from abuses of power and from the vulnerability that results from isolation from others; it enables them to participate effectively in society through the assertion of social and political power; it provides access to courts, administrative agencies, arbitrators, and other enforcement bodies; and it creates economic and political advocates for otherwise powerless people in the larger society. Freedom of association is the sine qua non of any free, democratic society.

Human resources management still puts a lid on conflict. Human resources textbooks, for example, disparage what is termed the "adversarial model" of U.S. labor relations as an obstacle to union-management cooperation. The human resources–business partnership values have so infused the workplace that it is unrealistic to talk about a clash of rights at the workplace because workers' rights have been submerged and diluted in a contrived "we are all one in the organization" unitarist ideology. The incompatibility of many basic human rights principles and human resources values, however, make it certain that the rights and interests of workers and employers do conflict in some fundamental ways.

The continued resistance of workers at all levels confirms that. Management has no chance of getting the loyalty and effort they want from workers without recognizing and respecting workers' human rights, particularly workers' right of freedom of association.

9

CRIMES AGAINST HUMANITY

Concluding Thoughts about Choosing Human Rights

The greatest evil in the world is the destruction or suppression of the humanity of human beings. In great part, this book is about how that evil is practiced at workplaces in the United States. Employers who maintain workplaces that require men and women and sometimes even children to risk their lives and endanger their health and eyes and limbs in order to earn a living are treating human life as cheap and are seeking their own gain through the desecration of human life. Those who engage in racial supremacy and other similar forms of discrimination treat others as if they are not fully human. Those who deny workers their right of freedom of association deny their humanity by making them servile, dependent, and powerless to protect themselves or to become involved in the decisions that directly affect their lives. Those who manipulate the behavior of workers to ensure that servility, powerlessness, and subordination are complicit in using workers as disposable commodities or as resources for others' gain.

These are inhumane acts that by their nature, scope, and duration constitute crimes against humanity. Under international law, crimes against humanity are defined as "particularly odious offenses" that seriously attack human dignity or inflict "grave humiliation or a degradation" on human beings. They are in-humane acts that cause "great suffering, or serious injury to body or to mental or physical health." They are not isolated inhumane acts, even if such an iso-lated act violated human rights, but are part of either a government policy "or wide practice of atrocities tolerated or condoned by a government or de facto authority." In other words, they must be "part of a widespread or systematic practice."[1]

These crimes have been committed at workplaces around the country be-cause so many workers are powerless and stand before their employers not as adult persons with rights but as children or servants dependent on the will and interests of their supervisors and employers. As an anonymous United Auto-mobile worker asked in a poem, "What is it about that entrance way, those gates to the plant?" What is it "that pierces you through and transform your being" and "commands 'for eight hours you shall be different'"? In sum, "What is it that instantaneously makes a child out of a man?"[2]

The tragic injustice is that so many working men and women have come to expect little or nothing out of life and are resigned to having little or no con-trol over their workplace lives. As this book demonstrates, that is because they have been denied, kept ignorant of, or led to believe that they do not need the rights that would not only protect them against those who have the power to harm them but also would free them of dependence on the will of others and enable them to participate in and influence decisions that affect their lives. The defenseless vulnerability in the face of great power that could do them harm is what saps the essence of humanity out of men and women and makes them compliant, long-suffering, and resigned.

What does it mean, for example, to be "goddamned niggers" in this country other than to be something less than human, an inferior grade of humanity, and so different that dominant whites segregate them? Although it is no lon-ger an era of lynching and attack dogs (renunciations of blacks' humanity and human rights), President Johnson was prescient as well as perceptive when he said over forty years ago that equal rights for African Americans was an issue that laid "bare the secret heart of America itself." Race still matters in the United States in determining the worth of human beings as well as in the distribu-tion of the society's benefits and burdens. The history is of white supremacy denying black people their full humanity. The current-day deleterious con-sequences of this history of segregation and degradation, moreover, are now being used as justification for renewed assertions of white superiority and the exclusion of blacks.

What better evidence is there of the ongoing suppression of the human spirit than in the separate and unequal "apartheid education" given to children in the most poverty-stricken and ghettoized "inner cities" in this country over fifty years after the Supreme Court rejected separate educational facilities for white and black children? Who would disagree "that the most deadly of all sins is the mutilation of a child's spirit?"[3] Yet, those who could do something to prevent that crime express no outrage about, take no action against, and even participate in the deliberate political and economic choices that devalue other people's children's human rights by treating them as disposable.

What black workers are experiencing today in cities across the country is not the result of impersonal forces over which no one had any control but, rather, the inevitable consequence of human choices made by federal, state, and local government, employers, unions, and many other organizations and groups to violate the human rights of black people or not to resist the violators and violations. Despite all the white-inspired furor about reverse discrimination, we have a system that after 330 or more years of affirmative action for whites has a built-in racial status quo and deep-rooted but only covertly expressed values that honor and reward whiteness.

White superiority in this country has not made life simply more difficult for African Americans; it has denied them even those minimal things without which it is impossible to develop one's capabilities and to live life as human beings. It was and is a denial of humanity and human rights. Rights are supposed to protect people from those who have the power to harm them. The great irony in U.S. labor history is that except for relatively brief interruptions and with rare exceptions, it has been the rights and freedoms of employers that have been promoted and protected, not the rights and freedoms of workers subjected to their power. From the beginning of this country, doctrines of property rights, freedom of contract, assumption of risk, contributory negligence, fellow servant, and employment at will were fashioned and used to aid and abet economic development to the suppression of workers' rights, including their right to organize, bargain collectively, and even their safety and health. The dominant free market philosophy, moreover, considered workers to be commodities to be priced in the market no differently than any other resource for production. All was depersonalized in this separation of morality from law and economics. Workers' rights were made dependent on the relative power of employers and employees to the serious detriment of most workers.

Even after the passage of labor legislation, however, the value presumptions of employer dominance and employee subservience continue to be the major influences on those who make U.S. labor law and policy. What their legislative, judicial, and administrative agency decisions have done is to sanction and expand employers' resistance to workers' exercise of their freedom of association. For example, the deregulation of employer representation election campaign speech, including captive audience speeches—coupled with decisions denying nonemployee union organizers access to employees on company property—have increased the ability of employers to use their economic job-control power to squash unionization efforts.

Human Rights Watch's report in 2000, aptly titled "Unfair Advantage," concluded that freedom of association is a right under sustained attack when workers in this country try to exercise it. Human Rights Watch also concluded that the U.S. government was failing its responsibility under human rights standards to protect vulnerable workers from employer violations of their freedom of association right.[4] As a member of the International Labour Organization (ILO), the U.S. government is obliged to take all necessary measures to ensure that workers are free to exercise their right to organize,[5] yet the government and employers are joined in violating that right. That the government merely permits such private employer power to be exercised does not excuse the government from intervening when that private power is used to violate the human right of freedom of association (or any other human right).

The freedom of association, however, involves more than workers organizing. Collective bargaining is an integral part of the freedom of association as recognized in international law as well as in the Wagner and Taft-Hartley Acts, which recognize workers' right to organize for the purposes of collective bargaining or other mutual aid or protection. The Canadian Supreme Court has recognized collective bargaining "as the most significant collective action through which freedom of association is expressed in the labor context."[6] It is the basis on which workers assert their right to participate in the business decisions that affect their lives. As the Canadian Supreme Court put it, recognizing that workers have the right to bargain collectively as part of their freedom to associate reaffirms the values of dignity, personal autonomy, equality, and democracy that are inherent not only in the Canadian Charter of Rights but also in international law.

The worth of the U.S. statutory recognition of the right of freedom of association for purposes of collective bargaining depends in great part on what subjects are jointly negotiated. Under Canadian labor law, employers and unions are obliged to bargain in good faith about all conditions of employment except those that could not legally be included in the collective agreement. In the

United States, however, the Supreme Court and certain National Labor Relations Boards (NLRBs) have freed management from the obligation to bargain about some of the most important entrepreneurial decisions with the greatest impact not only on employee working conditions but also on the existence of their jobs. Some of the most important of these decisions, moreover, have been based on value-laden dicta and speculation about the inviolability of management rights that have remained unchanged since common law judges chose and applied them long before the National Labor Relations Act (NLRA).

The goal of employers in the United States always has been to stay free of unions or, if unionized, to retain unilateral control over their workplace sovereignty. For U.S. employers, the freedom of association as expressed in union organizing and collective bargaining is an encroachment on their power that is to be resisted and discouraged. In other words, workplace democracy (in the form of worker participation in and influence on workplace decisions that affect their lives) and free enterprise are fundamentally incompatible. This is a flat-out rejection of the human right of freedom of association at the workplace. This is not merely a matter of union-management dispute, it is a fundamental human rights issue. Denial of the freedom of association at the workplace prevents workers from making claims of their human rights effective or even known and leaves them powerless and dependent on the interests of their employers and the state.

In great part, this is why so many aspects of human resources' objectives and methods violate workers' rights to freedom of association and their human dignity. Human resources exploits people's desire for approval combined with their fear of job loss to try to get them to submit voluntarily and, ideally, happily to employer control and to cooperate willingly in the pursuit of their employer's objectives. The essentially psychological behavior-influencing methods of human resources become manipulative and deceitful when they are intended to create the perception of employee participation without the reality of participation. They are also manipulative and deceitful when they are intended to make workers feel valued, trusted, and respected when, in fact, human resources professionals disavow employer loyalty to employees. While employers demand loyalty from workers, they want workers to be both dependable and disposable. The perception of participation is intended to be the employee motivator, not the superior employer–subordinate employee reality that remains unchanged.

This manipulation is particularly abusive of men and women who work in meaningless and dehumanizing jobs that involve the systematic waste of human life and bring humiliation and violence to the spirit as well as to the body. Some jobs are too small for the human spirit.[7] It is an affront to human life and human dignity to seduce men and women into being satisfied with such work. These situations present the clearest evidence of an unjust manipulation that uses human beings as things or objects—"organizational assets" or "human capital"—for others to use.

Underlying all of human resources—from scientific management to welfare programs to employment managers (managerialists), to personnel management, to human relations, to today's human resource management under its various names—is an antiunion animus. Many reasons, including the following, are given for persuading workers that they should not and need not exercise their freedom of association: there is no inherent conflict between labor and management; whatever conflict does exist is due to personal adjustment problems that are best resolved by insiders not union outsiders; unions cause trouble including strikes and job loss; management can give workers all that they need, so unions are unnecessary; what is good for the employer is good for the employee; workers and management form a community that benefits all but requires teamwork and employees' undivided loyalty to the enterprise; unions are needed only in the case of bad management and are unnecessary when management treats workers fairly. Human resources, in other words, fills the freedom of association gap. The only acceptable unions, therefore, are those that agree with management's goals and methods—in other words, unions that are no longer unions.

This is simply another approach to denying workers their freedom of association rights by excluding unions as a source of worker power and participation at the workplace. Despite its mythological image of being the internal champion for employees, human resources is, as it always has been, an employer tool to increase production and profits and to reinforce employer power and control at the workplace. Despite its soft-sell approach, human resource methods are designed to dilute and submerge worker rights into a contrived "we are all one in the organization" unitarist ideology. It leaves workers powerless.

There is another dimension to this human rights violation. The more badly informed people are about their own interests and rights, the more easily they can be fooled and misled and the less likely it is that they will seek active participation at the workplace level. Human resources methods and objectives also prevent workers from understanding their historical situation and the possibilities of overcoming existing injustice. In other words, the exploitive nature of the system is deliberately obscured or concealed as are the "courage and strength of ordinary people in the struggle to humanize it."[8]

Consequently, people are more likely to blame themselves for failures in a system where the odds are stacked against them. Human resources is a tool used to keep workers under employer control while at the same time keeping them smiling, diffusing their anger, and reconciling them with the status quo.[9] Human resources professionals—as well as their associates in academe who conceal what needs to be revealed for all to know or who sell their academic work and expertise as consultants to business—have served power. They have developed human resources "science" into an ideology of American business, individualistic and collective-free—that is, freedom of association–free.

Whatever employers, human resources professionals, or their academic associates believe or do, however, human rights are among what no one, including states and employers, ought to have the power to grant or deny. Employers in the United States, however, aided by human resources professionals, have arrogated that power unto themselves.

Among workers' rights as human rights, no aspect of work is more directly related to the sacredness of human life than the safety and health of men and women who labor. It is the right to life that is dependent on workplace health and safety. The economic history of this country, however, leaves no doubt that the lives of certain workers are cheap and have readily been sacrificed for economic development. Employer competitiveness, efficiency, property rights, and profitability have and do override the human rights of workers to physical security and safe and healthful workplaces.

There is no distributive justice in the distribution of benefits and burdens in that only certain workers are exposed to the most severe risks to their bodies and lives. From the earliest days of this country, moreover, immigrant workers and African Americans have borne a disproportionate share of the burdens resulting from the callous disregard of their health and safety at work. Their lives were cheap in making steel, digging coal, and working in the rail yards, and they continue to be cheap on jobs immigrant and black workers perform now in industries such as beef, pork, and poultry slaughtering and processing.

The right to life is embedded in every human rights declaration, covenant, and convention. It rejects human sacrifice for economic development; it places the highest value on a human life, and an eye, and an arm or leg or a hand; and it proclaims the absolute priority of human rights over economic and institutional interests.

When employers do nothing about known, preventable, predictable workplace risks that can cause death or serious injury to a worker, that is a deliberate choice, and any consequences are not mere misfortunes beyond anyone's control. When death is the result, it is murder at the workplace. Film Recovery Systems, Pymm Thermometer, Imperial Foods, and employers in the asbestos, lead, and cotton textile industries (discussed in Chapters 6 and 7), not only intentionally disregarded and were indifferent to death-causing preventable health and safety hazards but also covered up those hazards and exploited them for their own financial gain. The U.S. Congress, however, in the Occupational Safety and Health (OSH) Act considered employers' willful violations of occupational safety and health standards that result in the death of a worker to be misdemeanors subject to a maximum of six months in jail. Human life from this perspective is merely another resource and commodity in the marketplace.

It is deplorable that so many U.S. employers and their allies in and out of government exploit every opportunity to stay free of safety and health regulations. It is scandalous and tragic when they engage in decades-long cover-ups to hide from workers, government agencies, and the general public not only the health and safety hazards of their products and production methods but also their human costs. What some have called an incestuous relationship between businesses and the scientific community in and around academe is actually a criminal conspiracy. Bought scientists and their bought research not only facilitated cover-ups but also exposed thousands of workers to multiple health and safety hazards causing pain, suffering, and death among generations of working people.

Business still employs academic scientists and uses their studies to resist safety and health regulations and to deny responsibility for work-caused human suffering. One consequence of this approach is to place the burden of health and safety uncertainty on workers. Once again, workers are silent canaries and guinea pigs.

This same heavy burden is placed on workers, moreover, by courts, the Occupational Safety and Health administration (OSHA), and arbitrators. The participation of workers in the protection of their own safety and health would be, by human rights standards, an inalienable right. In the United States, however, weak regulatory agency and judicial enforcement of safety and health is combined with even weaker (almost nonexistent) worker self-enforcement of their own safety and health rights.

An employee's right to refuse hazardous work without retaliation, for example, is indispensable if workers are to control their own lives in regard to workplace health and safety. In the United States, however, in contrast to other countries such as Canada and Sweden, courts, administrative agencies, and arbitrators have defined permissible work refusal circumstances in a way that places the burden of justifying refusals on the employees. They also make that burden the most difficult to sustain by requiring objective proof. When human life is balanced against management of a business, courts, agencies, and arbitrators have chosen a standard that maximizes employers' control of employee discipline and, therefore, minimizes employee interference with management's control.

There is no need to rehash here the particulars of how that is done. The major point is that this pro-employer authority, pro-employer property rights standard confronts workers with an inherently unfair dilemma: to follow orders and work thereby risking life and limb or to refuse the order to work thereby risking discharge or other serious discipline. No decent society would permit human beings to be put in that position, particularly when economic necessity pressures so many to choose a job over their own health and safety more often than not with no or insufficient information about the health and safety hazard of what they are ordered to do. Workers' humanity and human rights to a safe and healthful workplace are disrespected whichever choice they make.

The violations of workers' human rights in the United States are pervasive: the treatment of human beings as commodities or resources of production; the maintenance of a hypocritical gap between workplace practices and publicly asserted principles and values; the destruction of the human spirit though assertions of racial and ethnic superiority-inferiority and meaningless and dehumanizing work; the separation of morality from economics; the denial of workers' right of self-determination through freedom of association; governmental protection of the rights and interests of the already powerful employers to the detriment of the rights of workers subject to that power; manipulation of worker behavior at the workplace to keep them under management's control and to blind and mislead them to their human rights; the sacrifice of human life for economic development; and the dominance of the overall value judgment that people exist for the economy rather than the other way around.

In every single aspect and in totality, these violations suppress the life within human beings. They constitute *crimes against humanity* because they are (1) odious offenses of long duration that attack human dignity and inflict grave humiliation or degradation on human beings, (2) inhumane acts that cause death, great suffering, or serious injury to body and mind, and (3) not isolated inhumane acts but part of a government policy including government toleration of employer human rights violations.

Although the workplace destruction and suppression of human life discussed in this book satisfy the definition of crimes against humanity on every count, the international law of crimes against humanity has not been applied to such workplace violations of human rights in the United States or anywhere else in the world. The original meaning of *crimes against humanity* was developed in the context of dealing with the law of armed conflict in the 1907 Hague Convention. The meaning was developed further after World War I and again after World War II, each time addressing war crimes. Crimes against humanity were established for the first time in positive international law in the Charter of the International Military Tribunal sitting at Nuremberg in 1945.[10]

Despite its war crimes roots, the concept of *crimes against humanity* is constantly developing and, therefore, always incomplete. Over the years, for example, the definition has expanded to include designated crimes committed in peacetime as well as in time of war. We are still in the early stages of the recognition of workers' rights as human rights, therefore, the implications of human rights at the workplace are only beginning to emerge. This book provides ample evidence that the concept of crimes against humanity is applicable to victims of human rights violations at workplaces as well as anywhere else.

The core cause of crimes against humanity is the subordination of the needs of society (including fundamental human rights) to the needs of the economy. Human beings in the United States have become accessories to and resources for the economic system. Economic interests have laid down their laws to society, and society has responded by accepting those laws as the dominant standards of good and evil. Society itself becomes an adjunct not only to a market system but to a market system that demands and purports to require self-regulating markets unrestrained by society: "Instead of economy being embedded in social relations, social relations are embedded in the economic system."[11] In other words, people exist for the ends of the economy rather than the economy being a means to provide a more fully human life for people.

There is little scientific or, therefore, deterministic about systems of economics, including free-market economics and Marxian economics, all of which posit deterministic laws. The market economies guarantee nothing, including economic growth or less poverty and certainly not social justice, even if its so-called laws are obeyed. Despite claims to the contrary, the unregulated market (and, as we have seen, sometimes even the regulated market) "protects the power of the rich and the resourceful and the clever, and allows them to triumph over the poor, the modest and the simple."[12] It is the responsibility of the government, rather than to empower the powerful further, to promote and defend the common good, and to defend the poor and powerless against violations of their human rights and other forms of exploitation. Granted, this appears to be a cry in the wilderness when the philosophical principles of the unregulated market have been the dominant values of U.S. decision makers and policy makers since the earliest history of this country.

Ironically, this ideology of free markets has dominated despite the fact that a free market has never existed in this country (or in any other country for that matter); it takes a substantial amount of state intervention to establish and maintain a market system. The self-regulating market is irreconcilable with democracy and human rights—if *democracy* means power-sharing and not merely the appearances of democracy. There is a contradiction between capitalism and democracy and human rights in part because hierarchically structured employer organizations exclude workers from sharing power in making the decisions that affect workers' lives.

But human beings do not become something less than human when they enter the workplace. That previously cited anonymous auto worker–poet expressed the polar incompatibility of human rights and human powerlessness when he wondered what it was that "instantaneously makes a child out of a man" when he walked through the gates, entered the plant, passed the guards, and took his place along the line.[13] His powerlessness and vulnerability at the workplace are a violation of his human dignity.

It is important that workers know what their human, statutory, and contractual rights are to raise their consciousness, to give them a rights context in which to assess their situations, and to see what they have in common with others in their workplace community. Mere awareness of or declarations of their rights, however, cannot empower them. Awareness of rights can, however, change workers' understanding of their situation. That includes understanding that there are no unalterable economic laws that dictate and determine their workplace existence and that all institutions in society are the embodiment of the alterable behavior of individuals.

What all people, including workers, must discover is that the structures in their economic world rest on peoples' own participation in that world and that, if they choose to exert a collective will, they could overcome existing injustice in ways that would bring about the full reality of their human rights to participate in the decisions that affect their workplace lives, to have safe and healthful workplaces, to be free of discrimination, and, in every way, to be subjects in control of their labor rather than objects, resources, or commodities to be used for economic gain. Therein lies the grievousness of the moral failure of employers who use their power to deny workers their right of collective action.[14]

Although workers are told that there is no inherent conflict between themselves and employers, that conflict has been at the center of modern history and remains the central problem of all societies around the world.[15] Throughout the dominance of the values of the self-regulating market, there has been a countermovement of protective legislation and labor unions motivated by values of self-protection from the destructive consequences of the unrestrained market, including the damage inflicted on the humanity of workers. (All participants in the market, including corporations, have sought to manipulate and control the market to protect their interests from its vicissitudes.)

Since the values of the market philosophy reach into all aspects of human life, however, the countermovement, to be effective, must amount to more than separate groups each pursuing their own self-interest. The implementation of human rights standards requires a new vision that transcends narrow self-interest. It requires a revulsion from evil and a moral outrage that inspires a universal recognition of the interdependence of *all* people and generates a worldwide counterforce against injustices everywhere.

As Gunnar Myrdal recognized almost five decades ago, "Internationally, the ideals of liberty, equality and brotherhood can be attained only by a political development towards a Welfare World." Organized interference in unregulated markets around the world "have to be internationally coordinated and harmonized if we want to re-integrate the world economy."[16] That goal was and is not only for dreamers. As Myrdal pointed out, after World War II many quite sober economists, political scientists, lawyers, and practical politicians expected and planned for intergovernmental organizations, including the ILO, to develop supranational constitutions to govern a world community. That is not going to happen tomorrow.

The reality of today is that despite globalization, laws governing the workplace and employer-employee relations have remained national. It does not follow, moreover, that these national laws should be abandoned. Rather, the objective should be to revitalize these laws by bringing them into conformity with international human rights principles and ensuring that they be enforced effectively. Domestic labor law reform is a key element of the promotion and protection of workers' rights even in a global economy.[17]

In addition to promoting human rights standards in U.S. workplaces, this book also attempts to reaffirm the moral superiority and democratic nature of the values embodied in the NLRA and the OSH Act. The provisions of those laws confirmed that workers were human beings—not mere resources—and that human beings were not to be submissive to employers, markets, or governments. Americans need to be reminded that these statutory provisions promoted individual rights and responsibility, social obligations, and a democratic approach to employment decisions and the allocation of scarce resources. These are democratic American values. Employment at will, on the contrary, is an American practice that violates those democratic values in a most fundamental way. It is a classic example of autocracy at the workplace.

Both the NLRA and the OSH Act sought to eliminate the vulnerability that leaves workers at the mercy of other people or supposedly impersonal economic forces—either of which can transform them from self-reliant participants in society into helpless victims. That these promises to workers have been broken is no reason to reject those promises; it is reason for rededication to keeping those promises. Those promises, moreover, have been broken not by some uncontrollable impersonal forces but by deliberate political and economic policy choices.

Over the years in this country, government has done well by capital. Yet, government encouragement and protection are essential to the promotion of human rights at the workplace. The real task, therefore, is to get the government back on the side of the powerless at workplaces all around the United States. As spelled out in several chapters in this book, the promotion and protection of workers' human rights require not only radical changes in our labor laws but also in the dominant values underlying the doctrines of our labor-management systems.

The objective is to bring U.S. labor laws into compliance with international human rights standards. The United States has a legal obligation under international laws as well as a moral obligation as a member of the United Nations (UN) and the International Labour Organization (ILO) to commit itself to the realization of human rights principles espoused by these organizations.

For example, the UN Universal Declaration of Human Rights, for which the United States voted, calls on all nations to promote human rights and to take "progressive measures, national and international, to secure their universal and effective recognition and observance." Among these human rights are the right to freedom of association (Article 20), the right to form and join unions (Article 23[4]), and the right "to just and favorable conditions of work" (Article 23[1]).

The International Covenant on Civil and Political Rights (ICCPR), which the United States has signed and ratified, commits each state party to ensure the rights set forth in the Covenant to all persons (Article 2), including the freedom of association, "the right to form and join trade unions for the protection of his interests." The International Covenant on Economic, Social, and Cultural Rights (ICESCR), which the United States has signed but not ratified, obliges each state party to "take steps" to achieve the "full realization" of rights recognized in the Covenant, including "just and favorable conditions of work" in particular to "safe and healthy working conditions" (Article 7) and the right of everyone to join trade unions "for the promotion and protection of his [and her] economic and social interests" (Article 8). Although the United States has signed but not ratified the ICESCR, as a signatory the United States is obliged by established international law "to refrain from acts that would defeat the object and purpose" of the Covenant.[18]

The Declaration of Philadelphia, annexed to the ILO's Constitution, recognizes the solemn obligation of the ILO (of which the United States is a member) "to further among the nations of the world programmes which would achieve," among other things, the "effective recognition of the right to collective bargaining," "adequate protection for the life and health of workers in all occupations," and human beings' right to material well-being and spiritual development.[19]

The ILO's Declaration on Fundamental Principles and Rights at Work, which the United States has adopted, says that "in freely joining the ILO, all Members have endorsed the principles and rights set out in the Constitution and in the Declaration of Philadelphia, and have undertaken to work towards attaining the overall objectives of the Organization to the best of their resources and fully in line with their specific circumstances." The Declaration also states that even those members that have not ratified the ILO Conventions dealing with the freedom of association and the right to collective bargaining (among other rights) "have an obligation, arising from the very fact of membership in the [ILO] to respect, to promote and to realize, in good faith and in accordance with the [ILO] Constitution, the principles concerning the fundamental rights set forth in these conventions."[20]

Because of the importance of the freedom of association, the ILO has established special machinery, the Committee on Freedom of Association (CFA), to address complaints of violations of labor union rights. The CFA has no enforcement powers, and its recommendations tend to be expressed in mild language. The United States, however, has taken the position that it has no legal obligation to the ILO Conventions it has not ratified, such as ILO Conventions nos. 87 and 98. The United States also contends that it has no legal obligation under the ILO Declaration on Fundamental Principles and Rights at Work, which it considers "a non-binding statement of principles" that "gives rise to no legal obligations."[21]

The CFA, in response, points out that its responsibility is "to examine complaints alleging violations of freedom of association whether or not the country concerned has ratified the relevant ILO Conventions." Its jurisdiction includes the United States, the Committee asserts, because as a member of the ILO, the United States "accepts the fundamental principles embodied in the Constitution and the Declaration of Philadelphia, including the principles of freedom of association."[22] The United States has acknowledged that it "respects, promotes and realizes" the fundamental principles and rights at work and claims that it is in "full compliance with any obligations it may have by virtue of membership in the ILO."[23]

As discussed in Chapter 4, the CFA found the U.S. Supreme Court's decision in *Lechmere* (holding that nonemployee union organizers would almost never have the right to enter employer property to communicate with unorganized employees) contrary to the principles set forth in ILO Conventions nos. 87 and 98. The Committee called on the U.S. government "to guarantee access of trade union representatives to workplaces, with due respect for the rights of property and management, so that unions can communicate with workers, in order to apprize them of the potential advantages of unionization."[24]

The Committee on Freedom of Association has also (1) expressed concern about the long-standing problem of delay in the U.S. labor law system and urged speedy handling of complaints;[25] (2) found that the NLRA did not treat workers and employers on a fully equal basis because it mandates the NLRB to seek an injunction against certain union unfair labor practices but not any employer unfair labor practices;[26] and (3) ruled that the permanent replacement of economic strikers meant that the essential right to strike was not fully guaranteed.[27] The CFA has also urged the U.S. government to bring its labor legislation for federal-sector employees into conformity with ILO conventions, particularly nos. 87 and 98. In addition, the Committee has also found state public-sector collective bargaining legislation "reasonably appropriate" in some states, "mixed" in some states, and nonexistent in others with some of those states banning it completely. The Committee requested the government:

> to draw the attention of the authorities concerned, and in particular in those jurisdictions where public service workers other than those engaged in the administration of the State should enjoy such rights, and that priority should be given to collective bargaining as the means to settle disputes arising in connection with the determination of terms and conditions of employment in the public service.[28]

Most recently, the CFA concluded that the Supreme Court's denial to un-documented workers of the NLRB's back-pay remedy for violations of the NLRA left the Board with remedial measures that provide little protection to undocumented workers "who can be indiscriminately dismissed for exercising freedom of association rights without any direct penalty aimed at dissuading such action."[29] The Committee also found that U.S. states that ban public-sector collective bargaining are in violation of ILO Conventions nos. 87 and 98 and, in regard to one of those states, North Carolina, requested that state to establish collective bargaining in the public sector.[30] In 2006 the Committee requested the U.S. government to engage in collective bargaining with workers' organizations over the terms and conditions of employment for the approximately 56,000 federal airport screeners in the Transportation Security Administration—except for matters "directly" related to national security issues.[31] In 2008, the Committee responded to the charge that the expansion of the definition of "supervisor" was depriving workers who are not supervisors of their collective bargaining rights. The Committee found that certain NLRB interpretations gave rise "to an overly wide definition of supervisory staff that would go beyond freedom of association principles."[32] Finally, in response to a complaint that a decision of the NLRB denying graduate teaching and research assistants at private universities the right to engage in collective bargaining, the Committee concluded that in so far as they were workers, these teaching and research assistants were entitled to the full protection of their right to bargain collectively over the terms and conditions of their employment—excluding academic requirements and policies.[33]

Over the years, there have been a number of proposed legislative changes intended to promote and protect workers' rights to organize and bargain collectively with their employers. They include proposals to increase the effectiveness of NLRB remedies; to crack down on the antiunion consulting industry; to lift prohibitions on secondary activity to permit unions to exercise solidarity around the world; to minimize employer coercive involvement in representation campaigns by the use of union authorization card certifications; and to guarantee employees who vote for a union (at least when their chosen representative fails to negotiate a first contract) a grievance procedure with binding arbitration.

Clearly, it will be a momentous task to bring U.S. labor law into conformity with established human rights principles. As difficult as it would be to correct the deficiencies in our current labor laws while preserving their strengths, human rights principles raise other challenges to U.S. labor law. The first is whether employers should be permitted to try to persuade workers not to exercise their freedom of association right. In addition to issues of employer job-control power and manipulation of workers' attitudes at the workplace discussed earlier, there is the contradiction of allowing employers to use their power over employees to discourage their exercise of the right that enables them to participate in the decisions that directly affect their lives. Permitting employers to resist the implementation of human rights at the workplace disparages human rights by reducing them to the level of other costs or considerations that employers make in the course of doing business.

All human rights documents affirm that everyone has the right to freedom of association. Despite this, the Taft-Hartley Act, as well as many state statues, expressly bar millions of workers from the law's protection of their right to organize and bargain collectively. Section 2 of the NLRA excludes resident and immigrant agricultural laborers (an estimated three million),[34] domestic service workers (an estimated one million), independent contractors, and low-level supervisors and managers. Among other consequences, these exclusions mean that employers can intimidate or even fire these workers if they attempt to exercise their freedom of association because they are not protected by the law. Those federal and state exclusions openly conflict with international human rights principles that affirm the right of every person to form and join trade unions and to bargain collectively.

Although the NLRA makes no distinction between a union with a majority or a union without a majority, the NLRB has interpreted Section 9(A) of the Act to say that when a union lacks a majority of the employees in a bargaining unit, there is no union. Unless there is a union that has support from the majority of employees, workers' human right to freedom of association is lost in a "black hole" of no union rights.[35] Bargaining collectively with a nonmajority union that bargains for its own members is protected widely in countries with systems of free collective bargaining. (A nonmajority union, among other important functions, could represent its members in the activation of OSHA's health and safety committees and support a worker's refusal to work. It could also provide protection against employment-at-will discharges.) In sum, nonmajority unions would bring at least some due process and democracy to the workplace.[36] As Charles Morris has written:

> Considering the need for employee representation today, including the need for representation in non-traditional organizational structures, the role of the minority union should be reaffirmed and reinvigorated. Without such unions, the right of association—such as would be protected by ILO Convention Nos. 87 and

98 were they applicable—becomes meaningless for employees who desire such association but are unable to persuade a majority of their fellow employees to join with them. In a democracy, the very essence of the right of association is its protection of a minority from the tyranny of a majority.[37]

These and other fundamental changes involved in conforming U.S. labor law and policy to international human rights standards will also require a change in the market philosophy value judgments underlying the current state of labor law as well as the decisions of the courts, agencies, and arbitrators. The necessary changes concern the value judgment justifying the dominance of exclusive management rights and the principles of freedom of contract when applied to the outcome of the collective bargaining process.

As detailed in this book, the management rights value judgment has dominated U.S. labor relations and law, and its continued dominance is a major block to the realization of workers' rights as human rights in this country. The right of workers to participate in the decisions affecting their workplace lives is most consistent not only with the principles of human rights but also with democratic principles. Instead, U.S. labor law has been interpreted and applied in ways that put federal government power in private employer hands by strengthening the managerial authority of employers who already have great power over their employees.

This raises possibly the most difficult challenge in bringing about change. Although the values of the Wagner Act were most consistent with human rights principles, that law incorporated the common law freedom of contract approach to collective bargaining negotiations. The freedom of contract doctrine as applied to the workplace in this country historically separated law from morals and ignored the power imbalance inherent in the employer-worker relationship. Congress added Section 9(d) in the Taft-Hartley Act to affirm that the mutual obligation of employers and unions to bargain in good faith did "not compel either party to agree to a proposal or require the making of a concession."[38] The Supreme Court has read that language to prevent the NLRB from setting the terms of collective bargaining agreements.[39]

The Supreme Court, using the freedom of contract doctrine, rejected an NLRB order to an employer, affirmed by a Court of Appeals,[40] to grant a contract clause even where it was undisputed that the employer was guilty of persistent bad faith bargaining intended to frustrate the making of a collective bargaining agreement. The Court of Appeals in that same case based its decision on what the Supreme Court acknowledged was an "equally important policy of the Act that workers' rights to collective bargaining are to be secured." The Supreme Court concluded, however, that "allowing the Board to compel agreement when the parties themselves are unable to agree would violate the fundamental premise on which the Act is based—private bargaining under governmental supervision of the procedure alone, without any official compulsion over the actual terms of the contract."[41]

The freedom of contract approach makes rights, including human rights, negotiable and, therefore, their very existence dependent on the relative bargaining power of employees and unions. This is a contradiction: Human rights are nonnegotiable. They are possessed by every person by virtue of being a human being, not by virtue of being a member of a union powerful enough to negotiate those human rights into an enforceable collective bargaining contract. Human rights are rights that no government or employer or union or any other body has the moral authority to grant or deny. The only use of power that is legitimate is that which promotes and protects human rights.

The implications of this contradiction between human rights and freedom of contract to determine which human right, if any, gets into enforceable collective agreements are vast. (One serious implication discussed in this book in Chapter 7 involves the arbitration of health and safety disputes where workers' rights are limited to what is set forth in a contract, whereas employer rights have extracontractual as well as contractual sources.)

It is not only labor arbitrators who do not understand workers' rights as human rights but also administrative agencies (such as the NLRB) and courts, including the Supreme Court. None of them utilize human rights standards in their decision making. Supreme Court Justice Ruth Bader Ginsburg remarked that the U.S. Supreme Court has shown no "readiness to look beyond one's own shores" when deciding cases.[42] One commentator called the resistance of U.S. judges to the use of human rights precedents from around the world even as guides, "legal isolationism."[43]

This is particularly ironic since U.S. judges had no hesitation early in this country's history in importing and using British common law principles when deciding issues of workers' and employers' rights. In addition, U.S. labor lawyers, particularly practitioners before the courts, administrative agencies, and arbitrators, have taken little notice of international law or international human rights law. One writer attributes this legal isolationism to the "belief of some American judges that foreign judicial attitudes are too liberal...and should be rejected as alien to the American mainstream."[44] The Supreme Court has been ridiculed for its failure to participate in a global judicial human rights dialogue.[45]

In a 1988 death penalty case, Supreme Court Justice Antonin Scalia rejected international decisions barring the death penalty, stating "We must not forget that it is the Constitution of the United States that we are expounding."[46]

This self-imposed isolation from any case precedent other than our own even as aids to decision making is head-in-the-sand foolish, ideology-blinded, and arrogant. As one writer asked, "Are the contemporary views of nations such as England and Canada, Germany and Japan (where we, after all, drafted their current constitutions) really more 'foreign' than the views of a group of white men who lived over two centuries ago, owned slaves and denied women the vote?"[47]

The U.S. judiciary, agency board members, labor arbitrators, and labor lawyer–practitioners with rare exception have voluntarily excluded themselves from the human rights movement. The true test of the sincerity of this country's publicly proclaimed commitment to human rights is whether it will ratify the human rights treaties developed by the UN and the ILO, including those workers' rights documents discussed in this book. These treaties have been accepted by the international community and have become customary international law. Nonratification means that international human rights standards have no binding legal standing to U.S. courts. That is why the U.S. Council for International Business (USCIB) has opposed ratification of ILO Convention 87 on the Freedom of Association and Protection of the Right to Organize.

Labor unions are indispensable to any movement to achieve worker human rights. To become a vanguard organization in a broader human rights movement, however, organized labor needs a new vision that will take it beyond what C. Wright Mills called "mere pork chop contentment."[48] Powerful institutions are needed to make rights effective. For too long, however, too many unions have operated by the market philosophy values of being concerned only with pursuing their own self-interest and maximizing economic returns only for their own members.

The end result was what has been called corporate liberalism in which unions were tamed "by recruiting and rewarding a labor leadership willing to deradicalize its own rank and file."[49] An ideology of labor-management cooperation was concocted to signal the end of labor-management conflict. Management and unions used the cooperation theme to justify an arrangement in which unions and their members were rewarded economically for providing "stability" to employers and union "statesmen" who denounced and suppressed labor militancy, particularly anything resembling codetermination. This arrangement, of course, left unions powerless to do anything in serious economic downturns except to agree to concessions to try to save jobs. Eventually, as we have seen, even the more progressive of the employer advocates of labor-management cooperation adopted union-free programs as well as human resource methods to control their employees.

The new vision would transcend narrow self-interest not only to act on behalf of all workers (including the unemployed) but also to promote the unity, well-being, and humanity of all people. Unions need to act and perceive themselves as what they truly are intended to be (and in some cases are): nongovernmental human rights organizations promoting freedom of association and safety and health, opposing invidious discrimination, proposing and supporting legislation that benefits all workers and their families, working on behalf of the unemployed and the poor, and striving for a system where workers are not resources for the economy but where the economy is designed to provide more human lives for all. In sum, organized labor is meant to be the great counterforce *against* economic and social injustice and the great force *for* human rights.[50]

That requires reorganizing labor and redistributing power for the sake of human rights and a just society. That makes it a moral endeavor as well.[51] The new vision will need a radical agenda not unlike the Congress of Industrial Organizations' (CIO's) at its best when it was a dynamic social as well as economic force representing "almost every left-of-center political tendency in the nation" including politically conscious militants who were the "shop stewards, the committeemen, the local union officers, and the regional directors who gave leadership to an underclass—immigrants or the sons and daughters of immigrants, African Americans, Appalachian whites, the unskilled and the uneducated— whose voice had long been mute."[52] It was a movement in which these workers could believe not merely a dues-in, benefits-out slot machine.

The CIO was also an organization that did not see itself as part of the management team. The values of the unregulated market philosophy as adapted by employers in this country as a business creed are inconsistent with the values underlying workers' human rights. What's good for the company is often not good for the company's workers—and that's when workers rights need enforcement. Labor history in this country has shown that workers cooperate in bringing about their own demise when they abandon their adversarial role, which allows management to use them as instruments of management policy. That kind of labor peace or labor-management cooperation or "stability" facilitates violations of workers' human rights. If adversarialism ends, so does workers' freedom of association. Workers then become dependent on their employers for whatever workplace rights they have. As said many times in this book, such dependency is contrary to the nature of human rights.

All of these changes and surely more not mentioned here are needed for workers' human rights to be respected and enforced at U.S. workplaces. If the violations of workers' human rights described in this book are understood for what they are—crimes against humanity—it should be obvious that this book is not about misfortunes that beset workers or their supposedly inevitable and unavoidable plight but instead about injustice caused by the deliberate choices of those with the power to make those choices.

Although it is not fashionable to say so in the objective and scientific world of academe, this book is about good and evil choices. The United States is not the best of all possible worlds. Our piece of the world, moreover, does not run by chance or by the dictates of some unalterable economic laws—so that in either event no one is responsible and no one can be blamed. The root of evil in all forms of crime against humanity is the "ability to erase the humanity of other beings and turn them into usable and dispensable things."[53] This ability, promoted by the free market economic philosophy prevalent in the U.S. workplace, turns human beings into instruments and seeks life "through the dehumanization of others."[54]

Social justice requires a transformation to a human rights–focused workplace. That transformation cannot occur without a change in the values that have led to the current state of workplace injustice. Martin Luther King, Jr., best described what that means when he called for a "radical revolution of values" that would begin a "shift from a thing-oriented society to a person-oriented society"; that would "cause us to question the fairness and justice of many of our past and present policies"; and that would "develop an overriding loyalty to mankind as a whole." Dr. King warned that "If we do not act, we shall surely be dragged down the long, dark, and shameful corridors of time reserved for those who possess power without compassion, might without morality, and strength without sight."[55] Dr. King pointed out, moreover, that structural as well as personal changes were required: "On the one hand we are called to play the Good Samaritan on life's roadside, but that will be only the initial act. One day we must come to see that the whole Jericho Road must be transformed so that men and women will not be constantly beaten and robbed as they make their journey on life's highway. True compassion is more than flinging a coin to a beggar. It comes to see that an edifice which produces beggars needs restructuring."[56]

It is time for this country to stop being hypocritical about workplace human rights and to stop trying to paper over our violations of workers' human rights with false claims that our employer-worker relations laws, policies, and practices are models for the world to follow. It is time to act to be a better nation and a better people.

NOTES

Introduction

1. From Patricia Werhane, *Persons, Rights, and Corporations* (Englewood Cliffs, N.J.: Prentice Hall, 1985), 127–28.

1. Justice and Human Rights

1. C. H. Perelman, *Justice* (New York: Random House, 1967), 3–4.

2. Paul Brest, "The Fundamental Rights Controversy: The Essential Contradictions of Normative Constitutional Scholarship," 90 *Yale Law Journal* (1981): 87.

3. Judith Shklar, *The Faces of Injustice* (New Haven: Yale University Press, 1990), 87.

4. Bernard Yack, "Jurisprudence and Political Theory: Injustice and the Victim's Voice," 89 *Michigan Law Review* (May 1991): 1348.

5. Leo Rosten, *Leo Rosten's Treasury of Jewish Quotations* (Northvale, N.J.: Jason Aronson Inc., 1988), 459.

6. J. R. Lucas, *On Justice* (Oxford: Oxford University Press, 1989), 180.

7. Joel Fineberg, "The Nature and Value of Rights," 4 *Journal of Value Inquiry* (Winter 1970): 252.

8. Jack Donnelly, *Universal Human Rights in Theory and Practice* (Ithaca: Cornell University Press, 1989), 12.

9. Michael J. Perry, *The Idea of Human Rights: Four Inquiries* (New York: Oxford University Press, 1998), 63–64, 71. Perry identifies the following as good for every human being: "affection, the cooperation of others, a place in the community, and help in trouble," and the following as bad for every human being: murder, imprisonment, enslavement, starvation, torture, homelessness, racism, and friendlessness.

He points out that these beliefs about what is good and bad for every human being "are widely shared across cultures." Ibid., 71.

10. *Arthur Miller's Collected Plays,* vol. 1 (New York: Viking Press, 1957), 180–181.

11. Ibid., 181.

12. Virginia Leary, "The Paradox of Workers' Rights as Human Rights," in *Human Rights, Labor Rights, and International Trade,* ed. Lance Compa and Stephen Diamond (Philadelphia: University of Pennsylvania Press, 1996), 22, 25.

13. Quoted in Bob Hepple, "Rights at Work," International Labour Organization, International Institute for Labour Studies (2003), 2.

14. Donnelly, *Universal Human Rights,* 26–27, 30.

15. Ibid., 26–27.

16. Ibid., 24. The International Bill of Rights is comprised of the Universal Declaration of Human Rights (UDHR); the International Covenant on Civil and Political Rights (ICCPR); and the International Covenant on Economic, Social and Cultural Rights (ICESCR). These documents are reproduced in Henry Steiner and Philip Alston, eds., *International Human Rights in Context: Law, Politics, Morals* (Oxford: Clarendon Press, 1996), UDHR: 1156–1160; ICCPR: 1161–1171; ICESCR: 1175–1181.

17. Steiner and Alston, *International Human Rights in Context,* 1159–1160.

18. Ibid., 1161.

19. 90 *Cong. Rec.* 55–57 (1944).

20. A. Glenn Mower, *Human Rights and American Foreign Policy* (New York: Greenwood Press, 1987), 39–40.

21. Henry Shue, *Basic Rights: Subsistence, Affluence, and U.S. Foreign Policy* (Princeton: Princeton University Press, 1980), 27.

22. Eleanor Roosevelt, quoted in *The Universal Declaration of Human Rights: A Magna Carta for All Humanity* (1997) at http://www.unhchr.ch/udhr/miscinfo/carta.htm.

23. John Houck, "Human Work and Employment Generation," in *Catholic Social Teaching and the United States Economy,* ed. John Houck and Oliver Williams (Washington, D.C.: University Press of America, 1984), 24.

24. Hepple, "Rights at Work," 16.

25. Houck, "Human Work and Employment Generation," 24.

26. Charles Wilber and Kenneth Jameson, *An Inquiry into the Poverty of Economics* (Notre Dame, Ind.: University of Notre Dame Press, 1983), 251.

27. Shue, *Basic Rights,* 30.

28. James Gross, "The Broken Promises of the National Labor Relations Act and the Occupational Safety and Health Act: Conflicting Values and Conceptions of Rights and Justice," 73 *Chicago-Kent Law Review* (1998): 384–385.

29. Shue, *Basic Rights,* 78.

30. Alfred Kazin, "The Way We Live Now," *The New York Review,* April 22, 1993, 4.

31. Judith Shklar, "Injustice, Injury, and Inequality: An Introduction," in *Justice and Equality Here and Now,* ed. Frank Lucash (Ithaca: Cornell University Press, 1986), 25.

32. Gore Vidal, "Two Immoralists: Orville Prescott and Ayn Rand," in *Rocking the Boat* (New York: Dell, 1963), 264.

33. Ayn Rand, *For the New Intellectual,* (New York: New American Library, 1961), 100.

34. Jacques Maritain, *The Person and the Common Good* (New York: C. Scribner's Sons, 1947), 81–82.

35. Robert N. Bellah, *The Broken Covenant: American Civil Religion in Time of Trial* (New York: Senbury Press, 1975), 84.

36. Lucas, *On Justice,* 68–69.

37. Hepple, "Rights at Work," 15.

38. Lucas, *On Justice,* 18.

39. John Donne, "Mediation XVII," in *The Complete Poetry and Selected Prose of John Donne and William Blake,* ed. Robert Silliman Hillyer (New York: Random House, 1941), 331.

40. John Steinbeck, *The Grapes of Wrath* (New York: Harper & Brothers, 1939), 570.

41. Errol Harris, "Respect for Persons," in *Ethics and Society*, ed. Richard DeGeorge (Garden City, N.Y.: Anchor Books, 1966), 122.

42. Shue, *Basic Rights*, 35–64.

43. Ibid., 19; Robert Johann, "Love and Justice," in *Ethics and Society*, 44–45.

44. John R. Donahue, "Biblical Perspectives on Justice," in *The Faith That Does Justice*, ed. John Haughey (Mahwah, N.J.: Paulist Press, 1977), 108.

45. Martin Luther King, "I've Been to the Mountaintop," in Paul Lauter, general ed., *Heath Anthology of American Literature*, vol. 2 (Lexington: D.C. Heath & Co., 1994), 2492.

46. Jacques Maritain, *The Rights of Man and Natural Law* (New York: Charles Scribner's & Sons, 1943), 47.

47. Mark Twain, *A Connecticut Yankee in King Arthur's Court*, in *The Complete Novels of Mark Twain* (New York: Harper & Row, 1936), 169, 187.

48. Ibid., 188.

49. Ibid., 193.

50. Thomas Cahill, *How the Irish Saved Civilization* (New York: Anchor Books Doubleday, 1995), 97.

51. Shklar, "Injustice, Injury, and Inequality," 26.

52. Martin Niemoeller, quoted in Bartlett's *Familiar Quotations*, 15th ed., ed. Emily Morison Beck (Boston: Little, Brown, 1980), 824.

53. Shklar, *Faces of Injustice*, 2.

54. Thomas Geoghegan, *Which Side Are You On?* (New York: Farrar, Straus & Giroux, 1991), 273.

55. Ibid., 274.

56. Shklar, *Faces of Injustice*, 112.

57. A. M. Rosenthal, "On My Mind," *New York Times*, November 6, 1992, A29.

58. Yack, "Jurisprudence and Political Theory," 1347; Donahue, "Biblical Perspectives on Justice," 108.

59. Donnelly, *Universal Human Rights*, 17–18.

60. Ibid., 18.

61. Steinbeck, *Grapes of Wrath*, 52.

2. "Without Distinction of Any Kind"

1. John Lewis, "Bloody Sunday," in *Voices in Our Blood*, ed. John Meacham (New York: Random House, 2001), 292, 297–301.

2. Ibid., 309.

3. Ibid., 310.

4. Michael Perry, *The Idea of Human Rights: Four Inquiries* (New York: Oxford University Press, 1998), 4–5.

5. See Richard Wasserstrom, "Rights, Human Rights, and Racial Discrimination," *The Journal of Philosophy* 61, no. 628 (1964): 625–641.

6. G.A. Res. 217A, U.N. GAOR, 3d Sess., 1st plen. mtg., U.N. Doc. A/810 (Dec. 10, 1948).

7. Dec. 16, 1966, 999 U.N.T.S. 171.

8. Dec. 16, 1966, 993 U.N.T.S. 3.

9. http://www.ilo.org/ilolex/english/iloconst.htm.

10. http://www.ilo.org/ilolex/cgi-lex/convde.pl?.

11. Alexis de Tocqueville, *Democracy in America* (New York: Vintage Books, 1945), 3, 13, 344, 372.

12. Gunnar Myrdal, *An American Dilemma: The Negro Problem and Modern Democracy* (New York: Harper Brothers, 1944).

13. *Report of the National Advisory Commission on Civil Disorders* (New York: Bantam Books, 1968), 1 ("Summary of Report").

14. Fred R. Harris and Roger W. Wilkins, eds., *Quiet Riots: Race and Poverty in the United States* (New York: Pantheon Books, 1988), 101–103.

15. Myrdal, *American Dilemma,* 5–6, 23.

16. Richard Kluger, *Simple Justice: The History of Brown v. Board of Education and Black America's Struggle for Equality* (New York: Knopf, 1976), 314.

17. C. Vann Woodward, *The Burden of Southern History* (Baton Rouge: Louisiana State University Press, 1960), 79.

18. Myrdal, *American Dilemma,* 658.

19. 163 U.S. 537 (1896).

20. C. Vann Woodward, *The Strange Career of Jim Crow,* 3rd ed. (New York: Oxford University Press, 1974), 81–82.

21. Brook Thomas, *Plessy v. Ferguson: A Brief of History with Documents* (Boston: Bedford Books, 1997), 1.

22. Ibid., 2, 5–6.

23. Ibid., 10–11.

24. Woodward, *Burden of Southern History,* 83.

25. Philip Dray, *At the Hands of Persons Unknown: The Lynching of Black America* (New York: The Modern Library, 2003), 16, 177, 219, 233, 384.

26. Woodward, *Strange Career of Jim Crow,* 107.

27. Winthrop Jordan, *White over Black: American Attitudes toward the Negro, 1550–1812* (Baltimore: Penguin Books, 1969), 418.

28. Kluger, *Simple Justice,* 116.

29. Benjamin E. Mays, "The Moral Aspects of Segregation," in *Voices in Our Blood,* ed. John Meacham (New York: Random House, 2001), 125.

30. 347 U.S. 483 (1954).

31. Ibid., 494.

32. "Convention on the Rights of the Child," in United Nations, *Human Rights: A Compilation of International Instruments,* vol. 1 (1994), 185. (Emphasis added.)

33. Jonathan Kozol, *Ordinary Resurrections: Children in the Years of Hope* (New York: Crown, 2000) 201.

34. Ibid., 218.

35. Thomas Sowell, *Black Education: Myths and Tragedies* (New York: McKay, 1972), 222–223.

36. Jonathan Kozol, *Death at an Early Age* (Boston: Houghton Mifflin, 1967), vii.

37. Jonathan Kozol, *Amazing Grace: The Lives of Children and the Conscience of a Nation* (New York: Crown, 1995), 186.

38. Howell Raines, "Grady's Gist," in *Voices in Our Blood,* ed. John Meacham (New York: Random House, 2001), 527.

39. See James A. Gross, "A Human Rights Perspective on U.S. Education: Only Some Children Matter," *Catholic University Law Review* 50 (2001): 919–956.

40. Ibid., 942–943.

41. Michael K. Brown et al., *Whitewashing Race: The Myth of a Color-Blind Society* (Berkeley: University of California Press, 2003), 10, 12. See also Dinesh D'Souza, *The End of Racism* (New York: The Free Press, 1995); Richard Epstein, *Forbidden Grounds: The Case against Employment Discrimination Laws* (Cambridge, Mass.: Harvard University Press, 1992); Tamar Jacoby, *Someone Else's House: America's Unfinished Struggle for Integration* (New York: The Free Press, 1998); Jim Sleeper, *Liberal Racism* (New York: Penguin Books, 1997); Shelby Steele, *A Dream Deferred: The Second Betrayal of Black Freedom in America* (New York: Harper Collins, 1998); Stephen and Abigail Thernstrom, *American in Black and White: One Nation Indivisible* (New York: Simon and Schuster, 1997).

42. Woodward, *Burden of Southern History,* 104.

43. Myrdal, *American Dilemma,* 208.

44. Klugar, *Simple Justice,* 306.

45. Brown, *Whitewashing Race,* 51.

46. Ibid., 25, 57.

47. Ibid., 163.

48. 347 U.S. 483 (1954).

49. Pub. L. No. 88–353, 78 Stat. 241 (1964), codified at 42 U.S.C. ¶ 1971 et seg. (1988).

50. Brown, *Whitewashing Race,* 44.

51. 38 U.S.C. 4104 (1944).

52. Brown, *Whitewashing Race,* 75.

53. Ibid., 76.

54. Ibid., 77.

55. Ibid., 78–79.

56. Ibid.

57. Ibid.

58. Ibid.

59. Thomas J. Sugrue, *The Origins of the Urban Crisis: Race and Inequality in Post War Detroit* (Princeton, N.J.: Princeton University Press, 1996) 3.

60. Klugar, *Simple Justice,* 51.

61. Myrdal, *American Dilemma,* 205, 304–305.

62. Sugrue, *Origins of the Urban Crisis,* 93, 99–100, 104, 112–114, 122.

63. Ibid., 100–102.

64. William H. Harris, *The Harder We Run: Black Workers since the Civil War* (New York: Oxford University Press, 1982), 140.

65. Jervis Anderson, *A. Philip Randolph: A Biological Portrait* (New York: Harcourt Brace Jovanovich, 1972), 296–315.

66. Sugrue, *Origins of the Urban Crisis,* 160–164.

67. Anderson, *A. Philip Randolph,* 329.

68. Sugrue, *Origins of the Urban Crisis,* 162–163.

69. Brown, *Whitewashing Race,* 90.

70. Fran Lebowitz, "Fran Lebowitz on Race," *Vanity Fair,* October, 1997, 220. As comedian Chris Rock put it: "There ain't no white man in this room that will change places with me—and I'm rich. That's how good it is to be white. There's a one-legged busboy in here right now that's going: 'I don't want to change. I'm gonna ride this white thing out and see where it takes me.'"

71. Cheryl I. Harris, "Whiteness as Property," *Harvard Law Review* 106, no. 1709 (1983): 1748.

72. Ibid., 1713.

73. Brown, *Whitewashing Race,* 4, 35.

74. Lebowitz, "Fran Lebowitz on Race," 222.

75. Brown, *Whitewashing Race,* 55.

76. August Wilson, *Radio Golf* (New York: Theatre Communications Group, 2007), 79.

77. Maya Angelou, "Creativity with Bill Moyers: Maya Angelou," directed by David Grubin (City: PBS Video/CU Educational Video, 1989).

78. Ibid.

79. Martin Luther King, Jr., "I Have a Dream," in *The Heath Anthology of American Literature,* vol. 2, 2d ed., ed. Paul Lauter (Lexington, Mass.: D.C. Heath, 1994), 2483, 2485.

80. Martin Luther King, Jr., "I've Been to the Mountaintop," in the *Heath Anthology of American Literature,* vol. 2, 2d ed., ed. Paul Lauter (Lexington, Mass.: D.C. Heath, 1994), 2488.

81. John Okada, *No-no boy* (Seattle: University of Washington Press, 1979), 134.

82. John Lewis, "Bloody Sunday," in *Voices in Our Blood,* ed. John Meacham (New York: Random House, 2001), 309–310.

3. The Market Economics Values underlying U.S. Labor Law

1. Robert Kuttner, "The Poverty of Economics," *The Atlantic Monthly,* February 1985, 83.

2. Lester C. Thurow, *Dangerous Currents* (New York: Random House, 1983), 139.

3. Kuttner, "The Poverty of Economics," 79.

4. Thurow, *Dangerous Currents,* 21.

5. Gunnar Myrdal, *Beyond the Welfare State* (New Haven: Yale University Press, 1960), 35.

6. Thurow, *Dangerous Currents,* xviii.

7. Kuttner, "The Poverty of Economics," 76.

8. Karl Polanyi, *The Great Transformation* (Boston: Beacon Press, 1957), 71.

9. Michael Novak, *The Spirit of Democratic Capitalism* (New York: American Enterprise Institute/ Simon and Schuster, 1982), 90.

10. Ibid.

11. Alan Brinkley, "The Problem of American Conservatism," *American Historical Review,* April 1994, 417.

12. Ibid., 416.

13. Friedrich A. Hayek, *The Road to Serfdom* (Chicago: University of Chicago Press, 1944), 204–205.

14. Ibid., 204.

15. Ibid., 205.

16. Lester Thurow, *The Zero-Sum Society* (New York: Basic Books, 1980), 129.

17. Charles K. Wilber and Kenneth P. Jameson, *An Inquiry into the Poverty of Economics* (South Bend, Ind.: University of Notre Dame Press, 1983), 78.

18. Thurow, *Dangerous Currents,* 222.

19. John Kenneth Galbraith, *American Capitalism: The Concept of Countervaluing Power* (1952; New Brunswick and London: Transaction Publishers, 1993), 28.

20. Friedrich A. Hayek, *The Mirage of Social Justice* (Chicago: University of Chicago Press, 1976), 66.

21. Francis Fox Piven and Richard A. Cloward, *The New Class War* (New York: Pantheon Books, 1982), 75.

22. Wilber and Jameson, *Inquiry into the Poverty of Economics,* 236–237.

23. James A. Gross, *Broken Promise: The Subversion of U.S. Labor Relations Policy, 1947–1994* (Philadelphia: Temple University Press, 1995), 285–286.

24. Polanyi, *Great Transformation,* 254.

25. Ibid., 256.

26. Ibid., 257.

27. Philip Selznick, *Law, Society, and Industrial Justice* (New York: Russell Sage Foundation, 1969), 8.

28. James A. Gross, "The Common Law Employment Contract and Collective Bargaining: Values and Views of Rights and Justice," *New Zealand Journal of Industrial Relations* 23, no. 2 (1998): 74.

29. Lawrence M. Friedman, *A History of American Law* (New York: Simon and Schuster, 1973), 17, 19.

30. Benjamin Cardozo, *The Nature of the Judicial Process* (New Haven: Yale University Press, 1921), 168.

31. Ibid., 13.

32. Ibid., 67.

33. Ibid., 161.

34. Ibid., 161, 167–168.

35. See Jeffrie G. Murphy and Jules L. Coleman, *Philosophy of Law: An Introduction to Jurisprudence,* rev. ed. (Boulder, Colo.: Westview Press, 1990), 33–55.

36. Morton J. Horowitz, *The Transformation of American Law, 1780–1860* (Cambridge, Mass.: Harvard University Press, 1977), xvi.

37. See Richard B. Morris, *Government and Labor in Early America* (New York: Harper & Row, 1946), 1–35, 55–91.

38. Horowitz, *Transformation of American Law, 1790–1860,* 208.

39. Selznick, *Law, Society, and Industrial Justice,* 124–129.

40. Morris, *Government and Labor in Early America,* 1.

41. Cardozo, *Nature of the Judicial Process,* 171.

42. Charles O. Gregory, *Labor and the Law,* rev. ed. (New York: W.W. Norton & Co., 1949), 87.

43. Horowitz, *Transformation of American Law, 1780–1860,* 254.

44. Morton J. Horowitz, *The Transformation of American Law, 1870–1960: The Crisis of Legal Ortho-doxy* (New York: Oxford University Press, 1992), 53.

45. Friedman, *History of American Law,* 14.

46. Ibid., 109.

47. Horowitz, *Transformation of American Law, 1780–1860,* 99.

48. Ibid., 71.

49. *Ryan v. New York Central Railroad,* 35 N.Y. 210 (1866).

50. Horowitz, *Transformation of American Law, 1870–1960,* 58.

51. Ibid.

52. Ralph Henry Gabriel, *The Course of American Democratic Thought* (New York: Ronald Press Co., 1956), 152–153.

53. Horowitz, *Transformation of American Law, 1780–1860,* 160, 184, 200.

54. Horowitz, *Transformation of American Law, 1870–1960,* 33.

55. 98 U.S. 45 (1905).

56. Horowitz, *Transformation of American Law, 1870–1960,* 29–30, 33.

57. Selznick, *Law, Society, and Industrial Justice,* 53, 57, 59.

58. Friedman, *History of American Law,* 486.

59. Horowitz, *Transformation of American Law, 1790–1860,* 255.

60. Gregory, *Labor and the Law,* 176.

61. Selznick, *Law, Society, and Industrial Justice,* 135.

62. Alan Fox, *Beyond Contract: Work, Power and Trust Relations* (London: Faber and Faber, 1974), 188.

63. 208 U.S. 161 (1908).

64. Ibid., 175.

65. Horowitz, *Transformation of American Law,* 50.

66. Gabriel, *Course of American Democratic Thought,* 209.

67. *Hammer v. Dagenhart,* 247 U.S. 251 (1918).

68. Gabriel, *Course of American Democratic Thought,* 276.

69. Ibid., 360.

70. Joseph Dorfman, "The Background of Institutional Economics," in *Institutional Economics: Veblen, Commons, and Mitchell Reconsidered* (Berkeley and Los Angeles: University of California Press, 1963), 33.

71. C. E. Ayres, "The Legacy of Thorstein Veblen," in ibid., 61.

72. Leon Litwack, *The American Labor Movement* (Englewood Cliffs, N.J.: Prentice Hall, 1962), 42–43.

73. Gabriel, *Course of American Democratic Thought,* 204.

74. Litwack, *American Labor Movement,* 36.

75. Melvyn Dubofsky, *The State and Labor in Modern America* (Chapel Hill: University of North Carolina Press, 1994), 38.

76. Ibid., 96–97.

77. Henry David, "Upheaval at Homestead," in *American in Crisis,* ed. Daniel Aaron (New York: Alfred A. Knopf, 1952), 162–163.

78. Milton Derber, *The American Idea of Industrial Democracy, 1865–1965* (Urbana: University of Illinois Press, 1970), 10.

79. Dubofsky, *The State and Labor in Modern America,* 55.

80. Ibid.

81. Milton Handler, *Cases and Materials on Labor Law* (St. Paul, Minn.: West, 1944), 22.

82. John Kenneth Galbraith, *The Great Crash* (Boston: Houghton Mifflin, 1961), 3.

83. James A. Gross, *The Making of the National Labor Relations Board: A Study in Economics, Politics, and the Law* (Albany: State University of New York Press, 1974), 147, 229.

84. James A. Gross, "Conflicting Statutory Purposes: Another Look at Fifty Years of NLRB Law Making," *Industrial and Labor Relations Review* 39 (October 1985): 10–11.

85. Pub. L. No. 74–198, 49 Stat. 449–50 (1935), codified as amended at 29 U.S.C. §§ 141–144, 167, 171–187 (1944).

86. Human Rights Watch, *Unfair Advantage: Workers' Freedom of Association in the United States under International Human Rights Standards* (New York: Human Rights Watch, 2000), 13.

87. Murphy and Coleman, *Philosophy of Law,* 90.

4. Property Rights over Freedom of Association Rights

1. James A. Gross, *The Reshaping of the National Labor Relations Board: National Labor Policy in Transition, 1937–1947* (Albany: State University of New York Press, 1981), 23.

2. Irving Bernstein, *Turbulent Years* (Boston: Houghton Mifflin, 1979), 790.

3. Gross, *Reshaping of the National Labor Relations Board,* 7.

4. Ibid., 17.

5. Ibid., 22.

6. Ralph Henry Gabriel, *The Course of American Democratic Thought* (New York: Ronald Press Co., 1956), 159.

7. Richard Hofstadter, *Social Darwinism in American Thought* (Boston: Beacon Press, 1944), 58.

8. Gabriel, *Course of American Democratic Thought,* 168.

9. Ibid., 160.

10. "Mr. Baer On Management Responsibilities," in *Unions, Management and the Public,* 3d ed., eds. E. Wright Bakke, Clark Kerr, Charles W. Anrod (New York: Harcourt, Brace & World, 1967), 213.

11. Gabriel, *Course of American Democratic Thought,* 168.

12. Lawrence M. Friedman, *A History of American Law* (New York: Simon & Schuster, 1973), 485.

13. Gabriel, *Course of American Democratic Thought,* 160.

14. George Figzhugh, *Cannibals All, or Slaves without Masters,* ed. C. Vann Woodward (Cambridge, Mass.: Belnap Press, 1988), xix.

15. Jacques Maritain, *The Person and the Common Good* (New York: C. Scribner's Sons, 1947), 81–82.

16. Elizabeth A. Fones-Wolf, *Selling Free Enterprise: The Business Assault on Labor and Liberalism* (Urbana: University of Illinois Press, 1994), 26.

17. Ibid., 6.

18. Ibid., 32, 190.

19. Ibid., 189, 199, 205.

20. Ibid., 195.

21. Ibid., 198.

22. Ibid., 87, 91.

23. Ibid., 76 (emphasis in the original).

24. Howell John Harris, "Industrial Democracy and Liberal Capitalism," in *Industrial Democracy in America: The Ambiguous Promise,* ed. Nelson Lichtenstein and Howell John Harris (New York: Woodrow Wilson Center Press and Cambridge University Press, 1996), 61.

25. Elizabeth A. Fones-Wolf, *Selling Free Enterprise,* 159.

26. Ibid., 41, 159.

27. Gross, *Reshaping of the National Labor Relations Board.*

28. Ibid., 108.

29. Ibid., 225. The official name of the Taft-Hartley Act is the Labor–Management Relations Act, 29 U.S.C. §§ 141-197 (1947).

30. House Committee on Education and Labor, "The Failure of Labor Law—A Betrayal of American Workers," 98th Cong., 2d sess., 1984, 1, 24.

31. James A Gross, *Broken Promise: The Subversion of U.S. Labor Relations Policy, 1947–1994* (Philadelphia: Temple University Press, 1995), 13–14.

32. Ibid., 273.

33. *NLRB v. Federbush Co.,* 121 F. 2d 954, 957 (2d Cir., 1941).

34. Robert F. Wagner, "The Wagner Act—A Reappraisal," 93 Cong. Rec. A895, A896 (1947), reprinted in 2 LMRA Legis. Hist. 935, 938.

35. 29 U.S.C. § 158(c) (1994).

36. Clyde W. Summers, "Questioning the Unquestioned in Collective Labor Law," *Catholic University Law Review* 47 (1998): 791, 806.

37. John Logan, "Representatives of Their Own Choosing?: Certification, Elections, and Employer Free Speech," *Seattle University Law Review* 23 (Winter 2000): 549, 566.

38. 324 U.S. 793 (1945).

39. Seamprufe, Inc., 109 N.L.R.B. 24, 32 (1954).

40. Ibid.

41. 351 U.S. 105 (1956).

42. Ibid., 112–113.

43. Jay Gresham, "Still as Strangers: Non-employee Union Organizers on Private Commercial Property," *Texas Law Review* 62 (1983): 111.

44. See, e.g., Fibreboard Paper Products Corp. v. NLRB, 379 U.S. 203 (1964) (pronouncing employers free of any obligation to bargain about managerial decisions "at the core of entrepreneurial control"); NLRB v. McKay Radio & Tel. Co., 304 U.S. 333 (1938) (pronouncing that employers were not bound to discharge those hired to fill the places of economic strikers in order to make places for those strikers).

45. Gresham, "Still as Strangers," 166 (emphasis in the original).

46. 502 U.S. 527 (1992).

47. Cynthia L. Estlund, "Labor, Property and Sovereignty after *Lechmere,*" *Stanford Law Review* 46 (1994): 305, 309.

48. *Lechmere, Inc. v NLRB,* 502 U.S. 527, 532 (1992).

49. Ibid., 539–540 (emphasis in original.)

50. Ibid., 540.

51. Estlund, "Labor, Property and Sovereignty after *Lechmere,*" 308.

52. Kate E. Andrias, "A Robust Public Debate: Realizing Free Speech in Workplace Representation Elections," *Yale Law Journal* 112 (2003): 2415, 2427.

53. 70 N.L.R.B. 802 (1946).

54. 96 N.L.R.B. 608 (1951).

55. 102 N.L.R.B. 1634 (1953).

56. 107 N.L.R.B. 400 (1953).

57. Ibid., 411.

58. Ibid.

59. James A. Gross, "A Human Rights Perspective on United States Labor Relations Law: A Violation of the Right of Freedom of Association," *Employee Rights and Employment Policy Journal* 3 (1999): 99.

60. NLRB v. Federbush Co., 121 F.2d 954, 957 (2d Cir. 1941).

61. John Logan, "Consultants, Lawyers, and the 'Union Free' Movement in the USA since the 1970s," *Industrial Relations Journal* 33 (August 2002): 202.

62. Ibid., 204.

63. Ibid., 205.

64. Ibid., 213.

65. Human Rights Watch, *Unfair Advantage: Workers' Freedom of Association in the United States under International Human Rights Standards* (New York: Human Rights Watch, 2000), 7.

66. Ibid., 8.

67. G.A. Res. 217, U.N. GAOR, 3d Sess., 1st plen. mtg., U.N. Doc. A/810 (Dec. 10, 1948).

68. Dec. 16, 1966, 999 U.N.T.S 171.

69. Dec. 16, 1966, 993 U.N.T.S. 3.

70. 31st Sess. (1948), 1 *International Labour Conventions & Recommendations* 435 (1992). ILOLex Database of International Labour Standards, http://www.ilo.org/ilolex/English.

71. 32d Sess. (1949), 1 *International Labour Conventions & Recommendations* 524 (1992).

72. ILO Declaration on Fundamental Principles and Rights at Work and Its Follow-up, adopted by the International Labour Conference, 86th Sess., Geneva, June 18, 1998.

73. Roy J. Adams, "The Right to Participate," *Employee Responsibilities and Rights Journal* 2 (1992): 94.

74. Edward E. Potter, *Freedom of Association, the Right to Organize, and Collective Bargaining: The Impact on U.S. Law and Practice of Ratification of ILO Conventions No. 87 & No. 98* (Washington, D.C.: Labor Policy Association, 1984), 42.

75. Case No. 1523, Complaint against the Government of the United States Presented by the United Food and Commercial Workers International Union (UFCW), the American Federation of Labor and Congress of Industrial Organizations (AFL-CIO), and the International Federation of Commercial, Clerical, Professional and Technical Employees (FIET), 75 (Series B) *ILO Official Bull.,* No. 3 (1992): 36, 40.

76. Ibid., 55.

77. Andrias, "A Robust Public Debate: Realizing Free Speech in Workplace Representation Elections," 2457.

78. Human Rights Watch, *Unfair Advantage,* 20.

79. Ibid., 21.

5. Expanding the Zone of Management Control

1. Donald E. Cullen and Marcia L. Greenbaum, *Management Rights and Collective Bargaining: Can Both Survive?* (Ithaca: New York State School of Industrial and Labor Relations, Cornell University, 1966), 13.

2. Neil W. Chamberlain, *The Labor Sector: An Introduction to Labor in the American Economy* (New York: McGraw-Hill, 1965), 342.

3. Ibid.

4. Howell John Harris, *The Right to Manage: Industrial Relations Policies of American Business in the 1940s* (Madison: University of Wisconsin Press, 1982), 96–97.

5. Chamberlain, *Labor Sector,* 344.

6. Ibid.

7. James B. Atleson, *Values and Assumptions in American Labor Law* (Amherst: University of Massachusetts Press, 1983), 122.

8. Harris, *Right to Manage,* 97; Chamberlain, *Labor Sector,* 347–350.

9. Cullen and Greenbaum, *Management Rights and Collective Bargaining,* 17.

10. Byron R. Abernethy, *Liberty Concepts in Labor Relations* (Washington, D.C.: American Council on Public Affairs, 1943), 9.

11. Harris, *Right to Manage,* 99.

12. Michael Novak, *The Spirit of Democratic Capitalism* (New York: American Enterprise Institute/ Simon and Schuster, 1982).

13. Ibid., 178–179.

14. 138 N.L.R.B. 550 (1962).

15. Ibid., 555, 558–560.

16. James A. Gross, *Broken Promise: The Subversion of U.S. Labor Relations Policy, 1947–1994* (Philadelphia: Temple University Press, 1995), 173.

17. Ibid.

18. Ibid.

19. Brief for the National Labor Relations Board, *Fibreboard Paper Products Corp. Petitioner v. NLRB,* in the Supreme Court of the United States, October Term, 1964, no. 14, p. 63. Cited in Gross, *Broken Promise,* 173–174.

20. Ibid.

21. Ibid., 22–23. (Emphasis added.)

22. Gross, *Broken Promise,* 174.

23. Ibid.

24. Ibid., 175.

25. "Decision of National Labor Relations Board in Case of Darlington Manufacturing Company, et al.," *Daily Labor Report,* no. 204, October 18, 1962, D-2.

26. *Darlington Mfg. Co.,* 139 N.L.R.B. 241 (1962).

27. Gross, *Broken Promise,* 175–176.

28. "Limits on Labor and Management," *Time,* April 9, 1965, 66.

29. Gross, *Broken Promise,* 176.

30. "Collective Bargaining Today—As Seen at the NLRB," address by Gerald Brown, *Daily Labor Report,* no. 52, March 18, 1965, D-2—D-3.

31. The details of this organized management resistance are discussed in Gross, *Broken Promise,* 200–214.

32. T. A. Wise, "Hill & Knowlton's World of Images," *Fortune,* September 1, 1967, 140.

33. Senate Subcommittee on Separation of Powers of the Committee on the Judiciary, *Hearings on Congressional Oversight of Administrative Agencies,* 90th Cong., 2d sess., 1968, 683–685, 688, 692.

34. 379 U.S. 203 (1964).

35. Theodore J. St. Antoine, "National Labor Policy: Reflections and Distortions of Social Justice," *Catholic University Law Review* 29 (1980): 540.

36. Clyde W. Summers, "Industrial Democracy: American's Unfulfilled Promise," *Cleveland State Law Review* 28 (1979): 36.

37. Atleson, *Values and Assumptions in American Labor Law,* 10.

38. Ibid., 2. Benjamin N. Cardozo, *The Nature of the Judicial Process* (New Haven: Yale University Press, 1921), 171.

39. Archibald Cox, Derek Curtis Bok, Robert A. Gorman, and Matthew W. Finkin, *Labor Law: Cases and Materials,* 14th ed. (new York: Foundation Press, 2006), 467.

40. Ibid., 468.

41. Ibid.

42. Ibid., 470.

43. Ibid.

44. Ibid.

45. Atleson, *Values and Assumptions in American Labor Law,* 126.

46. Cox, Bok, Gorman, and Finkin, *Labor Law: Cases and Materials,* 471.

47. *Textile Workers Union v. Darlington Mfg. Co.,* 380 U.S. 263 (1965).

48. Cox, Bok, Gorman, and Finkin, *Labor Law: Cases and Materials,* 254.

49. Ibid., 255.

50. Atleson, *Values and Assumptions in American Labor Law,* 140 (quoting Clyde Summers, "Labor Law in the Supreme Court—1975," *Yale Law Journal,* 75 (1965): 64–65).

51. Atleson, *Values and Assumptions in American Labor Law,* 141.

52. Ibid., 142.

53. 452 U.S. 666 (1981).

54. Cox, Bok, Gorman, and Finkin, *Labor Law: Cases and Materials,* 478.

55. Alan Hyde, "The Story of First National Maintenance Corp. v. NLRB: Eliminating Bargaining for Low-Wage Service Workers," in Laura J. Cooper and Catherine L. Fisk, eds., *Labor Law Stories,* (New York: Foundation Press, 2005), 302.

56. Cox, Box, Gorman, and Finking, *Labor Law: Cases and Materials,* 477.

57. Ibid., 478–479.

58. Atleson, *Values and Assumptions in American Labor Law,* 227, n. 90.

59. Cox, Box, Gorman, and Finking, *Labor Law: Cases and Materials,* 482.

60. Ibid., 483–484.

61. *Milwaukee Spring Division of Illinois Coil Spring Co,* 268 N.L.R.B. 601 (1984).

62. *Otis Elevator Co.,* 269 N.L.R.B. 891 (1984), 893, n. 5.

63. Jacques Maritain, *The Rights of Man and Natural Law* (New York: Scribner's Sons, 1943), 27.

64. See Sheldon Leader, *Freedom of Association: A Study in Labor Law and Political Theory* (New Haven: Yale University Press, 1992).

65. Tom Kahn, "Concluding Observations," in *Freedom of Association* (Washington, D.C.: AFL-CIO, 1998.)

66. Hyde, "The Story of First National Maintenance Corp. v. NLRB," 281.

67. Summers, "Industrial Democracy," 29.

68. Ibid., 34.

69. James A. Gross, "A Human Rights Perspective on United States Labor Relations Law: A Violation of the Right of Freedom of Association," *Employee Rights and Employment Policy Journal,* 3 (1999): 79.

70. Gross, *Broken Promise.*

71. Human Rights Watch, *Unfair Advantage: Workers' Freedom of Association in the United States under International Human Rights Standards* (New York: Human Rights Watch, 2000), 7.

6. Violations of the Human Right to Life and Limb

1. Emily A. Spieler, "Risks and Rights: The Case for Occupational Safety and Health as a Core Worker Right," in *Workers Rights as Human Rights, ed.* James A. Gross (Ithaca: Cornell University Press, 2003), 94.

2. Ibid., 104.

3. David Rosner and Gerald Markowitz, "Introduction," in *Dying for Work: Workers' Safety and Health in Twentieth-Century America,* ed. David Rosner and Gerald Markowitz (Bloomington: Indiana University Press, 1987), xi.

4. Ibid., xii.

5. Ibid.

6. Spieler, "Risks and Rights," 79, 226, n.2.

7. Thomas O. McGarity and Sidney A Shapiro, *Workers at Risk: The Failed Promised of the Occupational Safety and Health Administration* (Westport, Conn.: Praeger, 1993), vii.

8. Ruth Heifetz, "Women, Lead and Reproductive Hazards: Defining a New Risk," in *Dying for Work,* 167.

9. Dorothy Nelkin and Michael S. Brown, *Workers at Risk: Voices from the Workplace* (Chicago: University of Chicago Press, 1984), xiii.

10. David Rosner and Gerald Markowitz, "Research or Advocacy: Federal Occupational Safety and Health Policies During the New Deal," in *Dying for Work,* 88.

11. James B. Atleson, "Threats to Health and Safety: Employee Self-Help under the NLRA," 59 *Minnesota Law Review* (1975): 647.

12. David Michaels and Celeste Monforton, "Scientific Evidence in the Regulatory System: Manufacturing Uncertainty and the Demise of the Formal Regulatory System," 13 *Journal of Law and Policy* (2005): 21.

13. Nelkin and Brown, *Workers at Risk,* 182.

14. Crystal Eastman, *Work-Accidents and the Law* (New York: Russell Sage Foundation, 1910).

15. Ibid., 7, 11–12.

16. Ibid., 152.

17. Ibid., 13.

18. Ibid., 223.

19. Ibid., 225–226.

20. Ibid., 228–229.

21. McGarity and Shapiro, *Workers at Risk*, 332.

22. Nelkin and Brown, *Workers at Risk*, 178, 180–182.

23. Human Rights Watch, *Blood, Sweat, and Fear: Workers' Rights in U.S. Meat and Poultry Plants* (New York: Human Rights Watch, 2004), 1.

24. Ibid., 11.

25. Charles Levenstein and Gregory F. DeLaurier with Mary Lee Dunn, *The Cotton Dust Papers: Science, Politics, and Power in the 'Discovery' of Byssinosis in the U.S.* (Amityville, N.Y.: Baywood, 2002), 1.

26. Ibid., 8–9.

27. Charles Noble, *Liberalism at Work: The Rise and Fall of OSHA* (Philadelphia: Temple University Press, 1986), 101.

28. Adam Smith, *An Inquiry into the Nature and Causes of the Wealth of Nations*, ed. Edwin Cannan (1776; repr., Chicago: University of Chicago Press, 1952).

29. Robert Heilbroner, *The Worldly Philosophers: The Lives, Times and Ideas of the Great Economic Thinkers*, 6th ed. (New York: Simon and Schuster, 1986), 69.

30. Ibid., 70.

31. McGarity and Shapiro, *Workers at Risk*, 17.

32. See W. Kip Viscusi, *Fatal Tradeoffs: Public and Private Responsibilities for Risk* (New York: Oxford University Press, 1992).

33. Thomas O. McGarity and Sidney A. Shapiro, "OSHA's Critics and Regulatory Reform," *Wake Forest Law Review* 31 (1996): 604.

34. McGarity and Shapiro, *Workers at Risk*, 272.

35. Nelkin and Brown, *Workers at Risk*, 182.

36. Ibid., 92.

37. Ibid., 91.

38. John Stuart Mill, *Principles of Political Economy* (Fairfield, N.J.: Augustus M. Kelley, 1987), 388.

39. Mark Linder, "Fatal Subtractions: Statistical MIAs on the Industrial Battlefield," *Journal of Legislation* 10 (1994): 135–136.

40. McGarity and Shapiro, *Workers at Risk*, 275.

41. John Mendeloff, *The Dilemma of Toxic Substance Regulation: How Overregulation Causes Underregulation at OSHA* (Cambridge, Mass.: MIT Press, 1988), 33.

42. Daniel M. Berman, *Death on the Job: Occupational Health and Safety Struggles in the United States* (New York: Monthly Review Press, 1978), 23, 76–77.

43. Rosner and Markowitz, "Introduction," in *Dying for Work*, xv.

44. Anthony Bale, "America's First Compensation Crisis: Conflict over the Value and Meaning of Workplace Injuries under the Employers' Liability System," in *Dying for Work*, 48.

45. Human Rights Watch, *Blood, Sweat, and Fear*, 50.

46. Ibid., 52.

47. Ibid., 61–62.

48. James A. Gross, *The Reshaping of the National Labor Relations Board: National Labor Policy in Transition, 1937–1947* (Albany: State University of New York Press, 1981), 14.

49. Ibid., 15.

50. Ibid., 16.

51. Eastman, *Work-Accidents and the Law*, 187.

52. Ibid., 188.

53. Ibid., 186.

54. Bale, "America's First Compensation Crisis," in *Dying for Work,* 48.

55. Ibid., 39–40, 47.

56. McGarity and Shapiro, *Workers at Risk,* 23.

57. Levenstein, De Laurier, and Dunn, *Cotton Dust Papers,* 74.

58. Judson MacLaury, "The Job Safety Law of 1970: Its Passage Was Perilous," http://www/dol. gov/oasam/programs/history/osha.htm, (July 24, 2006), 6.

59. Noble, *Liberalism at Work* (quoting Occupational Safety and Health: Hearings on H.R. 14816 Before the Select Subcomm. on Labor of the House Comm. on Educ. and Labor, 90th Cong. 17–18 [1968] [testimony of W. Willard Wirtz]).

60. Pub. L. No. 91–596, 84 Stat. 1590 (1970), codified at 29 U.S.C. §§ 651–78 (1994).

61. Noble, *Liberalism at Work,* 95–96.

62. McGarity and Shapiro, *Workers at Risk,* 36.

63. Ibid.

64. 29 U.S.C. § 651 (1988).

65. See James A. Gross, "The Broken Promises of the National Labor Relations Act and the Occupational Safety and Health Act: Conflicting Values and Conceptions of Rights and Justice," *Chicago Kent Law Review* 73 (1998): 351–387.

66. Elizabeth A. Lambrecht Karels, "Make Employers Accountable for Workplace Safety! How the Dirty Little Secret of Workers' Compensation Puts Employees at Risk and Why Criminal Prosecution and Civil Action Will Save Lives and Money," *Hamline Journal of Public Law and Policy* 26 (Fall 2004): 129.

67. Sidney A. Shapiro, "Occupational Safety and Health: Policy Options and Political Reality," *Houston Law Review* 30 (1994): 39.

68. Karels, "Make Employers Accountable for Workplace Safety," 138.

69. Michaels and Monforton, "Scientific Evidence in the Regulatory System," 17.

70. For a full discussion, see Gross, "The Broken Promises of the National Labor Relations Act and the Occupational Safety and Health Act," 358–368.

71. McGarity and Shapiro, *Workers at Risk,* 93.

72. Ibid., 102.

73. Khalid Elhassan, "The OSHA Mission—Found and Lost: A Public Reminder," http://www. csrl.org/reports/osha.html (February 2000), Center for Study of Responsive Law, 8.

74. McGarity and Shapiro, *Workers at Risk,* 212.

75. Brett R. Gordon, Comment, "Employee Involvement in the Enforcement of the Occupational Safety and Health Laws of Canada and the United States," *Comparative Labor Law Journal* 15 (1994): 535.

76. Ibid., 536.

77. 29 U.S.C. § 666 (e) (1994).

78. See Anne D. Samuels, Note, "Reckless Endangerment of an Employee: A Proposal in the Wake of Film Recovery Systems to Make the Boss Responsible for His Crimes," *University of Michigan Journal of Law Reform* 20 (1987): 873–905.

79. Michaels and Monforton, "Scientific Evidence in the Regulatory System," 29–30.

80. *Getting Away with Murder in the Workplace: OSHA's Nonuse of Criminal Penalties for Safety Violations,* Sixty-sixth Report of the Committee on Government Operations, 100th Cong., 2d Sess., (October 1988), 1–2.

81. Ibid., 6.

82. Ibid.

83. Anthony Prince, "Hamlet NC Tragedy—Struggle for Safety Continues," *National Lawyers Guild Newsletter of the Labor and Employment Committee,* (October 2001): 1.

84. David Barstow and Lowell Bergman, "At a Texas Foundry, an Indifference to Life," *New York Times,* January 8, 2003, 1.

85. Ibid.

86. David Barstow and Lowell Bergman, "Family Profits, Wrung from Blood and Sweat," *New York Times,* January 9, 2003, 1.

87. Ibid.

88. David Barstow and Lowell Bergman, "Deaths on the Job, Slaps on the Wrist," *New York Times,* January 10, 2003, 1.

89. Ibid.

90. Ibid.

91. Robert Rabin, Eileen Silverstein, George Schatzki, eds., *Labor and Employment Law: Problems, Cases and Materials in the Law of Work,* 2d ed. (Eagan, Minn.: West Group, 1995), 555, 559–560.

92. David Rosner and Gerald Markowitz, "'A Gift of God'? The Public Health Controversy over Leaded Gasoline During the 1920s," in *Dying for Work,* ed. Rosner and Markowitz, 129–130.

93. Ibid., 130.

94. David Kotelchuck, "Asbestos; 'The Funeral Dress of Kings'—and Others," in *Dying for Work,* ed. Rosner and Markowitz, 195.

95. Atleson, "Threats to Health and Safety," 651–652, n. 19.

96. Ibid.

97. Charles Levenstein, Dianne Plantamura, and William Mass, "Labor and Byssinosis, 1941–1969," in *Dying for Work,* ed. Rosner and Markowitz, 221.

98. Berman, *Death on the Job,* 69.

99. Kotelchuck, "Asbestos; 'The Funeral Dress of Kings'—and Others," in *Dying for Work,* ed. Rosner and Markowitz, 203.

100. Levenstein, De Laurier, and Dunn, *Cotton Dust Papers,* 143.

101. Ibid., 144, 149.

102. Thomas O. McGarity, "Science in the Regulatory Process: On the Prospect of 'Daubertizing' Judicial Review of Risk Assessment," *Law and Contemporary Problems* 66 (Fall 2003): 165.

103. 509 U.S. 579 (1993).

104. Ibid., 592–593.

105. McGarity, "Science in the Regulatory Process," 168. See also David Michaels, *Doubt Is Their Product* (New York: Oxford University Press, 2008).

106. Michaels and Monforton, "Scientific Evidence in the Regulatory System," 34.

107. Ibid., 35.

108. Ibid., 40.

109. McGarity, "Science in the Regulatory Process," 224; McGarity and Shapiro, *Workers at Risk,* 263.

110. McGarity, "Science in the Regulatory Process," 171.

111. *Industrial Union Department, AFL-CIO v. American Petroleum Institute,* 448 U.S. 607 (1980).

112. Rabin, Silverstein, and Schatzki, *Labor and Employment Law,* 2d ed., 583–584.

113. Michaels and Monforton, "Scientific Evidence in the Regulatory System," 35–36.

7. The Value Choices of Courts, OSHA, and Labor Arbitrators

1. Paul Brodeur, *Expendable Americans: The Incredible Story of How Tens of Thousands of American Men and Women Die Each Year of Preventable Industrial Disease* (New York: Viking Press, 1973), 240.

2. *Getting Away with Murder in the Workplace: OSHA's Nonuse of Criminal Penalties for Safety Violations,* Sixty-Sixth Report of the Committee on Government Operations, 100th Cong., 2d Sess., October 1988.

3. Ralph Nader, "Address: Occupational Safety and Health Act," *Houston Law Review* 31 (1994): 9.

4. David Barstow, "U.S. Rarely Seeks Charges for Deaths in Workplace," *New York Times,* December 22, 2003, 1.

5. Anne D. Samuels, Note: "Reckless Endangerment of an Employee: A Proposal in the Wake of Film Recovery Systems to Make the Boss Responsible for His Claims," *University of Michigan Journal of Law* 20 (Spring 1987): 891–892.

6. Ibid., 892.

7. Nader, "Address: Occupational Safety and Health Act," 5.

8. Ibid., 10–11.

9. Kenneth M. Koprowitz, Note: "Corporate Criminal Liability for Workplace Hazards: A Viable Option for Enforcing Workplace Safety?," *Brooklyn Law Review* 52 (Fall 1986): 183–184.

10. *The OSHA Criminal Penalty Reform Act,* Hearing before the Committee on Labor and Human Resources, U.S. Senate, 102d Cong., 1st sess., on S.445 "To Amend the Provisions of the Occupational Safety and Health Act of 1970 Relating to Criminal Penalties and for Other Purposes," February 28, 1991, 54–55.

11. Ibid., 97, 99–100.

12. Ibid., 105–107.

13. Ibid., 110.

14. Thomas O. McGarity and Sidney A. Shapiro, *Workers At Risk: The Failed Promise of the Occupational Safety and Health Administration* (Westport, Conn.: Praeger, 1993), 322.

15. James B. Atleson, "Threats to Health and Safety: Employee Self-Help under the NLRA," *Minnesota Law Review* 59 (1975): 679–680.

16. McGarity and Shapiro, *Workers at Risk,* 329.

17. Daniel B. Klaff, "Evaluating Work: Enforcing Occupational and Health Standards in the United States, Canada and Sweden," *University of Pennsylvania Journal of Labor and Employment Law* 7 (Spring 2005): 639.

18. Randy S. Rabenowitz and Mark Hager, "Designing Health and Safety: Workplace Hazard Regulation in the United States and Canada," *Cornell International Law Journal* 33 (2000): 429.

19. Klaff, "Evaluating Work," 644.

20. Ibid., 648.

21. McGarity and Shapiro, *Workers at Risk,* 335.

22. 445 U.S. 1 (1980), n. 3.

23. Ibid., 10.

24. Ibid., 16–17, 21.

25. Ibid., 12.

26. Ibid., 4–5.

27. Ibid., 17.

28. Ibid., 17–22.

29. Ibid., 21.

30. 370 U.S. 9 (1962).

31. Ibid., 17.

32. Ibid., 16.

33. 29 U.S.C. § 143 (1982).

34. 414 U.S. 368 (1974).

35. Ibid., 384.

36. Ibid.,; *Gateway Coal Co. v. United Mine Workers of America et al.,* 466 F.2d 1157, 1159–1160 (3d Cir. 1972).

37. 414 U.S. 386; 466 F.2d 1162 (3d Cir. 1972).

38. Atleson, "Threats to Health and Safety," 670.

39. Ibid., 699.

40. Ibid., 694.

41. Paraphrasing: *NLRB v. Golub,* 388 F.2d 921 (2d Cir. 1967) (Circuit Judge Hays dissenting).

42. 466 F.2d 1157, 1160 (3d Cir. 1972).

43. 414 U.S. 368, 379 (1974).

44. Ibid.

45. Benjamin Cardozo, *The Nature of the Judicial Process* (New Haven: Yale University Press, 1921), 13, 168.

46. James A. Gross, "Value Judgments in Arbitration: Their Impact on the Parties' Arguments and on the Arbitrators' Decisions," in *Arbitration 1997: The Next Fifty Years,* Proceedings of the Fiftieth

Annual Meeting, National Academy of Arbitrators, ed. Joyce M. Najita (Washington, D.C.: Bureau of National Affairs [BNA], 1998), 218–219 [hereinafter *Arbitration 1997*].

47. Clinton S. Golden and Harold J. Ruttenberg, *The Dynamics of Industrial Democracy* (New York: Harper and Brothers, 1942), 42.

48. James A. Gross, "Incorporating Human Rights Principles into U.S. Labor Arbitration: A Proposal for Fundamental Change," *Employee Rights and Employment Policy Journal* 8 (2004): 5.

49. George Nicolau, "Presidential Address: The Challenge and the Prize," in *Arbitration 1997*, 3.

50. Jack G. Day, "Prologue" *Case Western Reserve Law Review* 39 (1989): 516.

51. James B. Atleson, *Labor and the Wartime State* (Urbana: University of Illinois Press, 1998), 71–72.

52. Katherine Van Wezel Stone, "The Post-War Paradigm in American Labor Law," *Yale Law Journal* 90 (1981): 1558.

53. See James A. Gross, "Substantive Due Process: The Standards for Judgment Must Also Be Fair," in *Arbitration 2002: Workplace Arbitration, A Process in Evolution,* Proceedings of the Fifty-Fifth Annual Meeting, National Academy of Arbitrators, ed. Charles J. Coleman (Washington, D.C.: BNA, 2003), 58–62 [hereinafter *Arbitration 2002*].

54. Harry Shulman, "Reason, Contract, and Law in Labor Relations," *Harvard Law Review* 68 (1955): 1016.

55. Gross, "Incorporating Human Rights Principles into U.S. Labor Arbitration," 8–9.

56. Ibid., 9.

57. Ibid., 9–10.

58. Richard Mittenthal and Richard I. Bloch, "Arbitral Implications: Hearing the Sounds of Silence," in *Arbitration 1989: The Arbitrator's Discretion during and after the Hearing,* Proceedings of the Forty-Second Annual Meeting, National Academy of Arbitrators, ed. Gladys W. Gruenberg (Washington, D.C.: BNA, 1990), 69–70 [hereinafter *Arbitration 1989*].

59. Barry A. Macey, "A Union Viewpoint," in *Arbitration 1989*, 82–92.

60. Susan B. Tabler, "A Management Viewpoint," in *Arbitration 1989*, 92.

61. Sylvester Garrett, "The Interpretive Process: Myths and Reality," in *Arbitration 1985: Law And Practice,* Proceedings of the Thirty-Eighth Annual Meeting, National Academy of Arbitrators, ed. Walter J. Gershenfeld (Washington, D.C.: BNA, 1986), 145 [hereinafter *Arbitration 1985*].

62. Robert Rabin, "Some Comments on Obscenities, Health and Safety, and Workplace Values," *Buffalo Law Review* 34 (1985): 727.

63. Garrett, "Interpretive Process," in *Arbitration 1985*, 148.

64. James A. Gross, "Value Judgments in the Decisions of Labor Arbitrators," *Industrial and Labor Relations Review* 21 (1967): 55.

65. James A. Gross and Patricia Greenfield, "Arbitral Value Judgments in Health and Safety Disputes: Management Rights over Workers' Rights," *Buffalo Law Review* 34 (1985): 645.

66. James B. Atleson, "Arbitration: The Presence of Values in a Rational Decisionmaking System," in *Arbitration 1997*, 226.

67. James B. Atleson, "Obscenities in the Workplace: A Comment on Fair and Foul Expression and Status Relationships," *Buffalo Law Review* 34 (1985): 716.

68. Ibid., 714.

69. Rabin, "Some Comments on Obscenities, Health and Safety, and Workplace Values," 730.

70. Gross and Greenfield, "Arbitral Value Judgments in Health and Safety Disputes," 645–691.

71. Ibid., 648. (citing Schulman's exceptions to his work first, grieve later rule: "When obedience to a management order would require commission of a criminal or otherwise unlawful act or create an 'unusual health hazard or other serious sacrifice' ").

72. Ibid., 651–652.

73. Robert E. Allen and Patricia Linenberger, "The Employee's Right to Refuse Hazardous Work," *Employee Relations Law Journal* 9 (1983): 268.

74. Gross and Greenfield, "Arbitral Value Judgments in Health and Safety Disputes," 652–653.

75. Ibid.

76. Ibid., 654.

77. The two cases are: *Public Service Co.,* 60 Lab. Arb. Rep. (BNA) 1017, 1026 (1973) and *Capital Building Maintenance Services,* 100 Lab. Arb. Rep. (BNA) 887, 890 (1993).

78. Gross and Greenfield, "Arbitral Value Judgments in Health and Safety Disputes," 656–657.

79. Ibid.

80. *Columbus Coated Fabrics,* 88-1 Lab. Arb. Awards (CCH) ¶ 8150, 3749 (1987).

81. *Lancaster Electro Plating,* 93 Lab. Arb. Rep. (BNA) 203, 206 (1989). For other cases, see Gross, "Incorporating Human Rights Principles into U.S. Labor Arbitration," 33, n. 162.

82. *Beth Energy Mines, Inc.,* 87 Lab. Arb. Rep. (BNA) 577, 581 (1986).

83. *A and C Transportation Trucking Co.,* 12 Lab. Arb. Information System (LRP) 1180, XI–531 (1985).

84. *Minnesota Mining and Manufacturing,* 85 Lab. Arb. Rep. (BNA) 1179, 1180 (1985).

85. *Rapid Transit District,* Lab. Arb. in Government (AAA), Nov. 15, 1998, ¶ 4090.

86. *Stein, Inc.,* 114 Lab. Arb. Rep. (BNA) 1374, 1377 (2000).

87. For cited cases, see Gross, "Incorporating Human Rights Principles into U.S. Labor Arbitration," 34, nn. 169–173.

88. *Pennsylvania Department of Public Welfare,* 86 Lab. Arb. Rep. (BNA) 1032, 1036–1037 (1986).

89. *Indianapolis Power and Light Co.,* 87 Lab. Arb. Rep. (BNA) 559, 560, 562 (1986).

90. For cited cases, see Gross, "Incorporating Human Rights Principles into U.S. Labor Arbitration," 35, n. 176.

91. *Amoco Oil Co.,* 87 Lab. Arb. Rep. (BNA) 889, 893–894 (1986).

92. *Lancaster Electro Plating,* 93 Lab. Arb. Rep. (BNA) 203, 206 (1989).

93. Ibid., 206–207.

94. Quoted in Harold A. Katz, "Discussion," in *Labor Arbitration and Industrial Change,* Proceedings of the Sixteenth Annual Meeting, National Academy of Arbitrators, ed. Mark L. Kahn (Washington, D.C.: BNA, 1963), 223 [hereinafter *Labor Arbitration and Industrial Change*].

95. Arthur J. Goldberg, "Management Reserved Rights: A Labor View," in *Management Rights and the Arbitration Process,* Proceedings of the Ninth Annual Meeting, National Academy of Arbitrators, ed. Jean T. McKelvey (Washington, D.C.: BNA, 1956).

96. Ibid., 119, 125.

97. W. Willard Wirtz, "Due Process of Arbitration," in *The Arbitrator and the Parties,* Proceedings of the Eleventh Annual Meeting, National Academy of Arbitrators, ed. Jean T. McKelvey (Washington, D.C.: BNA, 1958), 4 [hereinafter *The Arbitrator and the Parties*].

98. Ibid., 36.

99. Ibid., 5.

100. Ibid., 35.

101. Q. Willard Wirtz, "Arbitration Is a Verb," in *Arbitration and the Public Interest,* Proceedings of the Twenty-Fourth Annual Meeting, National Academy of Arbitrators, ed. Gerald G. Somers and Barbara D. Dennis (Washington, D.C.: BNA, 1971), 40 [hereinafter *Arbitration and the Public Interest*].

102. 29 U.S.C. § 206 (d)(1) (2000).

103. 42 U.S.C. §§ 2000(e) to 2000(e)-17 (2000).

104. 29 U.S.C. § 623 (2000).

105. 29 U.S.C. §§ 651–678 (2000).

106. Katz, "Discussion," in *Labor Arbitration and Industrial Change,* 229–230.

107. Matthew O. Tobriner, "An Appellate Judge's View of the Labor Arbitration Process: Due Process and the Arbitration Process," in *The Arbitrator, The NLRB, and The Courts,* Proceedings of the Twentieth Annual Meeting, National Academy of Arbitrators, ed. Dallas L. Jones (Washington, D.C.: BNA, 1967), 46 [hereinafter *The Arbitrator, The NLRB, and The Courts*].

108. Jean T. McKelvey, "The Presidential Address: Sex and the Single Arbitrator," in *Arbitration and the Public Interest,* 18, 28.

109. W. Willard Wirtz, "Arbitration Is a Verb," in *Arbitration and the Public Interest,* 41.

110. Julius G. Getman, "What Price Employment? Arbitration, the Constitution, and Personal Freedom," in *Arbitration—1976,* Proceedings of the Twenty-Ninth Annual Meeting, National Academy of Arbitrators, ed. Barbara D. Dennis and Gerald G. Somers (Washington, D.C.: BNA, 1976), 61, 65 [hereinafter *Arbitration—1976*].

111. James E. Jones, Jr., "Comment," in *Arbitration—1976,* 87.

112. David E. Feller, "Comment," in *Arbitration and the Public Interest,* 80–81.

113. David E. Feller, "The Coming End of Arbitration's Golden Age," in *Arbitration—1976,* 107.

114. Clyde Summers, "The Individual Employee's Rights under the Collective Agreement: What Constitutes Fair Representation," in *Arbitration—1974,* Proceedings of the Twenty-Seventh Annual Meeting, National Academy of Arbitrators, ed. Barbara Dennis and Gerald G. Somers (Washington, D.C.: BNA, 1975), 51 [hereinafter *Arbitration—1974*].

115. *Knauf Fibre Glass,* 101 Lab. Arb. Rep. (BNA) 823, 827–828 (1993).

116. Ibid., 828.

117. Emily Spieler, "Risks and Rights: The Case for Occupational Safety and Health as a Core Worker Right," in *Workers' Rights as Human Rights,* ed. James A. Gross (Ithaca: Cornell University Press, 2003), 94.

118. See Gross, "Incorporating Human Rights Principles into U.S. Labor Arbitration," 38–43.

119. Spieler, "Risks and Rights," 115.

120. Mark Harcourt and Sondra Harcourt, "When Can an Employee Refuse Unsafe Work and Expect to Be Protected from Discipline? Evidence from Canada," *Industrial and Labor Relations Review* 53 (2000): 689, 701.

121. Ibid.

122. Spieler, "Risks and Rights," 99–105.

123. Ibid., 101–102.

124. Jack Donnelly, *Universal Human Rights in Theory and Practice* (Ithaca: Cornell University Press, 1989), 12.

125. *United Steelworkers of America v. American Manufacturing Co.,* 363 U.S. 564 (1960); *United Steelworkers of America v. Warrior and Gulf Mfg. Co.,* 363 U.S. 574 (1960); *United Steelworkers of America v. Enterprise Wheel and Car Corp.,* 363 U.S. 593 (1960).

126. John E. Dunsford, "Arbitral Discretion: The Tests of Just Cause," in *Arbitration 1989,* 27.

127. "Discussion," in *Arbitration 1982: Conduct of the Hearing,* Proceedings of the Thirty-Fifth Annual Meeting, National Academy of Arbitrators, ed. James L. Stern and Barbara D. Dennis (Washington, D.C.: BNA, 1983), 63 (comments of Neil Bernstein).

128. Morton Gabriel White, *Social Thought in America: The Revolt against Formalism* (Boston: Beacon Press, 1957), 208.

129. Bertram Diamond, "Discussion," in *Labor Arbitration—Perspectives and Problems,* Proceedings of the Seventeenth Annual Meeting, National Academy of Arbitrators, ed. Mark L. Kahn (Washington, D.C.: BNA, 1964), 162 [hereinafter *Labor Arbitration—Perspectives and Problems*].

130. Stephen Reinhardt, "Comment," in *Labor Arbitration at the Quarter Century Mark,* Proceedings of the Twenty-Fifth Annual Meeting, National Academy of Arbitrators, ed. Barbara D. Dennis and Gerald G. Somers (Washington, D.C.: BNA, 1973), 204, 209 [hereinafter *Labor Arbitration at the Quarter Century Mark*].

131. Ibid., 216 (comments of William Gould).

132. Lewis Maltby, "Free Speech Rights in the Workplace: Employee Perspective," in *Arbitration 1996: At the Crossroads,* Proceedings of the Forty-Ninth Annual Meeting, National Academy of Arbitrators, ed. Joyce M. Najita (Washington, D.C.: BNA, 1997), 49.

8. Surreptitious Violations

1. Howell John Harris, *The Right to Manage: Industrial Relations Policies of American Business in the 1940s* (Madison: University of Wisconsin Press, 1982), 159.

2. Reinhard Bendix, *Work and Authority in Industry: Ideologies of Management in the Course of Industrialization* (New York: Harper & Row, 1956), ix, xi, 1.

3. Bruce E. Kaufman, "Employment Relations and the Employment Relations System: A Guide to Theorizing," in *Theoretical Perspectives on Work and the Employment Relationship*, ed. Bruce E. Kaufman (Champaign: Industrial Relations Research Association/University of Illinois at Urbana-Champaign, 2004), 47, 56; John W. Budd, Rafael Gomez, and Noah M. Meltz, "Why a Balance Is Best: The Pluralist Industrial Relations Paradigm of Balancing Competing Interests," in ibid., 197.

4. Bendix, *Work and Authority in Industry*, xi.

5. Ibid., x.

6. Joseph H. Baritz, *The Servants of Power: The History of the Use of Social Science in American Industry* (Middletown, Conn.: Wesleyan University Press, 1960), 209 (quoting C. Wright Mills).

7. Ibid., 210.

8. Ibid., 116.

9. Julie Kimmel, *Creating 'A Real Science of Human Relations': Personnel Management and the Politics of Professionalism* (Ph.D. diss., Ann Arbor: University of Michigan, 2001), UMI Microfilm 9993134, 42–43 (dissertation submitted to Johns Hopkins University Press for publication).

10. Ibid., 194–195.

11. Baritz, *Servants of Power*, 29.

12. Alan Fox, *Beyond Contract: Work Power and Trust Relations* (London: Farber and Farber, 1974), 193.

13. Bendix, *Work and Authority in Industry*, 276.

14. Kimmel, *Creating 'A Real Science of Human Relations,'* 45–46.

15. Bendix, *Work and Authority in Industry*, 277

16. Baritz, *Servants of Power*, 97–98.

17. Bendix, *Work and Authority in Industry*, 279.

18. Daniel Nelson, "Scientific Management and the Workplace, 1920–1935," in *Masters to Management: Historical and Comparative Perspectives on American Employers*, ed. Sanford M. Jacoby (New York: Columbia University Press, 1991.), 86.

19. Ibid., 87.

20. Ibid.

21. Bendix, *Work and Authority in Industry*, 286–287.

22. Baritz, *Servants of Power*, 30.

23. Bendix, *Work and Authority in Industry*, 281.

24. Baritz, *Servants of Power*, 30.

25. Fox, *Beyond Contract*, 196.

26. Kimmel, 25–26.

27. Daniel M. G. Raff, "Ford Welfare Capitalism in Its Economic Context," in *Masters to Managers*, ed. Sanford M. Jacoby (New York: Columbia University Press, 1991), 100.

28. Elizabeth A. Fones-Wolf, *Selling Free Enterprise: The Business Assault on Labor and Liberalism, 1945–1960* (Urbana: University of Illinois Press, 1994), 93.

29. Harris, *Right to Manage*, 17.

30. Fones-Wolf, *Selling Free Enterprise*, 92.

31. Bendix, *Work and Authority in Industry*, 273.

32. Kimmel, *Creating 'A Real Science of Human Relations,'* 67–69, 72, 78.

33. Raff, "Ford Welfare Capitalism in Its Economic Content," in *Masters to Managers*, 104.

34. John Godard, "The New Institutionalism, Capitalist Diversity, and Industrial Relations," in *Theoretical Perspectives*, 252.

35. Kimmel, *Creating 'A Real Science of Human Relations,'* 3, 6, 196.

36. Ibid., 140–141.

37. Ibid., 16.

38. Ibid., 174.

39. Ibid., 184.

40. Harris, *Right to Manage,* 163.

41. Ibid.

42. Richard C. S. Trahair, *The Humanist Temper: The Life and Work of Elton Mayo* (New Brunswick: Transaction Books, 1984), 4–5.

43. Kimmel, *Creating 'A Real Science of Human Relations,'* 127.

44. Ibid., 302–303.

45. Ibid., 6, 203, 226–227.

46. Ibid., 227.

47. Ibid., 255.

48. Baritz, *Servants of Power,* 197.

49. Ibid., 205.

50. Ibid., 197.

51. Ibid., 137–138.

52. Henry A. Landsberger, *Hawthorne Revisited: Management and the Worker, Its Critics, and Developments in Human Relations in Industry* (Ithaca: Cornell University, New York State School of Industrial and Labor Relations, 1958), 3, 7.

53. Ibid., 10–11.

54. Baritz, *Servants of Power,* 92.

55. Ibid., 88–89.

56. Ibid., 93; Landsberger, *Hawthorne Revisited,* 23.

57. Landsberger, *Hawthorne Revisited,* 25.

58. Ibid., 65.

59. Trahair, *Humanist Temper,* 262.

60. Baritz, *Servants of Power,* 96.

61. Trahair, *Humanist Temper,* 255.

62. See Elton Mayo, *The Human Problems of an Industrial Civilization* (New York: Macmillan Co., 1933); Elton Mayo, *The Social Problems of an Industrial Civilization* (Boston: Harvard University Graduate School of Business Administration, 1946); F. J. Roethlisberger and William Dickson, *Management and the Worker* (Cambridge: Harvard University Press, 1939).

63. Fones-Wolf, *Selling Free Enterprise,* 75.

64. Kimmel, *Creating 'A Real Science of Human Relations,'* 252, 272.

65. Bendix, *Work and Authority in Industry,* 318.

66. Ibid.

67. Baritz, *Servants of Power,* 188 (emphasis in original).

68. Trahair, *Humanist Temper,* 267.

69. Baritz, *Servants of Power,* 105.

70. Ibid.

71. Fox, *Beyond Contract,* 237.

72. Landsberger, *Hawthorne Revisited,* 31.

73. Kimmel, *Creating 'A Real Science of Human Relations,'* 265–267.

74. Fones-Wolf, *Selling Free Enterprise,* 74.

75. Landsberger, *Hawthorne Revisited,* 45 (quoting C. Wright Mills).

76. Baritz, *Servants of Power,* 201–202.

77. Fones-Wolf, *Selling Free Enterprise,* 108.

78. Gordon E. Jackson, *How to Stay Union Free* (Memphis: Management Press, 1978).

79. Ibid., 5.

80. Ibid., 2 (emphasis in the original).

81. Ibid., 15.

82. Ibid., 21–22.

83. Ibid., 10, 43.

84. Ibid., 45.

85. Ibid., 47.

86. Ibid., 50.

87. Ibid., 54.

88. Ibid., 58–59.

89. Ibid., 85.

90. Baritz, *Servants of Power,* 114.

91. Sanford M. Jacoby, "American Exceptionalism Revisited: The Importance of Management," in *Masters to Managers,* 194.

92. Fox, *Beyond Contract,* 341.

93. Mike Parker, "Industrial Relations Myth and Shop-Floor Reality: The 'Team Concept' in the Auto Industry," in *Industrial Democracy in America: The Ambiguous Promise,* ed. Nelson Lichtenstein and Howell John Harris (Cambridge: Cambridge University Press, 1993), 249.

94. Laurie Graham, *On the Line at Subaru-Isuzu: The Japanese Model and the American Worker* (Ithaca: Cornell University Press, 1995), 7.

95. Parker, "Industrial Relations Myth and Shop-Floor Reality," in *Industrial Democracy,* 267.

96. Ibid.

97. David Marsden, "Employment Systems: Workplace HRM Strategies and Labor Institutions," in *Theoretical Perspectives,* 86.

98. Graham, *On the Line at Subaru-Isuzu,* 3, 8.

99. Paul Thompson and Kirsty Newsome, "Labor Process Theory, Work, and the Employment Relation," in *Theoretical Perspectives,* 145.

100. Rick Delbridge, *Life on the Line in Contemporary Manufacturing: The Workplace Experience of Lean Production and the "Japanese" Model* (Oxford: Oxford University Press, 1998), 10.

101. Dave Ulrich, "Introduction," in *Delivering Results: A New Mandate for Human Resource Professionals,* ed. Dave Ulrich (Boston: Harvard Business School Publishing, 1998), 19.

102. Bruce E. Kaufman, "Toward an Integrative Theory of Human Resource Management," in *Theoretical Perspectives,* 325.

103. David Ulrich, "A New Mandate for Human Resources," in *Delivering Results,* 30.

104. Ibid.

105. Ibid., 38.

106. Ibid., 39.

107. Ulrich, "Introduction," in *Delivering Results,* 16.

108. Christopher A. Bartlett and Sumantra Ghoshal, "Changing the Role of Top Management: Beyond Strategy to Purpose," in *Delivering Results,* 138.

109. Ibid., 134–135.

110. James C. Collins and Jerry I. Porras, "Building Your Company's Vision," in *Delivering Results,* 146–147.

111. Ibid., 149.

112. Ibid., 149–151.

113. Margaret Butteriss, *Re-Inventing HR: Changing Roles to Create the High-Performance Organization* (Toronto: John Wiley & Sons, 1998), 16.

114. Bartlett and Ghoshal, "Changing the Role of Top Management," in *Delivering Results,* 134.

115. Collins and Porras, "Building Your Company's Vision," in *Delivering Results,* 155.

116. Bartlett and Ghoshal, "Changing the Role of Top Management," in *Delivering Results,* 138.

117. Richard W. Beatty and Craig Eric Schneider, "New Human Resource Roles to Impact Organizational Performance: From 'Partners' to 'Players,'" in *Tomorrow's HR Management: 48 Thought Leaders Call for Change,* ed. Dave Ulrich, Michael R. Losey, and Gerry Lake (New York: John Wiley & Sons, 1997), 69; Bruce R. Ellig, "Is the Human Resource Function Neglecting the Employees?" in *Tomorrow's HR Management,* 273.

118. Ulrich, "New Mandate for Human Resources," in *Delivering Results,* 30.

119. Beatty and Schneider, "New Human Resource Rules," in *Tomorrow's HR Management*, 69, 72.

120. Clifford J. Ehrlich, "Human Resource Management: A Changing Script for a Changing World," in *Tomorrow's HR Management*, 169.

121. Thomas A. Kochan, "Rebalancing the Role of Human Resources," in *Tomorrow's HR Management*, 128.

122. Butteriss, "Introduction," in *Re-Inventing HR*, x; Ulrich, "New Mandate for Human Resources," in *Delivering Results*, 29.

123. Robert H. Waterman Jr., Judith Waterman, and Betsy A. Colland, "Toward a Career-Resilient Workforce," in *Delivering Results*, 269, 271.

124. This is the most precise definition of this so-called social contract that I have seen. Thomas Kochan, "Rebalancing the Role of Human Resources," in *Tomorrow's HR Management*, 122. Most definitions talk loosely about how pursuant to that "contract" "both employees and employers saw a cradle-to-grave relationship in which there was a stable, predictable exchange of work for rewards, which included long-term employment" (David E. Bowen and Caren Siehl, "The Future of Human Resource Management: March and Simon [1958] Revisited," in *Tomorrow's HR Management*, 262–263).

125. Peter Boxall and John Purcell, *Strategy and Human Resource Management* (New York: Palgrave Macmillan, 2003), 64.

126. Bowen and Siehl, "Future of Human Resource Management," in *Tomorrow's HR Management*, 264.

127. Waterman, Waterman, and Collard, "Toward a Career-Resilient Workforce," in *Delivering Results*, 271 (emphasis added).

128. Luis R. Gómez-Mejia, David B. Balkin, and Robert L. Cardy, *Managing Human Resources* (Upper Saddle River, N.J.: Prentice Hall, 2001), 20.

129. Ibid., 202.

130. Ulrich, "New Mandate for Human Resources," in *Delivering Results*, 31.

131. Gómez-Mejia, Balkin, and Cardy, *Managing Human Resources*, 430.

132. Clyde Summers, "Employment at Will in the United States: The Devine Right of Employers," *University of Pennsylvania Journal of Labor and Employment Law* 3 (2000): 65, 66.

133. Ibid., 65–66.

134. Ibid., 65.

135. Ibid., 77.

136. Ibid., 78.

137. Raymond L. Hogler, "Employment at Will and Scientific Management: The Ideology of Workplace Control," *Hofstra Labor law Journal* 3 (1985): 27, 38–39.

138. George Bohlander and Scott Snell, *Managing Human Resources* (Cincinnati, Ohio: South-Western Educational Publishing, 2000), 550; Gómez-Mejia, Balkin, and Cardy, *Managing Human Resources*, 463.

139. Martin H. Malin, "The Distributive and Corrective Justice Concerns in the Debate over Employment at Will: Some Preliminary Thoughts," *Chicago-Kent Law Review* 68 (1993): 117, 146.

140. Gómez-Mejia, Balkin, and Cardy, *Managing Human Resources*, 463.

141. Bohlander and Snell, *Managing Human Resources*, 552–554.

142. Gómez-Mejia, Balkin, and Cardy, *Managing Human Resources*, 434–436.

143. Thompson and Newsome, "Labor Process, Theory, Work and the Employment Relation," in *Theoretical Perspectives*, 148.

144. Graham, *On the Line at Subaru-Isuzu*, 58.

145. Ibid., 97.

146. Delbridge, *Life on the Line*, 151; Graham, *On the Line at Subaru-Isuzu*, 8.

147. Kaizen, from the Japanese *kai (change)* and *zen (good)*, is captured in the phrase "always searching for a better way." Graham, *On the Line at Subaru-Isuzu*, 104–105.

148. Ibid., 97–98.

149. Parker, "Industrial Relations Myth and Shop Floor Reality," in *Industrial Democracy*, 249.

150. Ibid., 250.

151. Thompson and Newsome, "Labor Process Theory," in *Theoretical Perspectives*, 147.

152. Graham, *On the Line at Subaru-Isuzu*, 112.

153. Delbridge, *Life on the Line*, 190.

154. Graham, *On the Line at Subaru-Isuzu*, 112–113.

155. Parker, "Industrial Relations Myth and Shop Floor Reality," in *Industrial Democracy*, 262.

156. Graham, *On the Line at Subaru-Isuzu*, 138.

157. Ibid., 82.

158. Ibid., 104–105.

159. Parker, "Industrial Relations Myth and Shop Floor Reality," in *Industrial Democracy*, 266.

160. Graham, *On the Line at Subaru-Isuzu*, 106.

161. Ibid., 98.

162. Parker, "Industrial Relations Myth and Shop Floor Reality," in *Industrial Democracy*, 264.

163. Delbridge, *Life on the Line*, 192.

164. Ibid., 204.

165. Ibid., 59, 146; Parker, "Industrial Relations Myth and Shop Floor Reality," in *Industrial Democracy*, 266. Graham, *On the Line at Subaru-Isuzu*, 106.

166. Graham, *On the Line at Subaru-Isuzu*, 135; Parker, "Industrial Relations Myth and Shop Floor Reality," in *Industrial Democracy*, 273.

167. Graham, *On the Line at Subaru-Isuzu*, 135–136.

168. Parker, "Industrial Relations Myth and Shop Floor Reality," in *Industrial Democracy*, 128–129.

169. Ibid., 257, 265; Delbridge, *Life on the Line*, 176.

170. Boxall and Purcell, *Strategy and Human Resource Management*, 178.

171. John Godard, "The New Institutionalism," in *Theoretical Perspectives*, 231.

172. Roderick Martin and Greg J. Bamber, "International Comparative Employment Relations Theory: Developing the Political Economy Perspective," in *Theoretical Perspectives* 302.

173. Parker, "Industrial Relations Myth and Shop Floor Reality," in *Industrial Democracy*, 251.

174. Gómez-Mejia, Balkin, and Cardy, *Managing Human Resources*, 491.

175. Thomas B. Moorhead, "U.S. Labor Law Serves Us Well," in *Workers' Rights as Human Rights*, ed. James A. Gross (Ithaca: Cornell University Press, 2003), 137–138.

176. Bohlander and Snell, *Managing Human Resources*, 627; Gómez-Mejia, Balkin, and Cardy, *Managing Human Resources*, 503. The latter describes a "Union substitution/proactive human resource management strategy" as "a union avoidance strategy in which management becomes so responsive to employees' needs that it removes the incentives for unionization." Ibid.

177. Parker, "Industrial Relations Myth and Shop Floor Reality," in *Industrial Democracy*, 274.

178. Thompson and Newsome, "Labor Process Theory," in *Theoretical Perspectives*, 149.

179. Graham, *On the Line at Subaru-Isuzu*, 134; Parker, "Industrial Relations Myth and Shop Floor Reality," in *Industrial Democracy*, 273.

180. Delbridge, *Life on the Line*, 151.

181. Ibid., 194.; Graham, *On the Line at Subaru-Isuzu*, 117, 119, 120–121, 128.

182. Graham, *On the Line at Subaru-Isuzu*, 128.

183. Delbridge, *Life on the Line*, 128.

184. Ben Hamper, *Rivethead: Tales from the Assembly Line* (New York: Warner Books, 1986).

185. Ibid., 1–2.

186. Ibid., 2

187. Ibid., xiv, 132.

188. Ibid., 13.

189. Ibid., 167.

190. Ibid., 48.

191. Ibid., 112.

192. Ibid., 111–113, 155.

193. Ibid., 32.

194. Ibid., 174.

195. Ibid., 47.

196. Ibid., 146.

197. Ibid., 77, 151–152.

198. Ibid., 206.

199. Joseph Heller, *Something Happened* (New York: Alfred A. Knopf, 1974).

200. Ibid., 13–15.

201. Ibid., 19.

202. Ibid., 28.

203. Ibid., 22–23.

204. Ibid., 30.

205. Ibid., 54–56.

206. Ibid., 31.

207. Ibid., 29.

208. Gómez-Mejia, Balkin, and Cardy, *Managing Human Resources,* 316.

209. Henry Shue, *Basic Rights: Subsistence, Affluence and U.S. Foreign Policy* (Princeton, N.J.: Princeton University Press, 1980), 78.

210. Landsberger, *Hawthorne Revisited,* 28–47.

9. Crimes against Humanity

1. Rome Statute of the International Criminal Court (Public Information and Documentation Section, International Criminal Court: The Netherlands, http://www.icc-cpi.int); United Nations, "Preparatory Commission for the International Criminal Court," PCNICC/2000/INF/3/Add.2, July 6, 2000. "Crime against Humanity," Wikipedia, http://en.wikipedia.org/wiki/Crimes_against_humanity; M. Cherif Bassiouni, "Crimes against Humanity," http://www.crimesofwar.org/thebook/crimes-against-humanity.html.

2. Patricia Werhane, *Persons, Rights, and Corporations* (Englewood Cliffs, N.J.: Prentice-Hall, 1985), 127–128.

3. Jonathan Kozol, *Death at an Early Age* (New York: Bantam Books, 1967), vii.

4. Human Rights Watch, *Unfair Advantage: Workers' Freedom of Association in the United States under International Human Rights Standards* (New York: Human Rights Watch, 2000), 7–8.

5. ILO Convention 87, *Freedom of Association and Protection of the Right to Organise,* 1948, Article 11, http://www.ilo.org/ilolex/english.

6. *Health Services and Support-Facilities Subsector Bargaining Association v. British Columbia,* 2007 SCC 27 (2007), http://scc.lexum.umontreal.

7. Studs Terkel, *Working* (New York: Avon, 1972), xiii, 675.

8. Gregory Baum, ed., *Work and Religion* (New York: Seabury Press, 1980), 133–134.

9. Gregory Baum, "Religion, Emancipation, and Human Rights," in *Reclaiming Democracy,* ed. Marguerite Mendell (Montreal: McGill-Queen's University Press, 2005), 57.

10. Bassiouni, "Crimes against Humanity," http://www.crimesofwar.org/thebook/crimes-against-humanity.html.

11. Karl Polanyi, *The Great Transformation* (Boston: Beacon Press, 1957), 57, 71, 75, 111–112.

12. Gregory Baum, *The Priority of Labor* (New York: Paulist Press, 1982), 32.

13. Werhane, *Persons, Rights and Corporations,* 127–128.

14. Baum, *Priority of Labor,* 57; Gregory Baum, *Karl Polanyi on Ethics and Economics* (Montreal: McGill-Queen's University Press, 1996), 27–28.

15. Baum, *Priority of Labor,* 23.

16. Gunnar Myrdal, *Beyond the Welfare State* (New Haven: Yale University Press, 1960), 16, 172–173.

17. Lance Compa, "Wary Allies: Trade Unions, NGOs, and Corporate Codes of Conduct," *American Prospect,* Summer 2001, 9.

18. *Vienna Convention on the Law of Treaties,* Signed at Vienna 23 May 1969, entry into force 27 January 1980, Article 18 (http://www.oas.org/legal/english/docs/Vienna%20Convention%20Treaties.htm); Human Rights Watch, *Ill-Equipped: U.S. Prisons and Offenders with Mental Illness* (New York: Human Rights Watch, 2003), 206; Human Rights Watch, *Blood, Sweat, and Fear: Workers' Rights in U.S. Meat and Poultry Plants* (New York: Human Rights Watch, 2004), 18 n.32.

19. *Declaration Concerning the Aims and Purposes of the International Labour Organization,* http://www.ilo.org/ilolex/english/iloconst.htm.

20. *ILO Declaration on Fundamental Principles and Rights at Work and Its Follow-Up,* adopted by the International Labour Conference at its Eighty-sixth Session, Geneva, 18 June 1998, http://www.ilo.org/declaration/thedeclaration/textdeclaration/lang—en/index.htm.

21. Case No. 2460, Complaint against the Government of the United States presented by the United Electrical, Radio and Machine Workers of America (UE), supported by Public Services International (PSI), Report No. 344, (2007) [hereinafter Case No. 2460, Report No. 344].

22. Case No. 2524, Complaint against the Government of the United States presented by the American Federation of Labor and Congress of Industrial Organizations (AFL-CIO), Report No. 349 (2008), 17.

23. Case No. 2460, Report No. 344 (2007).

24. Case No. 1523, Complaint against the Government of the United States presented by the United Food an Commercial Workers International Union (UFCW), the American Federation of Labor and Congress of Industrial Organizations (AFL-CIO) and the International Federation of Commercial, Clerical, Professional and Technical Employees (FIET), Report No. 284 (1992), 17 [hereinafter Case No. 1523, Report No. 284].

25. Case No. 1467, Complaint against the Government of the United States presented by the United Mine Workers of America, the American Federation of Labor and Congress of Industrial Organizations (AFL-CIO), the Miners' International Federation, Report No. 262 (1989).

26. Case No. 1523, Report No. 284.

27. Case No. 1543, Complaint against the Government of the United States presented by the American Federation of Labor and Congress of Industrial Organizations (AFL-CIO), 74 (Series B) *ILO Bull.* No. 2 (1991): 15.

28. Case No. 1557, Complaints against the Government of the United States presented by the American Federation of Labor and Congress of Industrial Organizations (AFL-CIO) and the Public Services International (PSI), 76 (Series B) *ILO Official Bull.,* No. 3. (1992): 110–112.

29. Case No. 2227, Complaints against the Government of the United States presented by the American Federation of Labor and the Congress of Industrial Organizations and the Confederation of Mexican Workers, Report No. 332. (2003).

30. Case No. 2460, Complaint against the Government of the United States Presented by the United Electrical Radio and Machine Workers of American, supported by Public Services International, Report No. 344. (2007).

31. Case No. 2292, Complaint against the Government of the United States presented by the American Federation of Government Employees, AFL-CIO, supported by Public Services International, Report No. 343. (2006).

32. Case No. 2524, Complaint against the Government of the United States presented by the American Federation of Labor and Congress of Industrial Organizations, Report No. 349. (2008).

33. Case No. 2547, Complaint against the Government of the United States presented by the United Automobile, Aerospace and Agricultural Implement Workers of America International Union and the American Federation of Labor and the Congress of Industrial Organizations, Report No. 350. (2008).

34. Human Rights Watch, *Unfair Advantage,* 189.

35. Clyde Summers, "Unions without Majority—A Black Hole?" *Chicago-Kent Law Review* 66 (1990): 531–532.

36. Ibid., 545–546.

37. Charles J. Morris, "A Blueprint for Reform of the National Labor Relations Act," *The Administrative Law Journal of the American University* 8 (Fall 1994): 554.

38. 29 U.S.C. § 158 (1947).

39. *H.K. Porter Co., Inc. v. NLRB,* 397 U.S. 99, 106 (1970).

40. *H.K. Porter Co., Inc. v. NLRB,* 71 L.R.R.M. (BNA) 2207 (1969).

41. 397 U.S. 99, 108 (1970).

42. Ruth Bader Ginsburg and Deborah Jones Merritt, "Affirmative Action: An International Human Rights Dialogue," *Cardozo Law Review* 21 (October 1999): 282.

43. Michael Ignatieff, "Introduction: American Exceptionalism and Human Rights," in *American Exceptionalism and Human Rights,* Michael Ignatieff, ed. (Princeton, N.J.: Princeton University Press, 2005), 8.

44. Ibid., 9.

45. Anne-Marie Slaughter, "A Brave New Judicial World," in *American Exceptionalism and Human Rights,* 278, 290.

46. Ibid., 285.

47. Ibid., 296.

48. Nelson Lichtenstein, "Introduction to the Illinois Edition," in *The New Men of Power: America's Labor Leaders,* C. Wright Mills (Urbana: University of Illinois Press, 2001), xxvi. (Originally published in 1948).

49. Ibid., xxiv.

50. Baum, *Priority of Labor,* 49, 51, 73 (emphasis added).

51. Ibid., 49.

52. Lichtenstein, "Introduction to the Illinois Edition," xi.

53. Andrew Delbanco, *The Death of Satan: How Americans Have Lost the Sense of Evil* (New York: Farrar, Strauss, and Giroux, 1995), 192.

54. Ibid., 229.

55. Martin Luther King, Jr., "Beyond Vietnam—A Time to Break Silence," http://www.american rhetoric.com/speeches/mlkatimetobreaksilence.htm.

56. Ibid.

INDEX